35,00
80E

Stabilizing the Workforce

Recent Titles from Quorum Books

The Management of Business-to-Business Advertising: A Working
Guide for Small to Mid-size Companies
Stewart Halsey Ross

Company Reorganization for Performance and Profit Improvement: A Guide
for Operating Executives and Their Staffs
Stanley B. Henrici

Foreign Multinational Investment in the United States: Struggle
for Industrial Supremacy
Sara L. Gordon and Francis A. Lees

Optimizing Work Performance: A Look Beyond the Bottom Line
Martin Morf

Advertising Compliance Law: Handbook for Marketing Professionals
and Their Counsel
John Lichtenberger

Technology and Human Productivity: Challenges for the Future
John W. Murphy and John T. Pardeck

The Practice of Multinational Banking: Macro-Policy Issues and Key
International Concepts
Dara M. Khambata

Microcomputer Applications in Banking
Chun H. Lam and George H. Hempel

Evaluating Corporate Investment and Financing Opportunities: A Handbook
and Guide to Selected Methods for Managers and Finance Professionals
Sherman L. Lewis

Handbook of Management Control Systems
Ahmed Belkaoui

Currency Fluctuations and the Perception of Corporate Performance:
A Communications Approach to Financial Accounting and Reporting
Loretta Graziano

International Law of Take-Overs and Mergers: United States, Canada, and
South and Central America
H. Leigh Ffrench

The Foreign Debt/National Development Conflict: External Adjustment
and Internal Disorder in the Developing Nations
Chris C. Carvounis

GP8700849

STABILIZING THE WORKFORCE

A Complete Guide to Controlling Turnover

JAMES E. GARDNER

Q

QUORUM BOOKS
NEW YORK • WESTPORT, CONNECTICUT • LONDON

Copyright Acknowledgments

Figure 1 is reprinted from Mobley, William H., Stanley O. Horner, and A. T. Hollingsworth, "An Examination of Precursors of Hospital Employee Turnover," *Journal of Applied Psychology*, Vol. 63, No. 4 (1978), p. 410. Copyright©by the American Psychological Association. Reprinted by permission of the authors.

Table 1 is reprinted from Mowday, Richard T., "Strategies for Adapting to High Rates of Employee Turnover," *Human Resource Management*, Vol. 23, No. 4, (Winter 1984). Copyright©1984 by John Wiley & Sons, Inc. Reprinted by permission of the publisher.

Library of Congress Cataloging-in-Publication Data

Gardner, James E.
  Stabilizing the workforce.

  Bibliography: p
  Includes index.
  1. Labor turnover. I. Title.
HF5549.5..T8G34   1986   658.3'14   86-9394
ISBN 0-89930-167-3 (lib. bdg. : alk. paper)

Library of Congress Catalog Card Number: 86-9394
ISBN 0-89930-167-3

First published in 1986 by Quorum Books

Greenwood Press, Inc.
88 Post Road West, Westport, Connecticut 06881

Printed in the United States of America

The paper used in this book complies with the Permanent Paper Standard issued by the National Information Standards Organization (Z39.48-1984).

10   9   8   7   6   5   4   3   2   1

To those admirable ladies and
teachers of Jeannette, Pennsylvania,
whose like we shall not see again:
Katharine Baughman Seiler,
Ethel Landgraff Hubbard,
and Marian LeVier Hollendonner.

Contents

Tables and Figures

Preface

Turnover is not one subject; it is many subjects.

When I started looking into turnover, I was not fully aware of all the paths it would lead me into or the distances I should go down the paths. But I did sense, quite accurately, that the subject needed reexploring in the light of social and economic developments in the country, that it was now a larger subject than ever before and one of somewhat more pressing concern.

So I moved boldly into aspects of turnover my three decades of experience in training and personnel research had prepared me to discuss and, with trepidation, into those aspects which fell outside my academic and professional province or only peripherally into it.

I am not apologetic on this account. But neither am I presumptuous. I trust that the exploration will go on and that expertness in various realms of the subject will be brought to bear further on it.

My immediate purpose, I believe, has been served. I wished to speak, as a "human resources" practitioner, to other practitioners who carry the label of human resources personnel and the label of manager, to help them through better understanding of background and techniques to address a task of increasing importance to them. I have tried to do their legwork for them.

In the process I have had my burden eased by the cooperation, for which I am grateful, of a number of American corporations, of governmental personnel, and of the proficient staff of the library of the University of North Carolina at Greensboro.

Introduction

Many companies failed to take turnover seriously until recent years.

Managers tended to think that voluntary turnover was generally "bad," but many of them only addressed the problem when it hurt. The author recalls conducting an investigation of turnover causes several years ago in a number of plants in response to requests from plant managers who were losing skilled employees and were having trouble replacing them. The labor market was tight and jobs were plentiful. But by the time the survey was completed and the report was ready for discussion, business had dropped off and the managers were engaged in laying off employees. They were not very receptive to a discussion of causes of quits and resignations in the plants; their immediate concern was not to retain employees. They asked, typically, "Do you really want to talk about voluntary turnover now?" And they gave the report a polite but unenthusiastic hearing. Indeed, one of the managers refused to be put on the mailing list for a new diagnostic turnover report that evolved from the research project. But nothing beyond this relatively unpopular report emerged. And nothing new was done about causes of voluntary turnover, until another time of urgent need when new requests would be made for a study, or the individual manager would act on his pet theory about turnover.

Research efforts by industrial psychologists to explain voluntary turnover had not been lacking. A considerable body of findings and hypotheses was making its way into the professional journals. But it is doubtful that much of it came to the attention of operating executives, and there was scant evidence of its being applied in industrial companies.

Managers tended to think that involuntary turnover (layoff) was the expected and proper response to business declines and that it was an indication of their managerial acumen to make the response quickly, before excess labor cost turned up on the cost-accounting reports. There were other points of view that seemed to make the layoff decision easy: that layoffs were "a fact of life"; that layoffs were really an uncontrollable kind of turnover they were powerless to do anything about (and still run the business); and that, if the laid-off employees did not return when recalled, the local labor market would be a ready source for their replacements.

The economic situation has changed, and the changes compel managers and human resources personnel to reexamine their attitudes and actions regarding turnover. Structural changes in the American industrial system, world-wide competition, swift advances in technology, the increasing prominence of the service-producing industry, the particular nature of "modern" layoffs involving mass terminations and plant closings, social pressures for job maintenance, the characteristics of the labor force—all of these factors (and others) argue for the building of a competent workforce within a company and for measures to preserve it. The emphasis of our thinking should shift from scattered efforts to "combat" turnover to the positive objective of stabilizing the workforce, and our actions must shift from improvisations to personnel planning and the establishment of personnel policies and procedures that can lead to increased stability of employment.

The purpose of this book, then, is to take a fresh look at turnover, to make a case for stabilizing the workforce in a company, and to discuss how the objective of stabilization might be achieved. In keeping with this intent, we look first at the economic and human costs of turnover. Next, we consider voluntary turnover, reviewing what research and related experience can tell us about causation and then discussing the application of the "lessons" thus available to us—first the minimizing of employee withdrawals from the workplace and then the more positive undertaking of maximizing employee commitment to the organization.

Since voluntary turnover is only part of our concern, we turn to a discussion of the other half of the turnover control task—to minimize involuntary turnover. We explore the means of reducing the occurrence of layoffs and job loss and of ameliorating their consequences to employees when they do occur.

After examining labor sources (the labor force and the unemployed) as an essential basis for personnel planning, we address one of the major directions personnel planning should take—the establishing of a procedure by which a company can hold onto employees it has given greater assurance of job security. There is the need, in concert with measures to avoid withdrawals and maximize commitment, to establish hiring, placement, and promotional procedures by which the individual employees might acquire job competences and attain jobs which, within the plant job hierarchies, give prospects of optimal development and satisfaction. Thus, the objective of workforce stabilization is translated into an ongoing process.

The vantage point for surveying, in this book, what can be done to stabilize the workforce is that of a "human resources" practitioner who for years was concerned daily with the selection, promotion, and training of employees—and their retention, as well. It is beyond the purview and competence of this volume to make economic projections or, in regard to personnel stabilization policies, to discuss psychological testing theory in detail. But what counts heavily with a company is what its managers and practitioners can do, in a practical way, in the office and at the workplace to carry out company objectives, in this case to help stabilize the workforce, which we would strongly insist is a worthy corporate objective.

Whatever is accomplished in stabilizing employment may depend in significant part on the manager's basic view of employees. Are they a commodity, a resource, or what? There is little hope, whatever the framework of policies and procedures and company codes, if a manager or supervisor persists in the beliefs (to cite common examples) that employees who leave voluntarily are committing a virtually punishable affront to the company, and that hard times dictate submissiveness on the part of the employees, who "should be thankful they have a job." Such anachronistic attitudes are fading but are still found in the backwaters of employee–company relationships. This volume may help put to rest these and similar sentiments inimical to workforce stabilization.

Stabilizing the Workforce

1

Costs of Turnover

The costs of turnover—the economic and human costs—are an essential consideration in a company's decisions on personnel policy. The topic is necessarily broad. It includes effects of turnover on the company and on its employees, those who leave and those who stay; and it takes into account the consequences of both voluntary and involuntary turnover.

VOLUNTARY TURNOVER

In regard to voluntary turnover, there has been a considerable research treatment of the money costs of turnover, the effects on those who leave, the impact on the organization, and organizational responses. It should be noted at the start that clear-cut distinctions between the consequences of voluntary turnover and the consequences of involuntary turnover are difficult to make. In certain cases the effects are similar. For examples, there is possible turnover trauma for the employee in job change as well as job loss; and some of the same organizational costs occur in the recall of a laid-off employee and in the hiring of a replacement. Nevertheless, there is sufficient difference to justify separate discussion—though overlap may indeed be present.

Economic Costs

It is difficult to arrive at a broadly applicable figure on money costs of replacing an employee because of the varying items that go into the calculations and the differences between companies in types and skill levels of jobs and in selection and training procedures. But rather accurate estimates have been made in individual companies, and models have been developed for making them.

Estimates of turnover costs from a number of studies in the late 1970's and early 1980's ranged from $400 to $4,700 per employee (McEvoy and Cascio

1985). On the basis of data from five California companies, the estimated average turnover cost per employee—including both direct and indirect costs—was $4,596 (Hall 1981). In a study of 160 tellers in a midwestern bank, the cost of turnover per employee was calculated to be $2,522.03, including costs associated with replacement acquisition and training, unabsorbed burden, and lost profit (Mirvis and Lawler 1977).

A major textile company in the southeast calculated in 1981 that the cost of replacing an employee in an unskilled job was $198; in a semiskilled job (primarily machine operating), $1,136; in a skilled job (primarily maintenance), $9,157. These costs included employment costs; costs related to training programs, instructor training, and follow-up; costs involved in interviews by supervisors and initial orientation; and costs of actual training (pay for instructor and trainee). This last factor was a net figure making allowance for actual pay (representing output) earned by the trainee during training. The cost figures were considered conservative since they did not take into account a number of germane items, including increases in unit production cost and drops in quality.

Cascio (1982, 20–43) provides a measuring method (following a procedure developed by H. L. Smith and L. E. Watkins) that uses three major categories of costs: (1) separation costs (exit interviews, administrative functions related to terminations, separation pay, and unemployment tax); (2) replacement costs (communicating job availability, preemployment administrative functions, entrance interview, staff meetings, postemployment acquisition and dissemination of information, and contracted medical examinations); and (3) training costs (information literature, instruction in a formal training program, and instruction by employee assignment).

Hall's model for estimating turnover costs (1981) includes recruiting and employment expenses as direct costs and orientation and training expenses as indirect costs. In calculating productivity losses ("learning curve losses"), he suggests that managers estimate the new employee's percent of effectiveness in each third of the learning period for the particular job.

There are, then, useful frameworks that can serve as a guide for costing turnover. But each company will have its own somewhat unique set of cost factors, and the values attached to these factors will certainly be different; indeed, costs will vary considerably from plant to plant and from job to job within a company. Training costs, a substantial item in virtually all companies, tend to be especially variable, depending on wage levels and training arrangements. It is necessary to pin down the training costs to specifics. Where a vestibule system is used and no useful output occurs, it is easy to calculate training costs (primarily trainer and trainee wages). But the cost of on-job training, conducted at the workplace, is more difficult to calculate. The output of the trainee, which may be hard to measure and place a value on (particularly if piece rates are not used on the job), must be part of the formula—on the credit side. Some training plans employ a combination of vestibule arrangements and on-job arrangements. Complications in training and other cost factors, however, are not beyond the resources of a company to surmount. And the effort to identify turnover costs is certainly justified since responsible personnel policies require such data.

There is, of course, another side to the issue. It has long been recognized that not all turnover represents a loss for the company. The departure of disruptive employees and of poor performers (assuming that reasonable salvaging efforts have been made) can be accurately termed a gain.

Calculable economic benefits of turnover to the company derive from these factors: lower salaries and employee benefits for new hires; recovery of unvested pension contribution of those who leave; savings in vacation pay and sick leave; return on capital recovered from the preceding items, making funds available for reinvestment (Kesner and Dalton 1982, 72–76).

While it is advisable to take a balanced view of turnover and thus to recognize the presence of benefits as well as costs, it would be difficult to argue that in most organizations the economic benefits of turnover exceed the turnover costs. Turnover may be advantageous to the company in certain cases, but considering the workforce as a whole and particularly the potential value of stabilizing it, an effort to control turnover—in a discriminating way, to be sure—is clearly indicated.

Effects on Leavers

One may assume with justification that job changes of a voluntary kind generally work to the advantage of the leaver, but the issue of cost is not altogether clear-cut. Studies of the returns to employees of quitting and changing jobs have been relatively inconclusive, although a report (Kahn and Low 1982) found that employees who engaged in job search prior to quitting tended to realize an immediate wage payoff. Costs that are significant deterrents to quits appear to be those represented by the loss of pension and, to less extent, the loss of medical benefits (Mitchell 1983).

A list of potential positive results would include higher earnings, better movement toward career goals, a better-fitting and more intrinsically satisfying job, and heightened feelings of personal efficacy. But there are potential losses associated with advantages given up in the prior job, such as seniority and benefits, and the possibility of disillusionment and career regression. Assuming that the new job is validly advantageous, there is still the probability that the transition will be a stressful experience, disruptive perhaps of the old "support system," family relationships, and the spouse's career plans and progress.

There may be a psychological cost to the employee in making a job change, whatever the balance of economic considerations. Trauma arising from layoffs is well known, but change in job status is likely to be a trying experience whether it involves losing a job or shifting to a new job. Gaylord and Symons (1984) emphasize the need for treating the emotional aspects of job loss or job change; they find an individual's response to job loss or change to be determined by the elements listed below (in an abridged form):

1. The individual's ability to cope with stress and his personality structure.
2. The meaning of the job to the individual.
3. The context in which the change occurs. Was it voluntary or involuntary?
4. The extent and effectiveness of the individual's support network.
5. The age of the individual. Emotional distress is especially likely to accompany a change in midlife.
6. The dual-career issue between husband and wife. Change may affect the marriage's "equilibrium"(72).

Some assertive individuals may cope with the help of practical career and job-seeking guidance. But others, referred to by the authors as the "conflicteds" and the "can't copes," need crisis intervention treatment of a broader nature, involving not only the practical aspects of the loss or change but also the emotional aspects and the support network.

Effects on Organization

The effect of voluntary turnover on an organization cannot be encompassed by cost figures alone. The organizational impact goes beyond the measurable economic aspect.

Price's review of turnover studies led to these propositions, as having a medium amount of supporting data, concerning effects probably produced in an organization by successively higher amounts of turnover (1977, 93–109):

Successively larger proportions of administrative staff members relative to production staff members.

Successively higher amounts of formalization, up to a point.

Successively lower amounts of integration (degree of participation in groups).

It is proposed that increased turnover will probably produce an increase in administrative staff and formalization and a decrease in integration. The organization, in effect, will tighten up in the interest of control and efficiency, and the employee groups will lose cohesiveness.

In regard to turnover's impact on organizational effectiveness (the degree to which an organization achieves its goals—a concept distinct from productivity but probably related to it), Price concludes that the net balance will probably be found to be negative, although he recognizes differences in impact between organizations. He states that "the conventional wisdom is probably correct in its belief that turnover generally has a basically negative impact on effectiveness. And this negative impact is probably nonlinear" (1977, 119).

There is an interesting idea (which Price attributes to Donald B. Trow) that organizational effectiveness may be influenced more by the variability in turnover than by the absolute amount of turnover (117,118). An organization, it is suggested, may cope with predictable high turnover with such mechanisms as increased staff and formalization without a significant loss of organizational effectiveness. But such response and counterplanning may not be possible with variable, less predictable amounts of turnover, and organizational effectiveness may therefore suffer. If this hypothesis has substance, it would suggest the advisability of controlling turnover at least to the point of decreasing its degree of variability—as a minimal organizational effort.

Mobley's listing of possible negative consequences of turnover to the organization includes, in addition to the more obvious cost items (such as training and replacement costs and associated productivity losses), these consequences: disruption of social and communication structures, loss of high performers, decreased satisfaction among stayers, stimulation of "undifferentiated" turnover control strategies (1982, 32).

Mobley lists the following possible positive consequences of turnover to the organization: displacement of poor performers, infusion of new knowledge–technology via replacements, stimulation of changes in policy and practice, increased internal mobility opportunities, increased structural flexibility, decrease in other "withdrawal" behaviors, opportunity for cost reduction, consolidation, and reduction of entrenched conflict (33).

Mowday (1984) discusses a number of negative consequences that voluntary turnover might have for an organization and suggests adaptive strategies, relevant to the consequences, that an organization might take. Table 1 lists the proposed strategies and the negative consequences of turnover they address.

A basic step is to identify the impact the excessive turnover has on the organization. The strategies, to be effective, should match the impacts. Other managerial considerations in selecting strategies, in addition to prospective effectiveness, are feasibility (technological processes and layout may limit the redesigning of jobs, for example) and cost.

Managers will find Mowday's strategies worthy of study and possible application in appropriate circumstances. They should be aware, however, of the problem of timing. Attempts to increase employee commitment and to inform employees, for example, have limited chance of success if they are pushed to the fore in a situation of crisis after a long period of neglect. Explaining turnover in an effort to affect interpretations favorably is probably advisable, whatever the situation, if it is done without overstatements and misstatements. But unless information giving is a normal process in the organization, the perceptions of employees will be clouded by the question of management's motives in explaining turnover "all of a sudden."

INVOLUNTARY TURNOVER

A company will resort to layoffs (or staff reduction) as a response to economic difficulties, but the advantage gained thereby has its price—for the organization, for those who stay, and especially for those who are dropped from the payroll.

Table 1

Matching the Consequences of Turnover with Potential Adaptive Strategies

Potential negative consequences of employee turnover	Potentially relevant adaptive strategies
Operational disruption	Hire excess employees Regulate patterns of turnover Part-time and captive labor pools Training current employees Work rule changes Increase commitment among stayers Automation Job redesign Employee skills inventory Collect and analyze turnover data
Demoralization	Manage beliefs about causes of turnover Training current employees
Negative public relations	Manage beliefs about causes of turnover Continuous and long-term recruiting
Personnel costs	Training current employees Part-time labor pool
Strategic opportunity costs	Hire excess employees Training current employees Part-time labor pool Continuous and long-term recruiting
Decreased social integration	Increase commitment among stayers Job redesign

Economic Costs to Company

On economic grounds, layoffs can be costly to a company. A major actual cost is in unemployment compensation to laid-off employees, for which the company is taxed by the state at a percentage of payroll, the rate directly related to the company's layoff record.

Since unemployment compensation is a state-administered program, provisions may vary from state to state. In a typical case, regular benefits may be paid for 13 to 26 weeks. If there is an "on indicator" (the state-insured unemployment rate being unusually high for several months) and the worker has exhausted his regular benefits, extended benefits may be paid for up to 13 additional weeks. The extended benefits funded by the state are chargeable to the employers.

Some companies also provide supplemental unemployment benefits (SUB) funded by the companies. Notable examples of these are found in the automobile and brewing industries.

As set forth in the supplementary agreement between General Motors (GM) and the United Auto Workers (UAW) (dated September 21, 1984), the GM SUB plan provides three kinds of benefits: regular benefits for full weeks of layoff; short-week benefits for layoffs lasting part of a week; and separation payments when employment is terminated because of layoffs or total and permanent disability (*What you should know about your benefits* 1985).

Employees are eligible for regular benefits for a full week of layoff if they are laid off due to reduction in force, discontinuance of a plant or operation, temporary layoff, or inability to do work offered by the plant but ability to do other available work in the plant if more seniority were possessed. The employee must also have at least one year of seniority, give evidence of receiving a state unemployment compensation benefit (or of ineligibility for an acceptable reason), and have at least one credit unit or a fraction. Credit units are used to determine how long an employee can receive regular benefits according to his years of seniority. A credit is canceled for each regular benefit paid, and the maximum period of payment is governed by the seniority-based credits accumulated. An employee with less than ten years of seniority may accumulate a maximum of 52 credit units; with ten or more years of seniority, a maximum of 104 credit units.

The amount of the SUB is so devised that the employee will realize, from this benefit combined with state unemployment compensation and any earnings he may have, 95% of his weekly after-tax pay (minus $17.50 for work-related expenses). An example of the weekly benefit calculation in the case of a specific worker, as given in an employee benefits booklet:

An assembler with a spouse and two children living and working in Detroit, Michigan, is laid off commencing in April 1985, with an hourly rate of $13.07 (including cost-of-living allowance).

40 hours of gross pay	$522.80
Less: federal, state, local taxes and FICA	− 136.49*
Weekly after-tax pay	$386.31
95% of after-tax pay	$366.99
Less: Work-related expenses	− 17.50
Total income level for week	$349.49

*Based on the provisions of tax laws as of April
1985. Taxes in this example consist of
federal and Michigan taxes including City of
Detroit resident income tax.

The total income level for the week of $349.49 consists of a $197.00 state unemployment compensation benefit and a $152.49 SUB benefit.

Short-week benefits are paid to workers with one or more years of seniority
who had less than 40 hours of work or pay made available by GM in the week.
Eligible workers receive 80% of their straight-time pay, including cost-of-living
allowances, for each hour less than 40 for which no work was offered or pay
received.

Employees are eligible for separation payments if they have one year or more
of seniority and are laid off from GM for 12 or more continuous months (or are
terminated at or after age 60 without a monthly GM pension benefit, or become
totally and permanently disabled and are ineligible for a disability pension solely
because of insufficient years of credited service). The benefit amount is determined by multiplying the employee's base hourly rate by a number of hours
based on years of seniority (ranging from 50 hours for 1 year of seniority to
2,080 for 30 or more).

For long-service employees, GM provides additional benefits through a guaranteed income stream (GIS) program designed, as stated in the benefits booklet,
"to promote employment stability and avoid layoffs." The program encourages
GM to make jobs available to long-service employees on indefinite layoff and
provides benefits to eligible employees until jobs are found for them. These
benefits include GIS income benefits (after the employee has exhausted his SUB),
GIS insurance coverage, and GIS redemption payment (which an employee may
elect to receive, if made available by GM, in lieu of any future GIS benefits).

To be eligible, a laid-off employee must have 15 or more years of seniority
on the last day worked, or 10 or more years of seniority in the event of a plant
closing. There are requirements in regard to acceptance of GM job offers and
the seeking and acceptance of suitable employment elsewhere. The amount of
the benefit depends on length of seniority: for employees with 10 to 15 years,
the benefits are based on 50% of weekly earnings; the percentage increases by
1% for each full year of seniority beyond 15—up to a designated GIS maximum
benefit level.

The supplemental unemployment benefit provided by a brewing company,
through agreement with the International Brotherhood of Teamsters, parallels
the GM–UAW plan in some of its provisions. An employee is eligible (to cite
major requirements) if he has at least one year of service, is laid off because of
a reduction in the workforce that is not due to plant closing or to reasons beyond
the company's control, and is eligible for and receiving state unemployment
compensation benefits. Benefits for all full weeks of layoff are currently $60

and will increase to $65 on September 30, 1986. They begin with the fifth consecutive week of layoff and are payable for a maximum of 22 weeks. The length of the payment period will depend in individual cases on credit units accumulated; an employee is credited for 1 unit for each week of wages earned for actual work performed (up to 22 units). One credit unit is canceled for each supplemental unemployment benefit paid to the employee.

Companies incur other economic costs associated with layoffs in addition to their demonstrably substantial liability under provisions of state unemployment compensation plans and, in certain cases, their own supplemental unemployment benefit plan. There are supervisory and staff costs associated with the "processing" of employees as they leave the workforce and are recalled. Administrative arrangements vary from company to company, but a typical procedure requires the supervisor to notify the personnel department when employees are laid off and to inform the laid-off employee concerning benefits during the period of layoff (eligibility, arrangements for premium payments, etc.). The personnel office notes the layoffs in its records and includes these data in periodic summary reports of personnel changes. When the employee applies for unemployment compensation, the state Employment Security Commission office requires a form to be filled out by the personnel office concerning the facts of the layoff. When the laid-off employee is called back, he is "signed up" by the employment office and given a medical examination or partial examination.

In addition, the inevitable loss of some idled employees will require, of course, the hiring and training of new employees when the workforce fills up. The cost and difficulty of training replacements are perhaps more evident to the supervisor, who must struggle with the training, than to higher management. The effect of introducing newcomers into an experienced high-producing group can be especially devastating. The group must be reconstituted; replacing an experienced worker in such a unit can disrupt the finely meshed efficiency of the larger operation. To conceive of people in an effective production system as, in effect, interchangeable parts is highly naive. Moreover, employees who escape the layoff may feel put upon if there is pressure for production when the department is short handed and may suffer a loss of motivation which can carry over into the start-up period.

If an employee returns, particularly in case of a long layoff, there are requirements for retraining if a loss of skill has occurred. Fortunately, if the skill has been firmly established before layoff, a relatively short period of brushing up can usually serve for recovery from the loss. But the need for retraining is strong in the case of semiexperienced employees who have not been on the job long enough for "overlearning" to occur as an assurance of retention of skill. Much of the learning will have washed out with the passage of time and interference from other activities.

Rebuilding a decimated workforce after a long layoff is a monumental and highly expensive undertaking no matter how favorable the labor market.

Finally, layoffs will affect the profit-and-loss statement since fixed manufacturing costs will have to be absorbed by a reduced number of units of output.

Effects on Stayers

It is difficult to separate the impact of involuntary turnover on the organization from its impact on stayers since the stayers are the remaining personnel in the organization and in effect represent the organization. The effect of turnover is felt by them, as we shall discuss, and the organization's countermeasures are carried out by them or applied to them. The dilemma is that some of the very people who are retained and are expected to respond constructively to turnover, acting on behalf of the organization, are likely to suffer adverse effects (or perceive the situation as personally adverse) and to be psychologically unready to respond constructively.

When staff is cut for the purpose of reducing operational expenses and operations are commensurately reduced and total employee functions curtailed, the effect on employees who stay may be primarily anxiety over the possibility of being let out in a further cut. The effect is broader and more damaging if the operational rate remains the same and the reduced staff is expected to produce at the same level and carry out the same range of activities as the larger staff. Of course, in certain cases the organization will have been overstaffed and will be found to run as efficiently with a smaller workforce. In other cases overstaffing may not have been present. Companies typically engage in studies of cost reduction strategies, and if the evidence of overstaffing in relation to functions is valid (superficial analysis by consultants will not serve to establish it as such), the ill effects of the resulting cut may be minimized. In some instances, however, a company may simply specify a percentage reduction (say, 10% of staff) as a requirement and instruct its operating managers to effect the reduction. The burden on the separated employees may be eased by early retirement or termination settlements, especially in the case of salaried employees. But 10% must go.

The irony of personnel reductions which do not represent a judicious pruning of excess staff and which are not accompanied by a lowering of the total demand of work output is that the organization is then perceived pridefully by its top executives and board of directors as "running lean," whereas in truth it is understaffed and struggling.

"Learning to run lean" may be seen in some quarters as a positive outcome of turnover, but it has a fearful connotation for middle managers in many cases. As "veterans" of such episodes can attest, a likely effect, after an unproductive round of scuttlebutt, is heightened activity by the survivors in an effort to appear worthy of continued employment. Insecurity drives them forward for a time. But they soon find that despite extraordinary effort they cannot perform the functions and provide the services genuinely needed to keep the operational results up. They simply cannot cover the ground, or sustain the increased effort. In addition, they are often forced into performance of certain duties, since no one else is available now to execute them, that they have little interest in doing or have long ago lost skill in doing. Many of the additional activities required of experienced middle managers are demeaning to them.

The situation often results in frustration, poor morale, dissatisfaction, lowered personal and organizational efficiency, and interpersonal friction (brought on in part by uncertainty over who is responsible for what). Friction among stayers is unavoidable unless, in staff reductions, management carefully specifies changes in organizational structures and reporting and decisional arrangements and clarifies redistributed duties and responsibilities. Ambiguities result predictably in competition among staff members in the unofficial reshaping of jobs and staking out of provinces of authority. The less assertive stayers may retreat apprehensively to a concentration on functions they feel most comfortable and competent in performing. Whatever the course chosen by the staying managers, symptoms of stress appear among them and many of them look for a way out.

Across-the-board cuts in personnel which make little distinction among organizational units can be highly damaging to operational outcomes when they disrupt high-performance units of singular skill and cohesion.

When an experienced individual departs, the organization's store of expertness is correspondingly diminished. The later "infusion" of new knowledge through replacements may be considered a potential advantage of turnover; but the possibility of a net loss of expertness in the long run, when replacements are aboard, as well as in the short run should be taken into account. The most significant loss is likely to occur in expertness in the technology of the specific manufacturing processes, the consequences of which can have a direct bearing on operational effectiveness. Staff specialists such as accountants, industrial engineers, industrial relations specialists, and others can become immediately or quickly useful as replacements, indeed, on the basis of education alone. It is more difficult to replace the people who "know how to make the product." An awareness of the possible consequences of losing such people should inform layoff decisions. Corporate executives, attuned to other strategies in addressing problems, may underestimate the value of manufacturing skills and the importance of preserving those skills in tight economic situations.

"Running lean" has its risks, another one of which is the possibility that the organization may stimulate, through voluntary turnover as a reaction in the remaining workforce, the departure of more employees than contemplated in its planned reduction in force. It may have to run leaner than intended.

Although hourly paid leavers may not have the same advantages as salaried leavers, the hourly paid stayers, if under a union contract, may have more protection than salaried stayers. The contract will tie layoffs to operational levels. In addition, there are usually contract limitations on work loads, preventing the imposition of duties and output requirements beyond agreed-upon industrial-engineered standards. But security, satisfaction, and group cohesion remain matters of concern. And productivity may be a problem as well, particularly when work groups must be reconstituted and the coordination of activities and meshing of performance skills reestablished.

Of course, consequences to stayers may be favorable as well as unfavorable. Increased satisfaction, cohesion, and commitment may occur. New employees with fresh views may fill the gap in regard to interpersonal relations and operational effectiveness. And opportunities for advancement may be enhanced for the individuals who remain.

In some cases the effect may be minimal and the employees may proceed largely as before. The organization in such a case may find itself with stayers whose productivity and attitudes are better than those of the leavers; recent research appears to support this possibility (Wanous, Stumpf, and Bedrosian 1979). In addition, the stayers will typically include a core of long-service employees who have been productive and loyal over the years and can be expected to maintain their commitment to the company unless it alienates them with insensitive managing of the layoffs and the aftermath.

The impact is most likely to be a mixed bag of good and bad consequences, and difficult to interpret, as well. The stayers' reaction may depend on whether the turnover has been voluntary or involuntary. When layoffs have occurred, increased cohesiveness may develop, but it may represent a drawing together of employees who see themselves faced with a common threat. Improved performance may ensue but cannot be so readily construed as evidence of increased commitment; it may represent a reaction to a heightened sense of insecurity.

The prudent course for an organization is not to presume to know the precise impact of turnover on individual stayers but to accept the probability of adverse effects among them and to take countering action. Amidst the justifiable emphasis on steps to assist the laid-off leavers—a more urgent matter, to be sure—the organization cannot fail to address the concerns of the stayers. The continuing effectiveness of the organization may depend on it.

A number of actions of potential value are available to management for use with employees who remain after a layoff. It could:

1. Explain its layoff decision to employees, making a convincing economic case for the decision that also takes into account the effects on employees.
2. Demonstrate that the action does indeed assist the organization to weather the emergency situation it addresses; that is, confirm the wisdom of the decision through positive operational results, and inform the employees of interim progress.
3. Similarly, demonstrate that "sacrifices" that may be required of stayers are warranted and worthwhile. Highly committed employees may willingly assume an added work load but will expect good results to emerge eventually. A question asked by employees about running lean is: To what effect?
4. When changes in job content have been made, clearly define the revised job and expected role of the employee.
5. Open up job mobility and promotional possibilities for stayers and give related training; in effect, develop the stayers by increasing their range and depth of job skills. Such effort should be made to increase the employee's value to the company and his marketable skills generally so as to increase his chances of continued employability. It is unwise for the organization and demeaning to employees to take the callous view that the stayers should be "happy in these times just to have a job."
6. Take positive steps, primarily through training and reinforcement, to rebuild those high-performance groups disrupted by layoffs. As work groups are reconstituted,

management cannot reassign (or hire) employees on the basis of their acceptance of common goals and values since such a criterion would be difficult and probably illegal to impose. But the new group members could be chosen on qualifications and be thoroughly and quickly trained so that a lack of competency does not stand in the way of their acceptance as group members.

7. Issue a policy statement (or restate it) on layoffs, giving whatever reassurances of continued employment it can realistically give and indicating what it will do with laid-off employees to assist them in job placement and ease their burden.

8. Provide counseling for stayers who show signs of stress.

9. Have top-management personnel take active and visible roles in the efforts to address the emergency situation and, during the period of retrenchment, show restraint in the granting of perquisites and salary increases to top executives, thus assuring the stayers that everyone is in the fight together and no one is profiting from it.

10. Review the state of the relationship with key and long-service personnel who remain. If the values and goals of the organization are to be preserved, they will do the preserving; if carried forward, they must do the carrying. Through them, work values will be transmitted to newcomers. The time of layoffs is not a propitious time for attempts to elicit or substantially strengthen commitment, but most companies can rely on the constructive behavior of a dependable core of employees. Management should cultivate the relationship with these key people through such means as providing information and explanations to them and consulting with them on courses of action and on the way to proceed with the actions. Dissemination of information generally to the workforce is indicated, of course, but a closer collaborative relationship with key personnel is in order. A period of retrenchment may provide an opportune occasion for it.

Effects on the Unemployed

The consequences to laid-off employees are obviously more acute than the consequences to stayers, and the emotional problems are likely to be much more pronounced with job loss than with job change, although stress may occur, as indicated, in both cases. The potential damage to self-image is greater, and it is accompanied and aggravated by the loss of economic resources and security. This damage needs to be fully understood.

The cost to employees of layoffs resulting in long-term unemployment is hardly subject to dispute. The economic, social, and psychological consequences have been discussed at length in the literature. They are severe.

The Great Depression gave us stark lessons in the effects of unemployment. These effects were chronicled in literature and song, but a considerable volume of research was also focused then on the consequences of unemployment and enabled us to give generalized definitions to the consequences and to trace their course through stages of unemployment.

A summary of the early research (Eisenberg and Lazersfeld 1938) refers to such effects on the personality of the unemployed as threat to economic security, fear, feelings of inferiority, and loss of the employee's common sense of values and his prestige, self-confidence, and morale (359).

The progressive stages of reaction to unemployment are described in these terms: "We find that all writers who have described the course of unemployment seem to agree on the following points: First there is shock, which is followed by an active hunt for a job, during which the individual is still optimistic and unresigned; he still maintains an unbroken attitude. Second, when all efforts fail, the individual becomes pessimistic, anxious, and suffers active distress; this is the most crucial state of all. And third, the individual becomes fatalistic and adapts himself to his new state but with a narrower scope. He now has a broken attitude"(Eisenberg and Lazersfeld 1938, 378).

Of course, not all unemployed workers reacted the same or followed the same progression. Predisposing conditions affected attitudes of individuals. These factors were economic and social status (maladjustment greater at lower levels), age (greater maladjustment among older workers, but less likely to be "broken up" than middle group), sex (more distress among men), extent and impact of the depression, and length of unemployment.

The studies of the Great Depression also explored the effects on the family. There were indications that children of unemployed workers became emotionally unstable in somewhat the same way as the parents (a condition that probably contributed to lower school grades) and that the unemployed father suffered a loss of authority in the family.

The later research, focusing on more recent episodes of unemployment, confirms many of the early findings. But it gives additional insights into the psychological effects and especially their physiological manifestations (stress and its related physical symptoms) and looks further into the stages of the transition that follows job loss.

There is evidence that job loss is a stressful experience for most workers; that the stress of job loss and subsequent unemployment is associated with such psychological stress symptoms as depression, anger, irritation, and suspicion; that the risk factor for coronary heart disease may be expected to go up; and that other physical problems are likely to be significantly greater (such as dyspepsia, joint swelling, hypertension, and alopecia) as well as the incidence of suicides (Buss and Redburn 1983, 30). Drug use may also be high for acute conditions.

Stress may increase as the period of unemployment lengthens, but an important factor in the experience of stress is the social support given to the unemployed worker. Men who received relatively little support from wives, friends, and relatives (and did not feel they had many opportunities for being sociable) not only showed more depression and self-blame than those given adequate social support but had more days of illness and more health problems (cholesterol levels, ulcer activity) (Leff and Haft 1983, 12).

Komarovsky (1971) explored the effects of unemployment on the status of the husband in interviews with 59 families in which the husband, as sole provider, had been out of work for a year or more. She found, in a considerable proportion of the men, the same deterioration of personality (loss of emotional stability, breakdown of morale, irritability) found by other investigators; but she also noted such behaviors as drinking and unfaithfulness to the wife (66). Unemployment tended to lower the status of the husband and to undermine his authority as husband and his authority over his adolescent children.

When deterioration of family relationships accompanies unemployment, the prospect for adequate support at home is obviously dim.

A number of investigations have found a transitional cycle of changes in self-esteem associated with job loss and long-term unemployment, and there are similarities among the phases of the cycle identified by the studies (Hayes and Nutman 1981, 17). The initial phase appears to involve trauma, shock, denial, and immobilization (but accompanied by optimism in some cases). The next phase involves depression or pessimism, but may also be marked by an acceptance of reality. A later phase seems to be characterized by fatalism or inertia or adaptation to unemployment.

Certain graphic presentations of the transition show an upturn toward the end of the cycle, probably representing an adjustment associated with acceptance of the situation and a movement away from disabling depression. But the level of morale and self-esteem still appears lower than that of employed workers (Hayes and Nutman 1981, 14).

Deviations in a positive direction from the transitional pattern may occur in cases where such mediating factors exist as these (51–59):

The professional orientation (rather than company affiliation) of technical professionals, permitting a positive view of job loss as a "career break" (particularly among middle-career professionals).

Extensive publicity of the unemployment crisis (removing blame for unemployment from the individual).

Appreciation of idle time.

Strong financial position.

Low satisfaction with previous job.

Social support.

Opportunity and interest in engaging in training or unpaid alternate kinds of work.

"Legitimate" unemployment (perception of employee that job loss was beyond his control).

The manner in which the individual came to be unemployed (whether fired, laid off, left voluntarily, or retired) is another mediating factor.

It would be mistaken to conclude, however, that retirement presents relatively minor problems of adjustment. While being fired at work ranks high among significant life events, retirement is ranked almost as high, and perceptions of retiring have many unfavorable elements as well as favorable. Early retirement with a monetary settlement, a strategy used frequently by American managements in recent times to reduce personnel, needs close scrutiny for its effects on the self-esteem and psychological and physical well-being of the employee, and attention in regard to how the termination process was carried out and followed up.

While accepting the possibility of undesirable effects from retirement, generalizations are unwarranted. Individuals react and adjust differently. And not all consequences are intrinsically harmful. A recent study (Anderson 1985) relating retirement rules to postretirement health indicated that health (measured as the probability of survival) is likely to decline significantly if the mandatory retirement age is increased and employees therefore give additional time to the labor market.

A reading of the research literature on the effects of unemployment can be a somewhat depressing experience in itself and leads to a basic question: Can society deal effectively with the consequences of unemployment?

Fortunately, indications from the research point to actions that give hope of lessening the impact on employees. We can do something, for example, about social support—so important in the transition period. We may be able to provide unemployed workers with better support through family counseling, community interventions to offset social isolation, and opportunities for continuing contact with work associates. We may be able to reduce the early trauma and keep later stress under control through company outplacement programs using insightful approaches, and, as aspects of such programs, we can move the employee into constructive job search and training activities.

And, probably of most significance, job openings do now exist. It should be noted that the transition period from job loss during the U. S. Great Depression led typically to adjustments to unemployed status since there were very few jobs to go to. More recent charting of the transition involving British workers showed the same dreary path. But current American workers can realistically hope that the progression will lead ultimately to reemployment. Of the 5.1 million workers with three or more years of service who were displaced in the period 1979–1983, about three-fifths were reemployed by January 1984 (Flaim and Sehgal 1985, 3). There is hope for the displaced employee, but provisions for help are indicated. Outplacement services are obviously pertinent in today's situation.

Whatever is done should be informed by a knowledge of research and experiential indications. Not all training programs, for instance, can be expected to produce favorable results. Hayes and Nutman (1981, 136) list a number of conclusions regarding characteristics (rephrased here) of effective work orientation training programs: that they be related to a specific job; that they involve work experience, feedback on progress toward work-related goals, and immediate and positive reinforcement; that counseling and liaison be provided between the training and work setting; that resource personnel, with knowledge of the immediate work environment, be used as instructors; and that course content focus on work attitudes and work behavior rather than on general issues related to being unemployed.

Of course, the other side of the unemployment problem requires an effort to reduce the amount of unemployment. We need to work on both the prevention and the treatment aspects. But it appears obvious that effectiveness in dealing with the effects of unemployment will require that we keep the incidence of turnover at manageable size.

Company managements need to realize the full effects of their turnover decisions and to recognize their responsibilities toward their unemployed. There are signs of an increasing tendency to do so.

2

Research Indications on Voluntary Turnover

Since turnover research historically has placed major emphasis on voluntary terminations, a body of knowledge is available to us; and it would be useful to review the factors identified in the research as affecting voluntary turnover. We shall look at a substantial portion of the turnover research, specifically at a few major reports which summarize the literature and which attempt to read meaning into it and at a number of separate inquiries of recent origin. We shall give a brief statement of findings and then discuss them in detail.

In brief, this is what the research tells us:

A new taxonomy of turnover is emerging. It is aimed at isolating turnover that is controllable and harmful to the organization.

In the review of research studies by Porter and Steers (1973), a number of factors, under various headings, were found to be related to turnover: organization-wide factors (pay and promotion), work environment factors (including supervision prominently), job-related factors, and personal factors. The key issue appeared to be the meeting of employee expectations.

In Price's review (1977), these "determinants" of turnover were proposed: pay, integration (cohesiveness), instrumental company communication (information directly related to job performance), formal communication (information officially transmitted), and centralization (degree of concentration of power).

An updated review by Mobley and associates (1979) confirmed some of the conclusions from the earlier reviews but brought others into question. They conceive of voluntary turnover as individual-choice behavior and accordingly treat the individual as their unit of analysis.

Recent research has shifted from a pursuit of causation variables to an examination of the withdrawal process. The crucial state involves intent. Research also is focusing on commitment. Commitment seems to be related to both extrinsic (notably pay) and intrinsic factors. The sources of influence on the commitment of managers appear to change at various stages of tenure.

Turnover patterns (relationship among satisfaction, performance, and turnover) appear to be different between high and low performers and between voluntary and involuntary leavers. Late findings tend to disagree with earlier indications that leavers are superior performers.

There may be some common factors associated with turnover and absenteeism, but causation is not identical. And the "progressive" thesis (relating withdrawal to advancing stages involving lateness, absenteeism, and finally turnover) has not been proved.

DEFINING VOLUNTARY TURNOVER

At the outset, the point should be made that voluntary turnover is no easy subject to explore. There is a problem with the very definition. What kinds of terminations should be included in voluntary turnover, what left out? Obviously we should exclude layoffs. The remainder of the terminations might be characterized as voluntary in large part; but in order to take effective corrective actions, it is necessary to make a further distinction: between voluntary terminations adjudged to be "controllable" through managerial and supervisory actions and those considered "noncontrollable." Separations due to old-age retirement or the ill health of employees can hardly be included among controllable separations. Of the terminations that remain, quits and resignations comprise the largest categories, and they are usually considered as controllable. Yet it is amazing to discover how many quits and resignations are the result of personal situations unrelated to conditions of employment, such as marriage, moving of families, resumption of schooling, etc. Another distinction is useful in directing company actions: between "desirable" and "undesirable" separations (so-called functional and dysfunctional separations). Discharges should be viewed in terms of such distinction. Although regarded as "controllable," discharges can serve to eliminate disruptive employees whose performance is beyond repair and can therefore be considered as advantageous to the company. In addition, those quits involving employees whose performance is substandard are unlikely to be considered by the company as a regrettable loss it should strive to prevent.

Dalton, Krackhardt, and Porter (1981) suggest a highly discriminative taxonomy which classifies voluntary turnover as controllable or unavoidable and as dysfunctional (involving employees the organization wants to retain) or functional (involving employees negatively evaluated by the organization). Dalton, Todor, and Krackhardt (1982) suggest a taxonomy which divides voluntary turnover into functional and dysfunctional turnover and divides each of these into unavoidable and controllable. A reporting system based on these distinctions would be valuable to operating managers since it would serve to sharpen actions and focus them on pertinent populations and individuals. The author suggests, on the basis of his own experience, that organizations can devise discriminative turnover reports.

When a manager considers the research studies, he should bear in mind that they deal with voluntary turnover of somewhat varying composition. Nevertheless, quits and resignations can be confidently assumed to comprise the bulk of the voluntary turnover cases studied in the research, and managers can expect the indications from the research to be highly useful in addressing these kinds of separations.

SUMMARIES OF RESEARCH ON VOLUNTARY TURNOVER FACTORS

The Porter and Steers summary of research studies of turnover (1973) reached this general conclusion: "The major turnover findings of the review, when taken together, point to the centrality of the concept of met expectations in the withdrawal decision"(170). Expectations vary between individuals, but the summary indicates that, whatever they are, they must be substantially met if the employee is to remain.

Porter and Steers focus on the various factors making up the employees' expectations set and propose four general categories in which factors affecting withdrawal can be found: organization-wide factors, immediate work environment, job-related factors, and personal factors. They find enough evidence to conclude that important influences on turnover are present in each of the categories (156–167):

Organization-wide factors: pay and promotion.

Supervision (as an aspect of the immediate work environment): consideration, equity of treatment, recognition, and feedback.

Other work environment factors: size of working unit (the larger the size, the higher the turnover rate). (Concerning co-worker satisfaction or peer group interaction, the research indicates its potential importance in retention, but such findings are not universal.)

Job-related factors: perceived lack of sufficient job autonomy and responsibility (withdrawal tended to occur); role clarity (accurate role perception), favorably influenced retention. (Concerning job repetitiveness it appeared positively related to turnover, although such a conclusion may represent an oversimplification of the nature of the relationship and does not indisputably point to job enlargement or enrichment as the solution.)

Personal factors: greater age, longer service on the previous job, similarity between job requirements and vocational interests (turnover tended to go down); greater family size and responsibility in the case of women, extreme personality traits (turnover tended to go up).

Having concluded in their summary of findings that the decision to participate can be regarded as a process of balancing perceived or potential rewards with desired expectations, the authors suggest actions an organization might take to reduce turnover (172): maximize available rewards, consider cafeteria-style compensation plans, increase employees' accuracy of expectations concerning the job and the payoffs for performance.

With their admirable review, Porter and Steers moved beyond the findings of relationships between discrete factors and turnover to a conceptualization of "met expectations" as the process by which organizational factors impacted on the individual to produce satisfaction and influence the withdrawal decision. The withdrawal process came under additional scrutiny in later studies, notably by Price and by Mobley and associates.

Price's extensive study of the turnover literature (1977) produced a highly persuasive codification of the determinants of voluntary separations. The propositions he advances in regard to determinants (68–79):

1. "Successively higher amounts of pay will probably produce successively lower amounts of turnover"(68).

2. "Successively higher amounts of integration will probably produce successively lower amounts of turnover"(70). Integration is defined as the "extent of participation in primary and/or quasi primary relationships," the former being diffuse and emotionally involved, as in a rural family, and the latter specific and emotionally neutral. Terms often used in the literature pertinent to integration are "small group cohesiveness" and "informal organization."

3. "Successively higher amounts of instrumental communication will probably produce successively lower amounts of turnover" (73). Instrumental communication involves information directly related to job performance.

4. "Successively higher amounts of formal communication will probably produce successively lower amounts of turnover"(73). Formal communication involves information officially transmitted. "What is critical in reducing turnover," Price states, "is job-related information that is officially transmitted"(75).

5. "Successively higher amounts of centralization will probably produce successively higher amounts of turnover"(76). Centralization refers to the degree to which power is concentrated in an organization. The relevant literature often refers to "participation in decision making."

Price then addresses the crucial question: How do the determinants produce turnover? He sees two variables as intervening between the determinants and turnover: satisfaction, a social psychological variable, and opportunity, a structural variable (79–87). Price views satisfaction as a product of the five determinants and not, as widely regarded, as a determinant in itself. He sees an interaction effect between satisfaction and job opportunity outside the organization. "Dissatisfaction results in turnover only when opportunity is relatively high" (83). As intervening variables they operate differently; variations in satisfaction are produced by variations in determinants, but variations in opportunity are not produced by either the determinants or the level of satisfaction.

Figure 1
A Simplified Representation (by Mobley et al.) of Intermediate Linkages in the Employee Withdrawal Decision Process

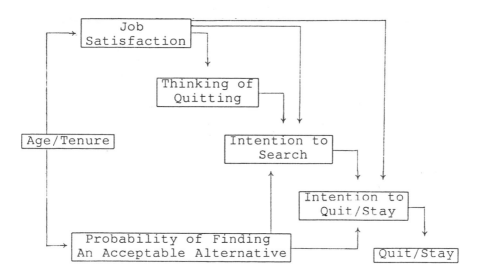

FURTHER STUDIES OF THE WITHDRAWAL PROCESS

Mobley and his associates have made significant progress in the further effort to understand the withdrawal process and have produced a series of models. Although the relationship between job satisfaction and turnover has been found to be consistently negative, as might be expected, the relatively small size of the correlation coefficients led Mobley, Horner, and Hollingsworth (1978) to conclude that further replication of the job satisfaction–withdrawal relationship would be less fruitful than an examination of the withdrawal process itself.

The model they proposed in 1978 lists a number of mediating steps (''cognitive and behavioral phenomena'') between the emotional experience of job satisfaction and actual withdrawal, as shown in Figure 1. In an evaluation of this ''simplified'' model conducted in a study of 203 hospital employees, which examined correlational strength among variables, they found that the factor having the single significant regression coefficient with turnover (among the variables studied) was intention to quit. The effect of overall job dissatisfaction was on thinking of quitting and intentions rather than turnover itself; moreover, the strongest coefficient for intention to quit was exhibited by intention to search, and the strongest coefficient for intention to search was with thinking of quitting (411–413).

The model was thus supported by the study in considerable part. It was recognized, however, that a prediction becomes more "trivial" the more closely the variable abuts the act; thus, the presence of a significant relationship between intention to quit and quit is of limited comfort to managers since it provides them with little opportunity at such late date to take preventive measures against the quit. The precedent relationships, however, do have the effect of opening the process to timely interventions.

It was also recognized that a quit may be an impulsive act involving none of the progressive steps in the model, a prospect specified in an earlier model developed by Mobley (1977). In the 1977 model,the Mobley intermediate linkage model, the links included (238) evaluation of existing job, experienced job satisfaction–dissatisfaction, thinking of quitting, evaluation of expected utility of search and cost of quitting, intention to search for alternatives, search for alternatives, evaluation of alternatives, comparison of alternatives versus present job, intention to quit–stay, quit–stay.

The Mobley, Horner, and Hollingsworth model of 1978 was appreciably confirmed in a study of National Guard members by Miller, Katerberg, and Hulin (1979) who concluded that their results were "consistent with those of Mobley and his associates and strengthen the empirical foundation of the simplified model. The relationships among withdrawal cognitions (intentions to leave and to search for a job, thoughts of quitting) and career mobility (age, tenure, job opportunities) in these data were consistent with the interpretation that satisfaction and career mobility influence turnover only through their influence on withdrawal cognition"(515).

Mobley, Griffeth, Hand, and Meglino issued later a new and more comprehensive model (1979), representing an effort to conceptualize the "individual-level" employee turnover process with a model consistent with the research literature. The new model (deriving in part from the review) is described by the authors as having these characteristics (516):

1. It is a model of individual-level turnover behavior. Individual differences in perceptions, expectations, and values are explicitly recognized. Further, individual differences in personal and occupational variables are included.

2. Perception and evaluation of alternative jobs are given explicit treatment.

3. The probable roles of centrality of work values and interests relative to other values and interests, beliefs regarding nonwork consequences of quitting or staying, and contractual constraints are specifically recognized.

4. The possible joint contribution to turnover of job satisfaction (present effect), job attraction (expected future effect), and attraction of attainable alternatives is proposed.

5. Intention to quit is considered to be the immediate precursor of turnover, with impulsive behavior and the time between measurement of intentions and behavior attenuating this relationship.

In the same article that contained the new model, Mobley and associates reviewed the turnover research studies conducted subsequently to the Porter–Steers and Price reviews. The updating review, as summarized (Mobley, Griffeth, Hand, and Meglino 1979, 513), found age, tenure, overall job satisfaction, and reaction to job content to be consistently associated (negatively) with turnover—in keeping with the Porter–Steers conclusions. Intention and commitment–attachment were consistently related to turnover and appeared to contribute more strongly to turnover behavior than did satisfaction and demographic variables (though conclusions as to relative contributions are tenuous because of the relatively small number of multivariate studies). Other findings (513):

Supervisory style and turnover: "modestly consistent support" for a negative relationship.

Relationship with turnover of promotion, pay, and peer-group relations: "inconclusive pattern of results."

Alternatives and turnover: "continues to be supported in aggregate-level studies, but has weak support at the individual level because it has been infrequently studied."

Met expectations and turnover: Direct support for the met-expectations hypothesis was found to be "weak," but the authors added, "Although realistic job previews have been shown to be a possible aid in reducing turnover, the psychology of this effect is not well understood."

Finally, the reviewers indicated that a great deal of variance is yet to be explained, that predictions are significantly enhanced by the inclusion of intentions, and that satisfaction is an "inadequate summary variable for capturing the effects of other demographic, organizational, or external variables."

Several variables contained in the new Mobley model (perceived job characteristics, personal employee characteristics, perceived alternative employment opportunities, intention of quitting job) and two added variables (confirmation of preemployment expectancies and organizational commitment) were tested by Michaels and Spector in a study of employees in a mental health facility (1982). Overall, the results supported the Mobley model. However, they did not confirm perceived alternative employment opportunities as a significant factor in the turnover process. The authors speculate that availability of other jobs "controls the behavior in concert with intention but not through intention" (58). In regard to the added variables, organizational commitment added, beyond satisfaction alone, to the predictability of intentions of quitting (an overlap between the constructs of commitment and intention was noted); but commitment did not predict intention or turnover quite as well as total satisfaction. Confirmed expectancy was found to be an antecedent of total satisfaction but not of organizational commitment, to correlate to some extent (r of .32) with intention but not with turnover.

The investigation of the steps in the pathway to turnover continues, particularly with regard to the models developed by Mobley or by Mobley and his associates. In connection with a study of the 1977 Mobley model, Hom, Griffeth, and

Sellaro (1984) proposed an alternative model that reorders the links somewhat; this revised ordering of constructs would have evaluation and comparison of the alternatives and quitting intention precede search intention and behavior.

Varied pathways may be hypothesized or found in the research. The expected cost of quitting, for example, may be most pertinent at the point when the employee is faced with an actual choice between the present job and an alternative, and a quit may occur only if the employee considers the alternative much more attractive (Hom, Griffeth, and Sellaro 1984, 163).

Martin and Hunt (1980) investigated intent to leave in a study conducted in two state highway departments, testing a "path-analytic social influence process model" which used five social power variables (expert power, referent power, reward power, coercive power, and legitimate power), two leader behavior dimensions (consideration and initiating structure), group cohesiveness, and job satisfaction. Among the findings, job satisfaction had a direct negative effect on intent to leave, and group cohesiveness had a direct positive effect on job satisfaction. But leader behavior did not affect intent, nor did group cohesiveness.

There is little doubt about the presence of a relationship between intent to change positions and turnover. A question that remains is whether variables influence turnover directly or through their impact on intention. A study of a large sample of accountants by Arnold and Feldman (1982) gave rise to a turnover model which shows the variables of age, job satisfaction, and organizational commitment affecting turnover through intention, but tenure and perceived job security exerting a direct influence on turnover, not through intention. Although the research involved a large (n = 654) and geographically widespread sample of accountants, the use of a single occupational group limits the generalization of the findings.

In a study by Waters and Roach (1979) of 132 female clerical employees, a measure of overall job satisfaction, intent about remaining with the company, and frequency of absences were correlated with terminations over a two-year period. Findings: The intent to remain and the frequency of absences added to the prediction of turnover. Job dissatisfaction did not add to the prediction for either year.

It would be useful to an operating manager to predict what will lead to what in the turnover process, but such prediction is of limited reliability at the present state of our knowledge and in individual cases. Fortunately, it is perhaps as important for him to be aware that a process is likely to take place (and in a number of instances may take the same general shape) and that he is likely to have time to act before the actual quitting occurs.

ABSENTEEISM AND TURNOVER

The relationship between absenteeism and voluntary turnover is apparently a rather complex matter not adequately explained by the "progression hypothesis" which posits absenteeism as a form of withdrawal precursory to the ultimate withdrawal represented by voluntary turnover. From the progression point of view, lateness may be considered a less severe form of withdrawal still, and the employee is often assumed to progress from lateness to absenteeism to turnover.

Lateness has not been the subject of much research study; absenteeism, though it has been under closer scrutiny, is still not well understood and not accurately predicted. Research methodology has not always been strong; the very measures of lateness and absenteeism have been questionable.

The Porter and Steers review of turnover and absenteeism (1973) indicated differences (as well as similarities) in factors related to turnover, on the one hand, and absenteeism, on the other. In a summary statement relating their organization-wide factors, work environment factors, job-related factors, and personal factors to absenteeism, Porter and Steers stated that enough evidence existed to conclude with "some degree of confidence" that increased unit size is directly and strongly related to absenteeism and to suggest (the evidence being tentative in this case) that opportunities for participation in decision making and increased job autonomy are inversely related to absenteeism (the scarcity of available research information on absenteeism tended to limit conclusions) (169). But they found these and a number of additional factors to be associated with turnover.

An Israeli study (Adler and Golan 1981) found that, with female telephone operators, job satisfaction and work tedium were generally significant predictors of lateness but not of absenteeism. In regard to prediction of absenteeism, Breaugh (1981) found in a longitudinal study of the 1977 absenteeism of research scientists that past absenteeism was a better predictor than the work attitudes of job satisfaction, job involvement, and supervisory satisfaction.

Adler and Golan (1981) throw doubt on the progression thesis with their finding that although lateness was more strongly related to unexcused absences than to medical absences, the relationship between lateness and unexcused absences was not progressive; they also speculate that the increasing absenteeism prior to termination noted in some studies may occur after the decision to terminate and may therefore not represent a process of progressive psychological withdrawal. In addition, they view lateness as a stable pattern of behavior, contrary to an earlier indication.

A later study of absenteeism–turnover progression was inconclusive; its findings neither supported the progression hypothesis strongly nor negated it (Gupta and Jenkins 1982). Indications of a progression were found in one organization under study but not in a second. Since the organizations (and related samples of employees) were significantly different (the first a 100-employee pet food-manufacturing plant employing 83% men and the second a bank organization of 20 branches employing 75% women), one may speculate that the search for universally applicable conclusions will be difficult indeed.

Wolpin and Burke (1985), after a study of the absenteeism–turnover relationship, argue "that there is no necessary relationship between absenteeism and turnover, and that measuring the relationship will tell us nothing about the processes of absenteeism and turnover. Therefore, we should not expect and even look for simple stable relationships between these two behaviors''(71–72).

A revealing study by Markham, Dansereau, and Alutto (1982) of temporal trends—within the period of the week and the year—of absenteeism for males and females showed the females to have higher rates of absenteeism generally than males. But the temporal trends, contrary to popular speculation, were largely similar for men and women. Within the week, both groups had relatively high absenteeism on Monday, showed a diminishing trend through Thursday, and had the highest rate on Friday. In terms of season of the year, the level of absenteeism for both groups was low in spring and fall and high in summer. The single difference in pattern occurred in winter, when absenteeism was low for men but somewhat high (though not as high as in summer) for women. The indications in this study that absenteeism for women is higher in the summer than in the winter does not confirm common-sense expectations.

FURTHER SEARCH FOR VARIABLES RELATED TO TURNOVER

Amidst the preoccupation with the withdrawal process, there has been a continuing search for organizational and personal variables related to turnover.

A study by Wanous, Stumpf, and Bedrosian (1979) of a substantial sample of new employees found organizational factors such as pay and training to be better predictors of job survival than individual variables such as race, age, sex, and education.

In a far-ranging examination of organizational, job, and personal characteristics in regard to their importance in explaining turnover, Koch and Rhodes (1981) found a number of variables significantly related to turnover of female factory workers: tenure, cycle time, poor leadership, communication flow, training time, family income, and satisfaction with pay.

The factor of pay was found to be more predictive of turnover when expanded to include pay administration variables (Weiner 1980).

Leadership behavior as an influence on turnover was investigated early by Fleishman and Harris (1962), who found a significant relationship between turnover (and grievances) and the leadership behaviors of ''consideration'' and ''structure.'' Low consideration and high structure were associated with high turnover but in a curvilinear way: Beyond certain critical levels, increased consideration and decreased structure had no effect. Taken in combination, consideration was the dominant factor; the findings indicated that ''high consideration foremen could increase structure with very little increase in grievances and no increase in turnover''(53).

A study by Skinner (1969) corroborated findings by Fleishman and Harris that high consideration was associated with low turnover rates and that the relationship was curvilinear (a consideration score above a certain point did not appreciably influence turnover rates).

The effect on turnover of realistic information given to new organizational members after the decision to join but before reporting was studied by Ilgen and Seely among new cadets entering the U. S. Military Academy (1974). The authors noted earlier findings of reductions in turnover when such information was given in advance of the decision to join the organization and suggested three plausible explanations: self-selection (some applicants decided not to join), increased commitment to the decision, and better preparation for coping with the situation. Their study tested the hypothesis that better preparation for coping could be achieved if new members were told what to expect after they decided to enter the organization (and voluntary resignations related to coping thus reduced). Comparing an experimental group of new cadets who received the information with a control group who did not, they did find a significantly smaller incidence of voluntary resignations in the informed group during a summer training period and before the first day of classes in the fall.

Realistic job previews used in the application procedure itself have come under considerable research scrutiny more recently and in the process have acquired the acronymic designation RJP. A number of studies have shown a relationship between RJPs and job survival. Perhaps the most comprehensive review to date of experiments on the effects of RJPs, a quantitative meta-analysis of 21 RJP experiments, led to this conclusion: "Specifically, RJPs appear to lower initial expectations about a job and the organization, to increase the number of candidates who drop out from further consideration for a job, to increase initial levels of organizational commitment and job satisfaction slightly, to increase performance (for audio-visual RJPs) and to increase job survival" (Premack and Wanous 1985, 712). There were very slight negative indications, based on fewer studies and people, concerning the applicant's perception of the company and his ability to cope with the job.

Despite the implications of the now-familiar acronym, RJPs can hardly be considered a standard procedure. Where they are used, considerable variation occurs from place to place in the subjects covered, the specificity of the information, the media employed (booklets, audio-visuals, word of mouth), the source of the information, the setting, and the audience. If the research is to be refined, future field studies will have to address the question of differential effects from RJP approaches of varying characteristics. Experience would suggest, however, that positive gains in turnover reduction (and possibly other benefits) are possible if the applicant is given a realistic view of the job. Experience would also suggest that primary reliance on printed material, audio-visuals, or other impersonal media to carry the message is not likely to be as effective as direct and personal communication with the applicant, including opportunity for give-and-take for purposes of clarification. It would appear, again on the basis of experience alone, that the acceptability of job information, as with feedback information, will depend significantly on characteristics of the information giver.

Finally, there is the issue of the relationship between job performance and turnover. The more numerous indications from research, as was suggested earlier, are that employees who leave tend to be the better performers, but the findings have arisen largely from studies of professional employees in service organizations rather than from studies of typical industrial workers, and they have not been consistent. Contradictory indications are noted in other studies, among the most recent being a study of female registered nurses in which those who left their jobs were not found to perform significantly better than those who stayed (Martin, Price, and Mueller 1981). This issue is far from being resolved; we need more evidence from studies of industrial samples and studies employing improved measures of performance.

It is advisable, in order to avoid drawing misleading conclusions, to make a distinction between voluntary and involuntary turnover when investigating the relationship between job performance and turnover. Wanous, Stumpf, and Bedrosian (1979), in their study of a sample of 1,736 newly hired employees in a variety of organizations, found that those who left voluntarily performed at a higher level than those who left involuntarily, but that both of these groups performed at a substantially lower level than those employees still on the job after seven months. Concerning job attitudes, the average for the voluntary leavers was lower than the average for the involuntary leavers, but these attitude averages of the leaving groups were both substantially lower than the average of those who stayed. In short, the stayers, on an average, performed better and had "better" job attitudes than the leavers; among the leavers, those who left voluntarily performed better but had less favorable job attitudes on an average than those who left involuntarily.

In terms of predictive relationships, the hypothesis that job performance would predict involuntary turnover and job attitudes would predict voluntary turnover was only partially supported by the study.

It would be of practical importance for a manager to know why high-performing employees voluntarily leave and to know if any difference exists in this regard between high and low performers. Spencer and Steers (1981) throw some light on this issue in a study of a sample of 295 hospital employees in which they probed the relationship between job satisfaction and voluntary turnover for employees rated high on performance and employees rated low. They found no significant differences, with respect to job satisfaction levels, between high performers who stayed and high performers who left. For low performers, the findings were not the same: Those who left were significantly less satisfied than those who stayed. In this study, as satisfaction increased, turnover decreased for low performers but remained relatively unchanged for high performers. The possibility that performance might be a moderator in the satisfaction–turnover relationship was suggested.

3

Addressing Voluntary Turnover: Minimizing Withdrawals

What can be done in an organization to minimize withdrawals of employees?

ORGANIZATIONAL FACTORS IN VOLUNTARY TURNOVER

It is fortunate that organizational factors, over which a company and its supervisors can exercise a substantial measure of control, have been found in the research to exert a significant influence over voluntary turnover, notwithstanding the acknowledged effects of personal and demographic factors lying beyond an organization's reach. The research, as we have seen, identifies such organizational factors as listed below. Supervisors have a direct hand in many of these.

Pay

Promotion

Aspects of training

Supervisory behaviors in regard to:

    Consideration

    Equity of treatment

    Recognition

    Feedback

Job characteristics involving extent of autonomy, control, responsibility, and independence

Job-related information, including clarification of the employee's role

Co-worker satisfaction (interaction with other employees)

The factors of pay, promotion, and training require organizational policies, but the administration of the related procedures is largely the function of the supervisor. The supervisor is directly involved, of course, in the so-called supervisory factors such as consideration, equity of treatment, recognition, and feedback. Although he does not unilaterally structure or restructure jobs—policy decisions are required in this matter—he can permit varying degrees of employee independence and control in the job, whatever its content. In addition, he is the major source of job-related information.

Employee satisfaction with co-workers is much further removed from organizational or supervisory jurisdiction than the other factors. Yet the degree of interaction among employees is dependent on whether a supervisor tends to curb or permit social interaction. The cohesiveness of employee groups is affected by supervisory style. And the satisfaction in belonging to a high-performance group is influenced by the placement and training functions performed by the supervisor or within his responsibility.

The thread of employee expectations appears to run through the factors; the extent to which an employee's expectations are met in regard to them provides a plausible rationale for employee persistence or withdrawal, even though it falls short of explaining it altogether. Of course, employee expectations (and perceptions concerning their fulfillment) are an individual matter. The failure to find independence and autonomy in the job (to cite one area of individual differences in expectations) would tend to move some employees—the achievers and those who want to exercise control—toward leaving the job. Employees of a different motivational–personality makeup would not be similarly moved.

Sometimes, however, an applicant does not accurately appraise the extent to which his expectations are likely to be met by employment in an organization. The company may have more or fewer rewards or different rewards than he contemplates. By providing realistic information, the company can set this matter straight, and the prospective new employee can then decide more rationally whether his expectations can be realized.

In addition, in the process of receiving information, the naive employee may modify his expectations and anticipate a sufficient fulfillment of the tempered expectations to bring him to a decision to come aboard. Of course, the decision equation should also include a clear idea, on the part of an employee, of what is expected of him.

ORGANIZATIONAL ACTIONS: A GENERAL FRAMEWORK

A framework of activities within which an organization can address employee expectations and perhaps meet them, then, would include the following:

1. Clarifying for the employee what he can expect of his employment in regard to rewards and satisfaction.

2. Clarifying for the employee what the company expects of him in return, that is, the kind of performance and behavior the rewards are contingent on.

3. Helping the employee to meet the company's expectations and to realize his own through adequate training that results in a high level of skill and brings the large rewards within the employee's reach.

4. Maximizing rewards so as to provide differing returns to meet the differing needs of individual employees.

If an organization works on the listed factors and employees generally find satisfaction in them, chances are increased that employees will stay.

But supervisors must be alert to signs of withdrawal in individual cases. Since dissatisfaction appears to give rise to intent and through stages of intent (to search, to leave) the employee comes to the act of quitting, supervisors may be given opportunity to ameliorate conditions giving rise to dissatisfaction and intent before the quit occurs if they can spot the early signs of withdrawal. But they may have to deal differentially with good and poor performers. The possibility exists that job satisfaction may have more influence on the staying or voluntary leaving of poor performers than of good.

In addition to interventions in the withdrawal process of the individual employee, a comprehensive management program to reduce withdrawals must also include measures to address the high-rate sources of voluntary turnover affecting many employees.

We shall discuss first the signs of withdrawal an organization might look for in the behavior of an individual and the possible actions, befitting the symptoms, the organization might take to forestall his quitting. Then we shall discuss the problem of "group defection"—the high incidence of turnover in work groups exposed to similar conditions in certain areas of the plant. Again, we shall be concerned with detection and ameliorative action, in this case action too late for the already departed employees but which may help us retain current and future employees.

SIGNS AND INTERVENTIONS INVOLVING INDIVIDUALS

Management's ability to intervene before an employee quits may be somewhat limited in terms of effective responses, but the venture need not be altogether blind. We may be able in some cases to identify an employee's behavior antecedent to quitting. What should a supervisor look for as a sign of an employee's intent to leave?

What happens outside the plant is largely hidden from the organization, and much of it may not be subject to legitimate inquiry by the organization. But what happens in the plant may provide helpful cues as to an employee's intent.

Job Performance

The employee's behavior in terms of job performance is an aspect of behavior constantly under the scrutiny of the supervisor. If job performance is a cue to intent to quit, the supervisor is in a position to detect it. Yet, the relationship between performance and intent to quit is not always clear and straightforward. For example, an employee who quits may well be a good performer and may remain so until the very end of his period of employment. There have been findings that those who leave are better performers than those who stay, although more recent studies have reported opposite results (Martin, Price, and Mueller 1981; Wanous, Stumpf, and Bedrosian 1979). A study of 420 credit managers from a large finance company indicated that those who were promoted performed better than those who quit and those who quit performed better than those who were fired (Wells and Muchinsky 1985).

It may not be considered a loss to have an "unsalvable" poor performer quit. The problem is to hold in place those employees whose performance warrants consideration for promotion and, more pertinently because they comprise the larger number, those employees whose performance is adequate or good but who are not necessarily promotable; and to ensure that those we designate poor performers and whose departure we may applaud are not performing below standard because of organizational factors, primarily our failure to provide adequate training. It is important that a supervisor sort this matter out.

It is important, too, that he appraise individual performance correctly. This is no mean task. It is particularly difficult in the case of employees who are in the advanced stages of developing job skill and are in a plateau period when objective evidence of improving performance, such as output, does not show up. The elements of skill in a complex job may need time for consolidation at several stages, and during such time the employee's state of skill may be underestimated by those who look at objective results and even by those who observe the performance itself. In regard to a perceptual-motor job, the observer must be insightfully aware of signs that the employee, for example, is beginning to shift for perceptual feedback to a more efficient sensory channel or system of channels. It is often found that an employee in a plateau period is in the process of shifting from visual to kinesthetic feedback, but is still holding onto the former and thus is not yet placing full reliance on kinesthetic feedback. The transition is difficult, but once he manages it, the performance is quicker and more productive. During the process, which is an essential process in skill development in certain jobs, the employee experiences frustration since signs of improvement are hidden even from him. Out of such frustration, as the author can testify from his studies of towel hemmers and hosiery loopers, thoughts of quitting may arise.

When the skill development has largely run its course and performance has stabilized, the supervisor can depend more reliably on output evidence (record of units produced within time periods, earnings on piece-rate jobs, for examples) as measures of performance. A requirement is that these measures be true indications of what the employee himself is doing and represent major outcomes of the performance, such as efficiency and quality. In certain machine-operating jobs, efficiency is the outcome of the combined efforts of machine operators and machine maintenance mechanics. And some measures, waste control as an example, while of some importance, do not stand alone or prominently as indices of performance. We tend, nevertheless, to rely on numerical indices, whatever they measure, because they provide us with such a convenient basis for judgment of performance. But only when they meet the tests of validity, significance, and pertinence can they adequately serve the purpose of performance evaluation.

The indices employed in performance evaluation should give an indication of how well balanced the performance is. Impressive results on one job criterion may be achieved at unacceptable costs on other measures, often those not so easily objectified. Example: high output neglectful of quality or without due concern for safety.

If valid objective indices are unavailable and cannot be contrived and a subjective appraisal of performance is therefore necessary, the appraisal should be based on an adequate observation of performance by someone who is expert in job methods and job execution. The supervisor is likely to know enough about the job to appraise observed performance, but adequate knowledge on his part is not always assured. Young supervisors or supervisors transferred from other departments will have difficulty recognizing signs of good or poor performance in a particular job, will indeed not know quite what to look for. Even those supervisors with significant experience in the particular department may be puzzled by the performance techniques employed by long-time employees in a particular job and may not even detect certain performance niceties. Supervisors who strongly advocate strict application of standard job methods are particularly in danger of misjudging the skill level of old-timers who invariably master "tricks" the industrial engineers never contemplated. But, assuming adequate job knowledge by the appraiser, there is still the need to observe long enough and often enough to get a genuine "fix" on performance. Dramatic examples and untypical segments of performance should not serve as a basis for evaluation.

With employees who have reached a stable level of performance and whose performance is adequately gauged—whether by measured results or observation—some fluctuation in performance is nevertheless inevitable and should not lead to a premature judgment that a permanent or significant change has taken place. Chance alone will account for some degree of variation, and supervisors should be aware of the dimensions of the aberration required for a conclusion that a significant change has taken place.

A significant change for the worse may or may not be antecedent to quitting. We need to find out what caused the change. Models for such analysis are readily available (Mager and Pipe 1970). Close observation and exploratory interviews, with employee input, provide an effective means for getting at the source of the trouble. Often the exploration of causes leads readily to a solution. If the investigation reveals a weakness of skill in some aspect of execution, training can be a relatively easy solution. A straightforward determination of causes and of corrective prescriptions is also possible if job conditions are adversely affecting performance. The problem is harder to probe and correct if poor motivation is hindering productivity, but in addressing such cases, the supervisor has a number of reinforcers at his command.

A common sign that a problem exists is untypical behavior on the part of the employee. If the employee has been a consistently good performer and the indices show a sudden significant drop, observation often reveals that the employee is spending more time away from the workplace than is his custom or is engaging in poor practices not earlier used. In the case of a highly skilled employee, the telltale signals may appear in the incidental or auxiliary or housekeeping aspects of the job rather than in the execution of the "production" job-tasks themselves. A truly skilled employee whose perceptual-motor habits are firmly established would be hard put to perform less skillfully than usual, in terms of deftness and speed, within the job task cycle. When the overall performance of such an employee suffers, his situation requires attention to prevent further deterioration of performance and to forestall any incipient move toward quitting that may arise from the employee's underlying difficulties.

The supervisor needs to identify those difficulties and arrange for ameliorative action. In this process he can be directive with the employee in specifying the evidences of a performance problem. If the indices are fair and the observations adequate, the employee is likely to accept the existence and dimensions of a problem; in many cases he is already acutely aware of trouble. But to arrive at causes and solutions, the supervisor is advised to use a participative approach. The employee needs to be given an opportunity to express himself and to become a partner in the problem-solving process. It is important that the course to be taken for improvement be acceptable to the employee, especially if it involves action on his part. If organizational obstacles are uncovered, the foreman should be prepared to make a commitment to remove them to the extent practical. There should be no doubt about who is to do what when an agreement on action is reached.

If a program of systematic and periodic performance reviews is carried out, many performance problems can be "handled" in that context. But suddenly untypical performance may need more immediate attention—and a monitoring system that will detect performance deterioration in its budding stage.

Performance Feedback

While poor performance in itself may be interpreted rightly in many cases as an early step in the withdrawal process, it is the feedback on performance that the employee's turnover decision is likely to hinge on.

Information on his employees' job performance is essential to a supervisor's management of his department in many of its aspects. While we have tended to focus our attention heavily on the effect of performance feedback on job performance itself, experience and research with the performance feedback–turnover relationship have indicated convincingly that a central question in an employee's turnover decision is simply, How am I doing? In regard to turnover, the subject of our concern, feedback on performance can affect an employee's turnover decision (Wells and Muchinsky 1985) and, one may reasonably conjecture, his intentions preliminary to the act of quitting.

Porter and Steers in their review of turnover factors referred to feedback as a supervisory factor (1973, 158). Price, in his discussion of formal communications as a turnover determinant, stated that officially transmitted job-related information is "critical" in reducing turnover (1977, 75).

Because feedback on performance may be the crucial issue in an employee's turnover decision, it is useful not only to consider the validity of the performance appraisal data, as we have done, but also the interrelated factors of acceptability, nature, content, and agent of the feedback.

It is pointless for the supervisor to collect data on employee performance strictly for his own information. Feedback on performance should reach the employee. Since feedback can come from numerous sources (Herold and Parsons 1985), it is important that the supervisor assume the role of feedback provider and that he take care to ensure that the feedback he gives is valid. It is unwise to allow the employee to infer how well he is doing; misperceptions can lead to false expectations. In the normal course of job skill development, we attempt— and advisedly so—to shift the burden of picking up feedback to the employee himself, and through our training we attempt to endow him with sufficient job expertness to assume this function. Ultimately, the performance must be largely self-sustaining, and it can become so through the employee's progressive ability to provide feedback and reinforcement for himself (or to find it for himself in the job task). Performance may thus be adequately served. But in regard to turnover decision, feedback from self may not be enough, even if it is accurate. The employee's tenure is not within his complete control. His own feedback cannot reassure him in this regard. The feedback may need a power source, may have to represent official cognizance, may have to be, in Price's terms, officially transmitted.

The supervisor is in position to be the official transmitter and is called upon to provide the feedback. But the effect of his feedback will depend upon its acceptability to the employee, and the issue of acceptability will turn in part on the characteristics of the supervisor (Ilgen, Fisher, and Taylor 1979). If his feedback is to be accepted, he will have to be seen by his employees as expert and trustworthy. They will more willingly respond, apparently, if the supervisor is a figure of some power who controls outcomes they consider of value. And they will tend to react more favorably to specific information he gives on performance than to general information.

The personality of the recipient is also a factor in acceptability of feedback and can account for individual differences in response to feedback. Employees who seek high achievement apparently need feedback related to competency;

those with high needs for affiliation are likely to be more receptive to feedback information concerning extrinsic rewards.

The nature of the feedback will also affect its acceptance. Negative feedback is less likely to be accepted than positive feedback and is likely to be perceived inaccurately.

Of all the feedback aspects, the content of the feedback—what actually is communicated—is likely to have the strongest influence on the employee's reaction; and advance planning of content, in regard to both topics and scope, is therefore highly advisable. For feedback to have maximum effect, it should be concerned not only with the employee's level of performance but, if the performance needs improving, with the basis of his difficulties and the remedial action that should be undertaken. An employee's intent may depend not only on whether the feedback is "good" or "bad" but also on what is going to be further required of him. He may react favorably or unfavorably to the measures to be taken for improvement of performance. Participation by the employee in the discussion may improve the chance that he will accept the solution. And adverse reaction to the feedback on a substandard level of performance may be offset if the employee conceives of the plan of action as a sincere and sufficient effort to help him.

Whatever information is given to him will give rise to expectations. If he sizes up the feedback as telling him he cannot expect to get out of the job the valued rewards earlier anticipated, he may indeed start down the turnover path. The feedback should therefore not omit the positive signs of performance (nor should it overstate them) when the good and bad aspects are intermixed. And a positive complexion can usually be given justifiably to constructive plans for improvement. Finally, where there is genuine hope for improvement, that hope should be communicated to the employee. With such measures, the employee's tendency to reject negative feedback may be substantially blunted.

Hope in itself is hardly enough, however, nor unsupported supervisory expectations of improved performance. The "Pygmalion effect" can apparently help to produce better performance on the job, although its reported successes have largely occurred in the classroom. But the supervisor's expectations, though of motivational value, give relatively undependable assurance of improved performance unless the employee is provided with the needed means of improvement beyond his effort alone. And a supervisor's expectations unsupported by somewhat reliable signs of improvement potential and a diagnostic effort to help the improvement along can lead to false expectations of performance success on the part of the employee, and to disillusionment, failing performance, and perhaps a decision to leave.

Complaints and Grievances

There are other aspects of work behavior, aside from job performance, that may show up as early warnings of potential turnover. Complaints and grousing may be precursors of quitting, especially if they are extreme or are uncharacteristic of the particular employee. A supervisor should be close enough to his employees to pick up the grumblings. Of course, formal grievances will come to his attention through established procedures. But the filing of a formal grievance is in some degree an indication of the employee's intent to stay; it might be considered a demonstration of the employee's interest in improving his situation rather than leaving it. The more ominous possibilities may lie in the rumbling undercurrent of discontent which never ascends to the level of formal grievances, and perhaps cannot be couched in those terms. Fortunately, the signs are usually evident to a supervisor who is attuned to the attitudes of his employees.

Again, it is necessary to get to causes, in this case to look behind the grievance or complaint to find out if there is substance to it. Formal grievances provide a machinery and time table for this process and the resolution of the problem. There is a similar need to analyze and resolve informal complaints. A supervisor who does not address the problem is inviting possible turnover. But he is equally at fault if he fosters employee expectations that he will act and then does not— or delays the intended action beyond the employee's threshold of tolerance or patience. Employees differ in the length of time they will tolerate an unresolved situation before taking steps to settle it—and the step taken by some may be to remove themselves from the situation while the supervisor is still sitting on it.

Shift Assignments

Shift of work assignment is frequently given by employees as the reason for quitting or contemplating quitting. There is no doubt that adjustment to night and rotating shifts is difficult for many employees. The physiological side of the problem involves the disruption of the circadian rhythms, fatigue, and various physical ailments, prominently gastritis. In addition, the shift may interfere with the employee's performance of his family role, and this difficulty may add to his physiological stress symptoms (Hood and Milazzo 1984). These conditions are likely to occur with employees on night shift and on a schedule of rotating shifts.

The rotating shift schedule appears to aggravate the shift problem. There is evidence that the general well-being of employees (mental health, job satisfaction, organizational commitment, and social participation) is better when shifts are fixed rather than rotated (Jamal 1981).

Of course, there are individual differences in reactions. But, in general, most workers prefer day work to night. And older workers appear to have more trouble adjusting to night work than younger employees.

Obviously, if a company could design a scheduling system which would allow workers to match their work hours with their personal and family needs, the problem of adjustment would be solved. The design most prominently advocated and used currently is a flexible schedule (flexitime). Yet there are practical limits to the application of flexitime, limits related to the type of process or service involved (not practical, for example, in continuous-process, multishift, or service-on-demand operations) and to company and union policies which have worked well in many respects and are not to be lightly abandoned. Moreover, the widely held expectation that flexitime would improve productivity has not yet been conclusively demonstrated in the limited studies conducted to date.

The improvement which is emerging in the studies is in employee morale. A Conference Board report (Gorlin 1982) indicated that almost all companies then using flexitime (not a very considerable number in America) reported improvement in morale. Field studies of flexitime appear to find increases in job satisfaction as a more likely outcome than improved performance or productivity (Orpen 1981; Narayanan and Nath 1982). However, there may be circumstances when productivity is increased with flexitime; a case can be made for flexitime when work group members share limited resources and lose time waiting for equipment to become available (Ralston, Anthony, and Gustafson 1985).

Since intent to quit may arise from dissatisfaction, the reported favorable effect of flexitime on satisfaction has meaning for managers seeking to head off the turnover decision. But, as indicated, they may find flexitime to be an impractical solution to the problem of shift adjustment which lies at the core of turnover decisions with many employees.

One method proposed for giving flexibility to the work schedule without overturning the seniority system is to facilitate shift-trading arrangements. This solution is more likely to find application with staff personnel than with line. Whatever the difficulty in manipulating schedules, however, there is apparently some merit in allowing an employee some influence in the matter; the adverse impact on family life of a nonstandard work day, for example, was found to be lessened in the degree the employee could control his work schedule (Staines and Pleck 1983).

Of wider utility and practicality in management's effort to address the problem of shift maladjustment as a force pushing an employee toward quitting would be a program to aid workers to adjust better to shift work by (1) informing them concerning what to expect when they go on a shift and the links between shift work and well-being and (2) counseling them with a view to exploring the possible mismatch between the work schedule and their personal and family situation and measures to cope with its adverse effects.

While symptoms of stress may arise from shift maladjustment, other causes may be at work. Symptoms of serious stress from whatever source are potential forerunners of turnover. There may be sources other than shift for conflict between family role and work role and for resultant stress. For example, it is a common complaint among housewives that husbands "bring their work home" and give inadequate attention to children and domestic matters. It is helpful in such cases for superiors to clarify what is expected of subordinates and, if necessary, to coach them in utilizing the regular work period more efficiently so as to accomplish what is expected in that period. Indeed, one of the main causes of stress within the organization itself is the superior's failure to remove ambiguity from the role of the employee.

Absenteeism

Since the statistical relationship between absenteeism and turnover is open to question and common causation not established, there is little assurance that absenteeism is precedent to voluntary turnover. Consequently, management's effort to curb absenteeism, while meritorious in itself, can hardly be expected to forestall quitting—although management would welcome such outcome if it occurred, if only as a byproduct.

Of course, in individual cases of disciplinary terminations for absenteeism, there is a direct connection between absenteeism and turnover. The typical disciplinary policy lists voluntary absenteeism as an offense subject, on the basis of repetition, to increasingly severe penalties (verbal warning, written warning, suspension, and discharge). The employee, aware of the procedural process, can in effect arrange for his own termination by repeated absences.

The presence of intermediate steps in the disciplinary procedure provides management an opportunity to explore the likelihood that the behavior in the individual case will shift from absenteeism to gestures toward quitting. Early in the game, when the beginning incident occurs, the supervisor in the process of giving a verbal warning to the employee can perhaps not only determine the reason (if he probes behind excuses) for the absenteeism but whether such reason points toward quitting. If he uncovers stressful job conditions or employment dissatisfactions often associated with quitting, addressing the situation may indeed have the effect of heading off a potential quit.

It may be found, as in the author's experience in a particular plant, that the absentees had no basis in dissatisfaction for leaving and indeed no inclination to leave. The plant in question was considered a good place to work, and one of the reasons was the management's leniency toward absenteeism. Absenteeism was considered a kind of fringe benefit; employees could take time off now and again with relative impunity. And so they took time off but with no thought of quitting.

This experience is not cited as typical; situations and people differ. The prudent course is to police absenteeism closely in an effort to curb it but also to detect signs of quitting. The disciplinary procedure itself is a good vehicle for this purpose.

The supervisor should be aware of constraints that may keep an employee in place; he should at least have knowledge of the labor market. The disgruntled employee who sees no prospect of other employment may continue to be a disciplinary problem but not to the extent of committing the offense that will result in his discharge. The supervisor may find it hard to uncover sources of dissatisfaction in such cases, but the effort is justified if the employee's job performance is satisfactory: when the job prospects improve and constraints are removed, the still-dissatisfied employee may be a prime candidate for entry in the turnover report.

Tardiness can be treated in the same manner as absenteeism. Supervisors should not assume that tardiness is a first step toward quitting, but should make an effort to probe for causes of the offense and in the process to identify any associated dissatisfactions of a kind that might lead eventually to quitting.

A Final Word on the Withdrawal Process

It should be pointed out that although withdrawal may be properly considered a process, there is no fixed progression of stages or inevitable steps down the pathway for every employee. An individual employee may show numerous signs of being on his way out but never reach the final act of quitting. Outside constraints including his personal circumstances and the availability of other and better jobs may lock him into an unsatisfactory situation. Or factors having nothing to do with the job or company may compel him to leave. Or he may quit in an impulsive, capricious act that abruptly collapses the neat course we had set out for him.

But there is a probability worth acting on: that with timely interventions within a company's realm of action, we can hold onto many good employees who otherwise would leave.

Periodic performance reviews provide a good procedural means of intervening when performance is a problem of possible relationship to turnover. But the periodic performance discussions can also give the supervisor insights into the employee's general situation—or can be expanded to give such insights—so that other sources of potential turnover can perhaps be identified. It is important in the periodic reviews to reexamine, in light of the employee's lengthening experience, the issue of what the company expects of the employee and what the employee expects of the company. That an employee's decision to leave may depend on his evaluation of a new prospect as being much more advantageous than his present job would seem to argue for reminding the employee periodically of the advantages he is enjoying—and realistically can aspire to—with his current employer. This is not an effort to persuade the employee to stay but to ensure that at least part of the decision equation—what he would be giving up—is perceived by him with reasonable accuracy. He may welcome, indeed may seek, the opportunity for a discussion of this matter before he moves to a decision. Since the decision to stay cannot be regarded as a permanent decision, the information-giving process must go on.

ADDRESSING GROUP PROBLEMS

Often a turnover problem is a group problem; turnover may represent the behavior of a number of employees in response to a common set of conditions.

If the turnover rate in a plant is high, it will usually be found that the rate arises largely from a concentration of cases in certain areas of the plant rather than from scattered cases involving isolated individuals.

Focusing the Effort

For efficiency in addressing such a problem, we need to focus our effort. We need to determine, by department and subdepartment and shift and job classification, where the pockets of high turnover exist and to identify the kinds of turnover present. Therefore, we need to start with turnover reports that give us diagnostic leads. And, of course, the reports must be timely, issued at quarterly or shorter intervals, so that we may strike before large damage is done.

A diagnostic report would begin by differentiating between turnover considered generally controllable by the organization (involving quits, resignations, discharges, layoffs for inability to perform job) and turnover beyond organizational control. But in order to home in efficiently on those voluntary terminations of a kind the organization can most confidently expect to do something about, it is useful to go further in the report to concentrate on quits and resignations and to pinpoint areas of high rate—by department, subdepartment, shift, and job classification. Reports providing this information can be readily devised and can be cranked out routinely by data-processing operations available in most organizations of significant size.

It is useful also to know where abnormal numbers of discharges are occurring. But discharges are relatively rare and not therefore an ideal subject for statistical reports. They can be analyzed and confronted as a separate problem involving individual cases. In this realm of necessarily finite endeavors—turnover representing only one of many organizational problems—the practical course is to focus on quits and resignations.

A format for a simplified version of a plant turnover report, showing quits and resignations by department for a particular period, is given in Table 2.

Those departments having disproportionate quits and resignations, more than expected on the basis of workforce size, could be assumed to be the loci of situations giving rise to voluntary turnover. Further analysis (the original report could have a finer breakdown) would identify the pockets of high withdrawal by subdepartments, shifts, and major job classifications or job types. Historical trends could be charted from the periodic reports, and divergences from trend lines could be additional evidence of problem spots.

Of course, this kind of report could be applied to various kinds of turnover. Quits and resignations could be combined if experience indicated little difference in causation. But resignations (involving the giving of notice to leave) are often attributable to personal causes beyond a company's control and unrelated to job conditions. Terminations for sickness and early retirements appear to be clear-cut turnover cases of a personal nature, but the incidences are perhaps worth

Table 2
Turnover Report on Quits and Resignations

	Total Plant	Dept. A	Dept. B	Dept. C
Employees				
Average Number	_____	_____	_____	_____
% of Total		_____	_____	_____
Quits				
Number	_____	_____	_____	_____
% of Total		_____	_____	_____
Rate*	_____	_____	_____	_____
Resignations				
Number	_____	_____	_____	_____
% of Total		_____	_____	_____
Rate**	_____	_____	_____	_____

examining for the presence of work-related factors. These kinds of terminations in certain cases represent a withdrawal from troubling or intolerable job situations.

Of course, it is necessary to move forward from report data, however diagnostic; once we know where the highest incidences of quits and resignations are occurring, we should proceed to find out why.

To probe for specific causes, perhaps the most fruitful procedure is to interview a sufficient sample of employees in the units (subdepartment and shift and especially the job classifications) in which the incidence has been found to be high. An ongoing program of so-called exit interviews can provide useful information on factors influencing voluntary separations, but in many instances the validity of such information has been disappointingly low. And in many cases of quits, it is often difficult to arrange an interview with the departing employee. A more effective procedure, it would appear, is to move into the job classification where the turnover rate is high and to interview current employees, addressing to them such questions as:

1. What is there about this job and working here that might cause employees to leave?

2. A number of employees have left here recently. As you understand it, why did they leave? (Assure respondents you do not seek names or confidential information.)

3. How do you feel about your job and working here?

These questions should serve to elicit information that will separate cases truly under the influence of the organization from those outside its practical control; and in regard to the former, they should point to specific causative factors that the organization and supervisors can address.

In many instances the problems will be found to lie in factors identified in the research studies. But close attention to the local situation, such as suggested above, is in order. A new aspect of one of the "common" factors may be uncovered or a unique factor may be found. In order to arrive at ameliorative actions pertinent to the situation and to avoid a shotgun approach, wasteful of effort and perhaps outside the mark altogether, it is necessary to bring the diagnosis at the end to a narrow precision.

As a procedure preliminary to the interviewing of employees in "pockets" of high turnover, it is advisable to examine the level of performance of employees who have quit or resigned within the report period. If the voluntary leavers are found to be mostly good performers, an extended probing in the interviews is indicated as well as a strong effort at ameliorating critical conditions. Obviously, the cost of turnover in such a case is heavy, and the problem needs to be addressed vigorously.

Information on levels of individual performance is usually available in a production department. If employees are on piece rate, earnings provide a ready index. In many cases a record is also kept on output in day-rate jobs. Quality indices related to individual performance are often available. The investigation should also secure the opinions of supervisors on performance. Some important aspects of performance may be outside the reach of objective measurement. In addition, in the absence of objective measures, subjective supervisory ratings may be the only source of performance evaluation.

Of course, it is advisable to secure the supervisor's opinions concerning the reasons for high turnover itself. Data from interviews with supervisors should be combined with data from employee interviews as a basis for arriving at conclusions concerning causes of high turnover. But, whereas the supervisor is usually an expert witness of job performance, there is a caution to be observed in ascribing validity to his statements on turnover causes. In some cases the supervisor is not in an open communicative relationship with his employees. Moreover, the employee who intends to leave may find it advantageous to keep this intent from the supervisor's notice. Finally, the supervisor himself may be part of the turnover problem, a situation he is not likely to be aware of or to admit if he is.

Example of a Focused Approach

To cite an example from the author's own experience, an investigation involving interviews with current employees and their supervisors of the reasons for voluntary terminations in high-turnover departments and job classifications revealed that some of the "classic" reasons were present but in a unique form:

Job characteristics were indeed a factor, but in terms of the fundamental nature of the job duties, the running conditions, and the variability of conditions.

Pay problems arose, but with specific reference to the relation of pay to types of duties, long learning periods, and nonstandard conditions.

Training was a problem area, but specifically in regard to enabling the naive employee to confront the workload requirements in a progressive way.

And so, on the basis of such information, we were in position to make recommendations germane to the specific problems:

A. Reexamining what could be done economically to remove some of the objectionable features of heavy and dirty jobs or to provide greater satisfactions in such jobs.
B. Making sure that our training efforts provided for:
 1. An adequate and progressive development of skill so that the trainee was moved into the full workload in a measured way and was not faced with the full job demands before he was ready. This objective argues for enough instructional attention early and late in the game and a close follow-up of the trainee's progress. Such action appears to be an essential aspect of any turnover reduction program.
 2. In multitask or multimachine jobs, a continuation or intensification of our efforts to:
  a. Determine whether certain jobs could be so structured as to (i) reduce the number of conflicting demands, or (ii) permit the individual to reach logical breakoff points in a task before responding to a conflicting task—and still preserve efficiency.
  b. Where conflicting demands remained, define more precisely the job organization aspect—the priorities among tasks and the means of making the most efficient use of time.
  c. Teach these organizational aspects well enough to prepare the trainee to tackle a sizable workload on his own before cutting him loose.
 3. A preparation of the trainee to cope with the variable and relatively unpredictable job conditions. Such an effort would require us to go beyond training new employees in job organization to the development and teaching of plans of attack for meeting abnormal conditions.
C. Continuing our efforts to control operating conditions to the extent practical so as to make the jobs more manageable.

D. Searching for more effective means of eliciting the necessary effort from the trainee during the learning period, especially in the piece-rate jobs requiring a long learning period.

4

Addressing Voluntary Turnover: Maximizing Commitment

It is a rather incomplete answer to a high rate of voluntary turnover to chase after employees who are approaching the mill exits, although an effort to intervene in the withdrawal process is indicated. A more positive approach is to concentrate on effecting or improving employee commitment. There is a process here as well as with withdrawal.

A LOOK AT FACTORS IN COMMITMENT

The process toward settled attachment has also come under research scrutiny. As early as midcentury, Rice and his associates, noting the statistical progression of turnover rates over a period of many weeks, came to view the process as comprising three phases through which groups of new employees pass (1950, 359):

1. The period of induction crisis, during which a certain number of casualties results from the first mutual interaction between the engaging company and the entrant group.
2. The period of differential transit, during which those who have survived learn the ways of life of the company and discover how far they have any place in it.
3. The period of settled connection, when those who have survived the first two periods take on the character of quasi-permanent employees.

The key word in the process of settling in, as currently viewed, appears to be "commitment."

The position that commitment is related to job satisfaction is strongly supportable. But the view is not universal, as evident from the study of insurance personnel by Wiener and Vardi (1980); they concluded that the organizational commitment was a "normative" process that may not be associated with job satisfaction, stating that "a loyal, dutiful, and self-sacrificing person may or may not be satisfied with aspects of his work and organization''(95). Moreover, the concept of commitment itself may require distinctions. O'Reilly and Caldwell, in a study of master of business administration graduates (1980), differentiated between attitudinal commitment and behavioral commitment (future tenure intentions), and on this basis they found a different pattern of relationships between commitment and factors involved in job choice. They found that job-choice decisions made on intrinsic factors (intrinsic interest in the job, opportunity for advancement, responsibility provided by the job, own feeling about the job) and for "internal" reasons are likely to be associated positively with feelings of satisfaction and attitudinal commitment, but that salary, an extrinsic factor, was positively related to future tenure intentions and negatively related to job satisfaction (559, 562). The suggestion that future attitudes and tenure may be affected by the way the job choice is made can be of practical value to managers and employment officers.

Although we must acknowledge the presence of employee predispositions and make note of different kinds of commitments, we can safely conclude that satisfied employees are more likely to move to a firm affiliation with a company than dissatisfied employees—and that the commitment, to have meaning for an employer seeking to stabilize his workforce, must appreciably involve tenure.

The importance of upward career mobility in an organization to an employee's commitment was pointed up in a study of employees in two large Southern California savings and loan associations (Scholl 1983). Career line variables such as mobility, opportunity, and size of salary increase were found to have the greatest impact on the "membership" decision. As factors in commitment and stability, these variables, the researcher concluded, should be examined in addition to such considerations as job design, salary, supervisory behavior, and structure of the unit.

Buchanan (1974), using a sample of 279 business and government managers, explored the relative importance of job experiences within the organization in influencing organizational commitment and the issue of how these experiences may vary in importance with time.

He noted the experience or factors identified as relevant to commitment in earlier studies: years of service to the organization, social interaction with peers or superiors in the workplace, job achievement, hierarchical advancement. In his own study, he viewed commitment as "a partisan, affective attachment to the goals and values of an organization, to one's role in relation to goals and values, and to the organization for its own sake, apart from its purely instrumental worth" (533). Methodologically, he measured commitment with an independent series of questionnaire items related to each of three components of commitment: "(a) identification—adoption as one's own the goals and values of the organization, (b) involvement—psychological immersion or absorption in the activities of one's work role, and (c) loyalty—a feeling of affection for and attachment to the organization"(533).

Mowday, Porter, and Steers reviewed a number of definitions of organizational commitment (1982, 20–26). For their purpose they define it as "the relative strength of an individual's identification with and involvement in a particular organization," and they characterize it conceptually by the factors of "(a) a strong belief in and acceptance of the organization's goals and values; (b) a willingness to exert considerable effort on behalf of the organization; and (c) a strong desire to maintain membership in the organization"(27).

Buchanan's research (1974) tested the relationship between experiences of managers who were at three different stages of their careers (first year, two to four years of service, five years or more) and the measure of their commitment. The experiences found to account most heavily for the variance in the commitment scale with each tenure group (542):

Stage 1: group attitudes toward organization, first-year job challenge, loyalty conflicts.

Stage 2: self-image reinforcement, personal importance, first-year job challenge, organizational commitment norms, group attitudes toward organization.

Stage 3: group attitudes toward organization, expectations realization, work commitment norms, fear of failure (negative relationship).

In the discussion of his findings, Buchanan makes a number of insightful observations which could be helpful to organizations in view of the importance to their continuing prosperity, indeed to their survival, of the strong commitment of their managers. As often noted, organizations tend to be concerned primarily with the commitment of new managers and to concentrate their commitment-building activities in the first few months of employment as part of an orientation or induction program. Such efforts may be superficial, indeed, in contrast with the importance of the work group's attitudes and of the initial work assignment— significant factors found by Buchanan. Early attempts at indoctrination may influence the factor of loyalty conflict specified by Buchanan, but he has a cautionary word concerning influence attempts: "Guidance is sought and accepted, but recruits apparently are skeptical of and sensitive to the organization's efforts to influence their attitudes and values. Influence attempts exceeding an individual's threshold of tolerance may well be counterproductive"(543).

But an organization is likely to neglect the matter of the continuing commitment of its managers of longer tenure, particularly in its middle-level managers, on the assumption, apparently, that commitment is somehow assured because they have stayed, although there is usually enough contrary evidence to indicate a need for attention if one would only look for it and appraise it correctly when it is found. Buchanan's research and related discussion of findings are of special value to organizations in that they address the often-neglected issue of the commitment of longer-service managers as well as new managers.

An organization practice popularly associated with the commitment of managers to a company is the movement of managers, by transfer or promotion, from one geographic location to another. Brett (1982) conducted a significant study of the relationship between job transfer mobility and well-being, contrasting a mobile sample of managers transferred within the United States by corporations with three comparison samples of stable managers. The study did not deal with the commitment of managers to the organization, but it may have implications in that regard. Brett's findings certainly throw a new light on the thesis that mobility damages the family's well-being. The aspects of well-being explored by Brett included self, standard of living, family life, marriage, work, and social relationships. She found very few differences between mobile and stable people. Indeed, mobile employees and their wives were found to be more satisfied with their lives, families, and marriages. But mobile employees and their wives were less satisfied with social relationships.

If stable social relationships are important to a family, it may be reluctant to affiliate with a company that frequently reassigns employees from one plant location to another—or has a reputation for arbitrarily or capriciously moving its employees about.

The reputation of a company in various regards is a factor in commitment that has been little touched by research. If a commitment means casting one's lot with a company, the company itself—as it is and as it is perceived by the individual—is an unavoidable part of the equation. A close look at the company is therefore indicated if we are to understand, in its many dimensions, the basis for commitment.

There is a community evaluation at work as well as (and related to) the attitudes of individuals. Some companies are generally regarded in the community as "good" places to work and some are not. The appraisal arises from such considerations as pay levels and benefit plans, but it may have a broader base than monetary rewards, though these are highly compelling. Is there an assurance of security through continuing employment, or does the company have a history of ups and downs involving layoffs and rehirings? Product demand is a germane issue here, but the individual and community are less aware of cyclical sales trends than of the layoffs occasioned by them.

Some companies are recognized as having better working conditions than others (a clean place rather than a dirty place to work, a safe place rather than a hazardous place, a place where employee safety is emphasized rather than minimally provided for). Some companies are regarded as better than others in supplying tools and equipment "to get the job done" and in maintaining and updating the machinery.

And some companies are seen as treating employees with more consideration than others. In the author's experience, job applicants were attracted to one company's mills in preference to another company's mills in situations where pay, benefits, and physical working conditions were equivalent. The preferred company had a reputation for fairness, openness, and considerateness. The other company was regarded as "hard" and arbitrary and unsympathetic to employee complaints and grievances. Much of this attitude derived from the supervisor's manner of dealing with employees, but upper management was also seen as hard driving and somewhat ruthless. In this company, workloads assigned to employees were regarded in the community as unfairly heavy.

Word also gets around in a community concerning the effort a company makes to train its employees.

Certain applicants—probably more in this era than in earlier times—apply ethical standards in approaching a commitment. They are reluctant or unwilling to join an organization whose products or services they consider as harmful or potentially harmful to society. They raise the question: What immediate or ultimate outcome will I be contributing to? And if they regard the outcome— the use of the service and the utilization or consumption of the product—to be morally objectionable, they will seek other employment.

Probably more applicants are influenced by the quality of the product than by its nature and utilization. Is the product (if a consumer item) one I would be proud to have in my home? Is it durable; is it well designed? Is the product one I would take pride in helping to manufacture? Does the company take pains to ensure quality of the product? It was revealing to the author to discover the reaction of management and supervisory applicants to a tour of the company's rug mill. To see and feel the richly designed rugs and carpeting and to watch the fabric emerge from the looms were unmistakable evidences to them of an outstanding product. But the "clincher" was to show the applicants the work of the "burlers" who meticulously sewed in by hand the rare tufts the loom had failed to weave in. Virtually no one could detect the location of the missing tufts, on either the surface or the back of the rug, but the burlers ensured by their minute inspection and skilled needlework that the product was "perfect." Such astounding attention (termed superfluous by many visitors) to quality made a profound impression on the applicants. The common reaction among them was a strong expressed interest in affiliation with a company that took such pains to make the product "right." Even in the absence of direct contact with the product, applicants are likely to be attracted by a company that has a community and/or industry-wide reputation for quality.

A significant part of a company's reputation in the community as good or bad arises from the extent of the company's expression of corporate citizenship. Is the company's contribution strictly economic, related to payrolls and taxes alone? Or does the company contribute as well to civic programs, the cultural life of the community, and the educational opportunities of the people—not only through its encouragement of employee participation but also as a corporate entity through sponsorship, endowments, scholarship grants, direct monetary contributions, etc.? In addition, what is its record in matters of ecology? In pollution control specifically?

Particularly in small towns, the appeal of a company may benefit from the physical presence of its local executives (or corporate executives in headquarter towns) in the community. In the author's experience, a company's store of goodwill in the community diminished when the chief executive officer, who had established residency in the town, had been active in community affairs, and was a familiar figure on Main Street was replaced upon retirement by a manager who commuted to his office and was rarely seen downtown. The company was then perceived as more remote and impersonal and less aware of community problems and less responsive to them.

Without the good opinion of the community, a company will be hard put to inspire commitment among its new employees. It is unlikely to command admiration and loyalty and pride of membership among them if it cannot command public respect.

COMPANY ACTIONS TO FOSTER COMMITMENT

Whatever the basis for taking a job with a company, the appeal may wane as time goes on. If the reputation of the company was a compelling influence, which may well be the case before experience works its effect, the company in the long run may not be perceived as possessing all the favorable characteristics first envisioned. And if the applicant's decision arises from an anticipated major advantage, the actual return may turn out to be less than expected, or not as important to the applicant as he first thought. A dramatic example of this was observed by the author in a town in which a high-paying organization established a plant, competing for employees with a traditional industry that had a significantly lower pay scale. Primarily for the higher pay, a substantial number of skilled mechanics and young supervisors left the established plants and took jobs of lower skill in the new company. Some stayed; pay can powerfully affect tenure. For others disillusionment set in when they weighed the higher pay against the unchallenging work they performed in earning it; these trickled on back to their skilled occupations in the old plants at a lower rate of pay.

One must be wary, of course, of generalizing. The response of an employee to various employment influences is an individual matter, related to the nature of the person and his circumstances. Indeed, strongly favorable beginning predisposition may repel disillusionment and a change of mind no matter what is experienced. One must take individual differences into account. A wise stance is to take whatever beginning steps give hope of resulting in a significant degree of commitment, but to avoid regarding commitment as a permanent state and take additional steps to nourish it as the employment period lengthens.

Early Steps

Management's efforts to foster a commitment should begin early. It is useful in the hiring process to give the prospective employee a realistic preview of the job, emphasizing job content, job conditions, performance requirements, and potential rewards. The process should make clear the connection between what the company expects of the employee and what he can expect of the company—

specifically the contingency between rewards and performance. In addition the company should explain what assistance will be given to the new employee to help him to achieve the performance level that will bring the indicated rewards. A discussion of future prospects is also in order.

The major requirement is realism. The idea is to bring about, in the applicant, as objectively accurate a perception as we can manage. With realistic perceptions of the job, the applicant will have more realistic expectations. And more, he will be in a better position to estimate how well the job fits him and to make a more reasoned decision on whether to accept or reject the job offer. If the hiring procedure involves the applicant, as well as the company, in a decision-making process (and we should encourage his weighing of the pros and cons), we can be better assured of a resolve, at least to himself, that he will make an effort to master the job, that is, to take the route leading to increased involvement.

In order to make a reasoned decision to join the organization, the applicant also needs to know what may lie beyond the immediate job. Again, realism of perception is the objective, so the information the company gives on this point should represent a realistic view of opportunities and a realistic appraisal of what the individual applicant might aspire to. Admittedly, realistic information on career prospects is more difficult to give than a realistic statement concerning the immediate job, but the company should make as straightforward a statement on future possibilities as it can support. A danger lies in overcommitting and raising unreasonable aspirations.

Induction efforts are needed in the case both of new employees who have had experience in other companies and of young applicants who are just entering the labor market. In the first case, the task is to keep the employee's previous experience, particularly if it was unfavorable, from coloring his attitude toward his current employer and to head off the transfer of work habits unacceptable in the new job. He should base his employment decision on a realistic view of characteristics of the new company and the prospective new job (advantages and requirements in performance and conduct). We should help by providing adequate information. Any early commitment that takes shape should arise from an accurate perception and evaluation of the new situation divorced from the employee's previous job experience and the related expectations that tend to persist but are no longer really applicable. A problem among naive applicants is that many of them have unreasonably high expectations. We should try through the use of information to scale down the expectations to realistic levels. But with these young applicants special care must be taken to make clear the concept that rewards are contingent on performance, since the lesson that rewards must be earned may not have been learned by them in their experience. The problem is compounded when unrealistically high expectations are accompanied by low qualifications (despite a relatively high level of formal education). An especially strong training effort is indicated. But developing commitment in this group may take considerable time and patience.

Since a company, in the interest of commitment, is concerned with having its new employees share the values and objectives of the organization, it is useful to inform them concerning those values and objectives, and to do it early.

Companies have not always bothered to give such information openly to new employees, but have tended to rely instead on their general reputation to carry the message. In addition, the framing of a statement on company values and goals is a difficult task. The statement can easily become overblown, filled with pious and virtuous declarations. But a number of companies have recently issued codes of corporate values and objectives. Since they have such a broad application, they cannot be very specific; but they can be meaningful to employees if couched in straightforward language. Again, realism is in order. The new employee is joining a secular enterprise, not a church. And the statement must be capable of demonstration or fulfillment; that is, an employee's experience in the company should confirm the validity of the code.

The aim of the code should not be overtly to indoctrinate but simply to state what the company stands for and make the statement in a way understandable to employees. Acceptance is up to the employee; an attempt to "sell" him is likely to be counterproductive (Zemke 1985).

Specific difficulties are invited if the company code espouses specific managerial tactics or techniques, such as management by objectives and team arrangements (corporate committees, task forces, etc.), which may not have universal application in the organization or the effectiveness of which has not been definitely established by hard evidence. The very nature of a credo is belief, but in the secular enterprise of running a corporation, faith alone will not serve to ensure that a particular tactic will work to the advantage of company and employees.

Again, difficulties can be expected if the code incorporates a somewhat unitary point of view concerning dealings with employees. There is a tendency in recent codes to accept employee-centered approaches involving autonomy, participation, challenging work, individual growth, etc., as the "right" way to proceed. While the Theory Y treatment may be effective in many situations and with many people, it is not always effective; and in unfavorable economic or operational circumstances which threaten the well-being and indeed the survival of the plant—times of crisis or emergency—a more directive approach is indicated. The prospects and consequences of changing situations need to be taken into account in drafting a company code.

In addition, whether the code deals with tactics or underlying points of view, there is always the nibbling doubt that the word has effectually reached all of the first-line supervisors, or that the word truly reflects the supervisors' views and is consistent with lessons they have learned from hard experience, or that if the supervisors really believe, they can act accordingly.

The employees will be more strongly influenced by managerial actions than by words; and they will tend to lose trust in a company whose policies and procedures are not consonant with the articles of the code and whose managers and supervisors do not execute them, even if consonant, in the pledged manner. Especially in a pledge of security of employment, management can easily overreach in practical terms and subject itself to employee charges of hypocrisy.

Management may make the valid point that the code represents goals rather than actuality and that it should be excused if the effort falls short of the objective. But employees are not likely to make these distinctions and may conclude that if it is in writing, it is supposed to exist, now.

Many of the organizational factors influencing withdrawals can have a direct or indirect effect on commitment. And many of the effects can occur or begin early.

Early socialization can influence certain new employees to stay on if the association with other employees is a satisfying experience. But the expectation that early socialization will result in acceptance of organizational objectives and a related high level of employee performance may be misguided. The new employee is likely to adopt the values and attitudes of the work group, and these must be consistent with organizational goals and values if the organization is to benefit. In such case, the commitment to the group may be, in practical terms, a commitment to the organization. But negative attitudes of work groups can stand in the way of the development of organizational commitment on the part of new group members.

It is not uncommon to find work groups whose work standards are low, as evidenced by slovenly work and poor output, and whose attitude toward management and the company is reflected in cynical and disrespectful comments which exceed the bounds of good-natured critical banter found in any group. The author has observed numerous examples of the early disillusionment of new employees arising from their exposure to the negative attitudes of the work group they were first placed with. It is useful for a company, in view of social influences on new employees, to be aware of employee attitudes and work behavior and, if there is a choice, to introduce new employees into high-performance groups which, in terms of work behavior at least, display a commitment to the company objectives of efficiency and quality. But such placement carries with it the responsibility for giving the kind of training to the newcomer that will permit him to acquire a high level of skill in reasonable time and to develop high standards of performance so that he can become a fully functioning and accepted member of the group.

Pay (along with the employee's perception of it) can be a strong influence on employee performance, especially if it is clearly contingent on performance. It can be a major source of satisfaction and a major deterrent to turnover. There is evidence that the level of pay as a basis of job choice decision can influence tenure intentions, which may be considered as one kind of commitment (O'Reilly and Caldwell 1980).

The appeal of the early assignment and its challenge to the new employee are likely to affect tenure intentions and inclinations toward commitment. Positive attitudes can arise from doing something considered personally worthwhile on the job and from contributing significantly to the operation in which the employee is first involved.

Early experience of some degree of performance success in the first job is apparently needed; evidence of early achievement may be required to keep the employee's uneasy and uncertain effort alive in the introductory or probationary period. Of course, an induction program can help the employee adjust to job demands, other employees, and the job environment at large; checklists of information and induction schedules should be carried out in the context of a continuing effort to inform the employee in matters that concern him and a continuing effort to give information on performance and to update the issue of employee expectations and company expectations. And if the employee is given off-the-job preliminary "orientation" before job assignment, the period should not be prolonged so as to delay unduly the employee's opportunity to engage in useful work and to experience success in it.

The key activity of a company in the new employee's achievement of early performance successes is training. Simple gestures will not serve in a matter so crucial to commitment. Adequate attention, adequate instruction based on solid learning principles, and competent instructors are all needed. And a skillful use of feedback is an essential ingredient. For the purpose of aiding early learning, feedback should relate to minute aspects of job task execution with reference to the trainee's good and poor responses. Specificity and immediacy enhance the value of feedback; and the competency of the giver of feedback (supervisor or instructor) and the respect in which he is held will influence the acceptability of the feedback. And the more positive the feedback, the better. This kind of feedback is part and parcel of the learning process early in the game. The burden of providing the feedback may be shifted to the trainee himself as skill develops, but he needs our strong help at the beginning.

Trainees appear to invite and accept learning-targeted feedback and to see it as helpful to the development of job skill. (Later, when feedback takes the form of a general evaluation of job performance, acceptability may become more of a problem.) But neither feedback nor any other single training technique in itself can be assumed to influence commitment. It is reasonable to expect, however, that the sort of training that launches a trainee toward genuine skill and gives evidence of effecting such development is ripe ground for commitment to grow in.

The supervisor, of course, is an influence from the beginning since he is the agent or director of the early activities involving the newcomer—the assigning, inducting, training, giving of feedback, reinforcing, etc. In addition, he is the embodiment of the organization, particularly in the early stages of an employee's period of service. Whatever he does adds up to an early perception of him on the part of the employee which colors the attitude toward the organization. The supervisor should show a concern for the employee from the very start, but a largely employee-centered approach at the beginning is hardly indicated. The naive employee needs to be taken by the hand. A rather directive approach that structures employee expectations—that will "maintain role differentiation and let followers know what to expect" (Stogdill 1974, 419)—would appear to be a highly pertinent kind of supervisory behavior early in the new employee's employment period.

In order for the supervisor to gain the respect of newcomers, job competency appears to be a requirement. Incompetent supervisors can blunt a new employee's movement toward organizational commitment.

Since the supervisor may serve as an exemplar for new employees and his attitude toward the company may rub off on them, it is important that the supervisor himself give evidences of commitment. In this connection it is useful to keep in mind the characteristics of leaders of high-performing systems, as identified by Vaill (1982): They put in extraordinary amounts of time, have very strong feelings about attainment of the system's purposes, and focus on key issues.

Fairness and objectivity in the supervisor's evaluation of the new employee's job performance are of great concern to new employees in the probationary period when job rights are at issue. It is also possible that the explanation for the employee's success or failure in the early employment period can affect his tenure decisions. A recent study of hotel room attendants indicated that attributing early performance to luck leads to early turnover (Parsons, Herold, and Leatherwood 1985). It is suggested that supervisors, in giving early feedback, encourage employees to attribute poor performance to effort and successful performance to ability and effort. The supervisor who fails to dispel the idea of luck as an explanation may lose the trust of the employee and may not provide the employee with enough feeling of achievement to ensure his persistence. Of course, the supervisor should take care that, in the interest of retaining the employee, he does not make false attributions.

If poor early performance is correctly attributable to adverse working conditions that make the job unmanageable despite the new employee's effort and satisfactory learning progress, all organizational measures to induce commitment are likely to be fruitless. As an absolute requirement, the job must be "runable" to begin with.

Sustaining the Commitment

Experience—in addition to research findings—gives ample evidence of difficulties in sustaining or strengthening commitment once the employee is through the early period of his employment. But something can be done.

As in the beginning, individual differences, particularly in regard to motivation, must be taken into account as a crucial factor in the sustaining of commitment. For some, the beginning commitment is so strong that it is relatively unshakable, even by adverse experience in the job. For others, the commitment is too tenuous to withstand the first threat of disappointment. But for probably the majority of new employees, there is a sufficient commitment to hold them in place for at least a short period of time, and the commitment is subject to strengthening or weakening on the basis of progressive experience on the job. The typical intent is to "have a go at it" and to see what develops.

The employment decision, as indicated, is likely to be the result of a sizing up of the advantages the company has to offer the applicant in his current circumstances as he perceives them. Another ingredient in the decision may be the reputation of the company, again as the applicant perceives it. An employee is usually sufficiently motivated to stick around long enough to find out if his expectations are confirmed or to look for signs of imminent realization. An organization may have time, therefore, to firm up the employee's incipient commitment.

The continuation of training is an obvious step. It is through the acquisition of job skill that many of the prospective rewards—greater pay, job tenure, promotional opportunities, etc.—become available to the employee. Training, if well done, can bring such rewards quickly within the employee's grasp. Poor training, in contrast, can delay the rewards beyond the patience of the employee or his willingness to endure.

In addition, the acquisition of skill itself is an intrinsic reward of value to most employees.

The strengthening of the commitment, however, may depend on how the training is carried out. It is primarily up to our training to hold the employee to the learning task until the rewards accompanying competency are realizable and a sustainable skill emerges. But the process itself can aid or hinder commitment. It is important for the trainee to experience reinforcement of progressively higher achievements so that the motivation is sustained. It is important, in the same regard, that he experience successes along the way. With reinforcement consistently contingent on improving performance and with experiences of success, the employee has a good chance of gaining confidence in facing later challenges to learning and, if the modeling is skillful and observant of high standards of performance, of acquiring high standards as a requirement for his ultimate self-reinforcement later on. In addition, the training should address itself to the progressive stages of skill development and to the specific learning difficulties experienced by the individual employee. This kind of training process can be expected to influence commitment favorably. And, as indicated, the rewards it brings can confirm early expectations—an apparently indispensable factor in commitment.

Feedback after the training period will be concerned primarily with evaluations of total job performance and should occur at periodic intervals so spaced as not to lose the effect of relative immediacy. The difficulties of performance appraisals have been exhaustively documented in the literature. A major consideration, of significance in commitment, is the acceptability of the evaluation in terms of the information given and the source of the information. In the first instance the issues are the validity of the job criteria and related measures of performance (are they true indices of job performance?), the validity and adequacy of the data on the employee's performance (do the data truly represent what he has done in the significant aspects of the job?), and the fairness of the appraiser's conclusions. The appraiser serving as the source of the evaluation, the immediate supervisor in most instances, should be considered expert and have the respect of employees if his feedback is to find acceptability.

The importance of career development to commitment should serve to move the appraisal process in the direction of (1) diagnosing performance difficulties in the current job and exploring means of improvement so that the employee is helped maximally to master the job and (2) reviewing anew the discussion of future prospects and what they are contingent upon.

Essential to an employee's continuing opportunity for effective performance on the job are satisfactory running conditions (involving tools, equipment, mechanical condition of the machinery, control of predictable adverse job situations, ambient conditions, nonconflicting tasks or job requirements, minimum of interference, etc.). Job enrichment may be a worthy objective of management, but management's more basic responsibility is to keep the job performable.

Enriched jobs can reduce turnover in some cases (McEvoy and Cascio 1985), but it must be recognized that these do not have the same appeal to all employees. The larger issue is the advisability of redesigning jobs on the basis of a hypothetical model for maximizing performance and satisfaction. It is commonly hypothesized that job characteristics such as skill variety, autonomy and participative opportunities can lead to greater work motivation and higher performance levels. Such outcomes apparently can be expected from employees who seek growth and control. And a company which restructures jobs in this way may benefit from a sense of commitment on the part of such employees. It is difficult to withhold some measure of loyalty from a company which provides powerful intrinsic rewards (or the possibility for them) of value to the particular individual.

Job enrichment, it may be posited, would have greater effect if the enrichment were done participatively. A recent study casts doubt on this hypothesis. With a sample of 76 desk receptionists, employee participation was not found to enhance the effects of enriched work (Griffeth 1985). Both appeared to affect turnover in the study group. But there were differences in other effects: Job enrichment resulted in improved scores on four of the six personal outcome measures (related to growth satisfaction and overall general satisfaction), participation on one. And employee participation in the enrichment process did not make enriched work more effective.

In the interpretation of the findings in this study, the admitted weakness of the participative "manipulation" used by the researcher needs to be taken into account. The intervention was a 90-minute meeting with employees for discussion of ways to enrich the job. Its ineffectiveness as a moderator raises the question: Do results from participation depend on the strength of the participation? In what (and how many) contexts? How much? How executed? At the least, varying degrees of participation should be more closely examined for relationships with variations in results.

Beyond the employee's beginning experience, some of the same factors— work group attitudes and job challenge, for example—continue apparently to work their influence on commitment. And other aspects of experience come into play—perhaps "self-image reinforcement" and "expectation realization," as suggested by Buchanan's study (1974). What will most strongly influence an employee as job service lengthens is largely an individual matter, but it is a matter that can be examined periodically. A means at the disposal of most organizations is an attitude survey which can probe such questions as: How do you feel about working on this job? In this department (or operation)? In this company? Such surveys can serve as a repeated monitoring device and are particularly useful in identifying problems of possible harm to commitment that are common to a number of employees. Insights into the attitudes of individuals can be further gained in the periodic performance reviews.

Noting the research indications that higher reported levels of commitment are likely to be associated with increasing length of service in an organization, Mowday, Porter, and Steers (1982, 65–66) suggest the following explanations, abridged here:

1. That longer tenure is likely to result in more desirable positions for the employee in terms of challenging job assignments, autonomy, and extrinsic rewards.

2. That the employee's increasing investment in time and energy as length of service increases makes it difficult for him to leave the organization.

3. That increasing length of service brings increasing social involvement in the organization and community.

4. That increasing tenure may decrease the employee's job mobility in regard to his specialized skill (of limited utility elsewhere) and his age.

5. That increasingly positive attitudes toward the organization may occur with lengthening service as the employee's way of rationalizing the sacrifice of other important life goals.

An employee's extension of his tenure with an organization may be explained by these factors, but they are not altogether convincing as explanations of increasing commitment if commitment involves more than tenure. Investment of time and effort, justification for forgoing other goals, and development of non-transferable job skills may serve to tie an employee to an organization but appear to have too negative a connotation to ensure an approving and supporting attitude toward the organization. In some cases of long tenure, the employee hangs on somewhat resignedly and does not come to a peaceful resolution of his doubt about "whether it was all worthwhile." Indeed, he may come to blame the organization for his supposed lost opportunities.

It would appear that something positive must occur as job service lengthens, such as gaining a coveted job or valued extrinsic rewards (the first item listed above), to ensure that the employee identifies himself with the organization and gives his loyalty to it. Commitment, so defined, is more likely to occur if the employee perceives the organization or its agents to be instrumental in the advantageous happenings or circumstances. Obviously, passage of time in itself cannot be depended upon to foster commitment. And the degree to which the employee reconciles himself to his situation is not always a dependable measure of commitment. The organization should be engaged in actions, such as those discussed in this chapter, that appear to have the potential, at least, of increasing commitment as job service increases.

Affiliation with athletic teams or other public groups associated with or sponsored by the organization is a potential source of commitment that has not been adequately explored. Although we have tended to deride company-sponsored athletic teams—and justifiably so—as having insignificant effect on job performance, we have failed to consider the possible effect on company loyalty. This effect is likely to be enhanced if the team identified with the department or plant or company is a winner. The loyalty to companies among team members and fans evident in industrial athletic leagues is often an impressive phenomenon. It is also apparent that the strongest feelings are generated by teams genuinely manned by regular employees rather than by "ringers" hired specifically for their athletic prowess.

One is led to wonder whether commitment can be enhanced by "winning" work teams operating within the organization. The author recalls from his youthful job experience the high regard in which the "top" blow shop was held throughout the glass plant. It produced the best ware and the most ware of all the shops in the factory and in the glass-manufacturing community at large. It was the champion and proudly claimed as "ours" by all employees in the plant. It was easy to feel committed to a company which somehow—perhaps by mere chance—produced this exceptional work team.

Perhaps in high-performance work units lies one of the keys to company commitment. Pride of membership develops in such units. We may not be warranted in assuming that such pride will be generalized, but we can hypothesize that the group members themselves are appreciatively aware of the company which provides them with the setting for working their wonders.

IDENTIFYING WITH COMPANY VALUES AND GOALS

The total effect of all of the factors discussed to this point may or may not add up to commitment. A necessary ingredient—indeed, the heart of commitment—is the individual's belief in and acceptance of the values and objectives of the organization. To enhance an individual's identification with company goals and values (a process referred to as "internalization"), several means have been hypothesized: "a clear specification of the rationale of organizational goals and values, sharing the rewards of organizational goal attainment, and involvement in goals processes''(Mobley 1982, 74).

In the process of identification, the employee is presumed to take responsibility not only for his own performance alone but for organizational performance. As part of a model of the determinants of organizational motivation, Lawler (1985, 14) hypothesizes that people can be led to feel responsible for organizational performance through such organizational design features as economic education, egalitarian perquisites, the existence of a flat and lean organization structure, various participative structures (such as work councils), and self-managing teams. Such design features will contribute to a felt sense of responsibility for organizational performance, it is supposed, because ''they create conditions where the individual can actually influence the direction an organization takes and its performance level''(14).

The idea is that employees will be motivated to organizational performance when they perceive valued rewards associated with organizational performance. Intrinsic rewards, it is posited, will be tied to organizational performance when employees feel responsible for that performance (through means stated above) and when they also have knowledge of organizational performance and it is meaningful to them. Extrinsic rewards, it is hypothesized, will be seen as tied to organizational performance when employees ''understand a pay system which actually rewards them for increases in organizational performance and when they have knowledge of organizational performance''(Lawler 1985, 13). A design feature related to extrinsic rewards is a participative gain-sharing plan.

In this manner, through intrinsic and extrinsic rewards, it is hypothesized that motivation for organizational performance can occur. But it is recognized that not everyone values the indicated rewards equally. The individual who experiences intrinsic satisfaction is likely to value personal growth, competence, and the use of his abilities, a characteristic more typical of highly educated people than lesser educated.

If one accepts on faith the participative model of organizational motivation or sees it as the wave of the future (made inevitable by higher educational levels in the population and the advances in technology), this paradigm will make eminent sense. But if one seeks to base his view of the participative approach to organizational performance on hard evidence of effectiveness in the here and now, one must pause to examine what participation and related structural designs can realistically be expected to achieve.

Leadership studies do not justify unqualified support of participative management. Some directive approaches are needed for employee satisfaction and productivity. Goal setting can apparently stand as an effective tool without participation of the employee in this process (Latham and Marshall 1982). And perhaps the same can be said for job enrichment (Griffeth 1985). The situation and the individual need to be appropriate for the participative approach.

In addition, managers and employees may not conceive of participation in the same way, and the effects of the manager's supposedly participative actions may be correspondingly unpredictable. We tend to consider participation in terms of what the manager intends rather than what the employee experiences. A study of participative decision making involving 264 employees of a large social service organization (Harrison 1985) indicated that, for the subordinate, the quality and quantity of the communication with the superior were important characteristics of the ''participative environment''; the results suggested that ''superiors enacting appropriate communication behaviors may be defined as participative by subordinates regardless of their stated intent. The opposite may also be true: superiors not enacting these behaviors may not be defined by subordinates as participative regardless of their intent''(113).

Assuming that we can define participation (and the subordinate's role in it), how do we teach it? Obviously, we must teach interpersonal skills to the managers and supervisors, an art in which few prospective mentors within or outside the organization are genuinely adept. And restructuring the organization to permit participation does not guarantee it will occur, and certainly not that it will be effective.

A basic question remains: Can commitment be made to occur in bureaucratic organizations? It has certainly occurred in the past in many instances, although the tales of disaffection have tended to capture the attention of organization scholars. It is conceivable that an employee could feel responsible for organizational performance without participative and autonomous structures and the other related design features purporting to result in high involvement. Might it occur on the basis of the employee's knowledge of organizational results and of his contribution to them?

What is really necessary to tie individual performance to organizational performance? The prospect of work groups or teams working cooperatively and harmoniously to produce organizational results and sharing in the resultant gains is an appealing one. But there are inherent difficulties which are obvious to industrial practitioners. To begin with, the manufacturing processes (and products) by their very nature may not lend themselves readily to group performance. To restructure the processes to permit a cooperative team attack may be excessively costly if not an unrealistic project altogether. In addition, the problem of assigning tasks to group members, in a situation where job boundaries can be loosened, may not be satisfactorily solved by ''self-management'' within the group. Clarification of roles is important for employee performance and satisfaction alike, even when the role is to be a temporary one, and a somewhat directive hand is useful. Finally, the requirement of equity in the sharing of gains from the group endeavor is hard to achieve and maintain, whatever the process of deciding who gets what.

To assume that practical operational problems can be best solved by participative processes and that the group members will be happy with the solutions is naive and an invitation to disillusionment. It is hard to accept this hypothesis, except in a tempered way, because group outcomes and the related rewards, for the essential purposes of learning, feedback, and reinforcement, must somehow be associated with individual performance. Relative individual contributions to the outcomes must be clear. And extrinsic rewards—in terms of sharing gains— should be reflective of the individual's contributions and contingent on them.

In many cases we can establish structural designs and contrive administrative arrangements to provide the best milieu for the success of participative management, but the acceptability of the approach by the workforce is not ensured. Acceptability is an unrealistic hope if we attempt to construct an egalitarian system in which distinctions among individual inputs and individual rewards are largely eliminated.

There is a dilemma involved in the size of the work group and the measure of performance or outcome associated with the group. The larger the group, the more significant its performance outcome to organizational outcome at large. But the larger the group, the less significant the role of group members. Obviously, the total workforce of a plant of substantial size represents too large a number to comprise a team. The same is true of most factory departments and subdepartments. The members, to make up a team, should work jointly—with some division of labor—to produce a product or advance a manufacturing process. Obviously, a half-dozen machine tenders performing the same operation side by side do not represent a work team. And some common and valid measure of group accomplishment must be available or capable of being devised. In practical terms, teams are most appropriately established at cost centers—points in the manufacturing process for which standard costs can be established, including labor costs, and actual costs and efficiency rates calculated. These groups are likely to be relatively small in size, and the performance outcomes from such a group a relatively small factor in the outcome of larger organizational units such as the department or the plant.

The problem of organizational commitment through the group approach is complex. In a situation where work teams are widely employed, loyalty to the individual team (and a sense of responsibility for its performance) would appear to be the first manifestation of commitment. In plants that are not group oriented, group loyalties do develop, but direct and individual attachment to the organizational entity would appear to be more plausible.

Those who propose that the internalizing of company values and goals can be achieved through the use of participative work groups can find a convenient model in the Japanese system of management and specifically in the Japanese quality circles. But one must examine the Japanese approach critically before concluding that it will work with American employees. Ensuring that work groups will accept company goals as consistent with their own interests and will work cooperatively to achieve those goals represents more of a problem in the United States than in Japan.

Organizational commitment is high among Japanese workers. This commitment is an expression of (may indeed be considered synonymous with) the Japanese worker's heavy dependence on the organization. There are reasons for this dependence, as Cole (1979, 243–250) points out:

Lack of alternate options for satisfying needs (and related factors such as the structuring of work relations to focus on group accomplishment; the dependence, apparently rooted in the family social pattern, of the work group on the foreman; relative inadequacy of governmental programs for solution of life problems).

Relative weakness in the capacity of workers to organize in opposition to employers.

Japanese heritage of values, ideology, and practices.

Cole suggests, however, that dependency per se is not adequate "for an internalization of organizational goals to take place so that the individual identifies his personal success with organizational success"; and he speculates on additional means (250). Employer dependability (in providing rewards and contributing to the solution of life problems) and employee participation would seem to be instrumental in the process of "internalization." A problem that lies ahead, however, is whether Japanese managers, while expanding the scope of employee participation to strengthen worker commitment to organizational goals, can confine participation to limited production-related decisions and avoid a threat to managerial prerogatives.

It is obvious that duplicates of the major factors associated with organizational commitment among Japanese workers are not found in the United States. There are more alternative means for satisfying needs here; worker organizations wield more power, and there is a decidedly different heritage (there are many heritages, in fact) of values and ideology. A basic point of difference is that American workers do not seek life fulfillment through work to the same degree as the Japanese.

Consequently we must search for our own means of integrating the goals of the work group with those of the organization. This issue may boil down to a consideration of what makes work groups cohesive and productive. Among the indications from research studies of American groups are a number which bear on this issue (Stogdill 1974).

In regard to performance,

Role structure, including differentiation of roles, is required in order for a group to engage in effective task performance (246).

Group performance suffers if the rate of turnover, both in leadership and in membership, is high (246).

Groups tend to accept as leader the member showing abilities and characteristics that facilitate the accomplishment of the group task (412).

"The greater a member's responsibility for goal attainment, the stronger his commitment to the goals" (270). Leaders show more concern than followers for group success, exhibit stonger commitment to the group goal, and work harder for group success than followers (270, 271).

In regard to cohesiveness,

"The greater the differentiation of function, the greater the interdependence and unity of the group . . . " (243).

"Groups develop norms that define appropriate conduct of members," and they bring pressure for conformance on those who deviate; the more cohesive the group, the greater the pressure for conformity it exerts (270).

Acceptance of a leader by the group is increased "if he identifies himself with the membership group rather than with external reference groups"; however, if the leader in a structured hierarchy identifies with superiors in the organization, he tends to be rated more effective (270).

Cohesiveness can obviously work either in a company's interests or against it, depending on the extent to which the group's goals coincide with company goals. A leader in a truly cohesive group apparently serves both as a true leader, for accomplishment of group goals, and as a "social" leader, for maintenance of the group. An industrial supervisor can serve in such a dual role if he accepts group norms and values and if the group's performance goals agree with the company's. It is a precarious position to function in.

As a practical course, he makes an effort to elicit good task performance from the group without fragmenting it. He is not consciously concerned with the process of "internalizing" company goals; he makes the assumption that company goals are accepted if employee performance is "good" according to company criteria. Fortunately, there are indications from leadership studies that he can take certain kinds of actions that will have positive effects on both productivity and cohesiveness. Stogdill's conclusion warrants emphasis at this point: The leadership behavior of structuring employee expectations is consistently related in a positive way to productivity and cohesiveness (as well as follower satisfaction) (1974, 419).

A supervisor can be assured of good performance and evidences of commitment from a work group that has a favorable attitude toward the company and is responsible and cohesive. But if, on the basis of these characteristics, he relies on the group for operational decisions, he must be wary of the group's possible escalation of its "commitment" to a course of action that is failing. Responsibility felt by the members for the decision and the very cohesiveness of the group may be at the base of the problem (Bazerman, Giuliano, and Appelman 1984). Group members tend to feel committed to the group and to the group's decision and so may decide to push forward on the same tack and make further investment in the nonproductive action. (This same tendency toward escalation may be found in individuals responsible for decisions.)

In attempting to reduce the escalation of poor group decisions, the supervisor should be careful not to diminish the cohesiveness of the group. An advisable course is to train the group in decision making and specifically in evaluating the relevancy of past outcomes to future decisions.

Other factors will be at play, to be sure, but perhaps one of the major clues to eliciting the commitment of the work group to organizational goals is the structuring behavior of the supervisor. He may well permit participation in order to increase employee cohesiveness and satisfaction, but the expectation that increased productivity will then ensue is not well founded; we can be more confident of such outcome if the supervisor is structuring in regard to employee roles and expectations. In the process, cohesiveness need not suffer.

An effective work team in a factory simply cannot be an undifferentiated mass of people under the loose commission to apply the training they have commonly received. The foreman will need to employ structuring skills as well as participative skills in order to lead his group constructively toward operational objectives of value to the organization. Indeed, his organizational task will require more than structuring in terms of employee roles and expectations; he will have to mold into a coordinate whole a group of disparate individuals—dependent and independent people, high achievers and low, high interactors and low, high aspirants and low (and those at other points on these scales of characteristics), people of varying abilities and backgrounds, those who seek fulfillment in their work and those who seek it elsewhere.

An experienced foreman in a U. S. factory is likely to be adept at coordination in the sense of scheduling and synchronizing the output from individually performed jobs. Coordination of the activities and efforts of employees engaged jointly in carrying out a task or assignment is a somewhat different function with which many foremen are relatively unfamiliar. They could therefore benefit from training in group processes, training of a kind usually referred to as team building. Unfortunately, training in this activity, as in participative practices, is a venture into performance aspects in which trainers are least proficient.

Modeling and giving feedback and reinforcement may indirectly assist the group members to "internalize" company goals in the sense of assisting them to acquire and observe high standards of performance based on the organization's criteria. These are activities a foreman is likely to be familiar with, but a major requisite for effectiveness in this role is competency. Even when group and company goals coincide, a foreman is not likely to be accepted genuinely as a leader if he is incapable of contributing significantly to the attainment of the goals. Nor is he likely to be perceived as effective by his employees if he has little or no clout with his superiors.

The presence of group attitudes in Buchanan's findings (1974), cited earlier, further confirms what we already know from numerous studies and experience in various contexts and with various populations about the effects of group attitudes on individuals. What is pertinent here is the prospect, supported by evidence in the Buchanan study, that group attitudes can be instrumental in the individual's identifying with company goals. The observance of high performance norms among other employees can help elicit from the new employee a high level of performance (and help the incorporation of high standards by him) conducive to the realization of company goals. Whether identification with company goals is consciously experienced or not by the employee, high performance of benefit to both the employee and the company can ensue; group conformity will help ensure it if the group's goals are consistent with the company's. But we are also aware that social pressure from disaffected employees can be a negative influence detrimental to the individual's performance and to whatever organizational commitment it may represent.

Social pressures as a means of committing new employees to a company's productivity goals would appear to be useful primarily in already established high-performance units.

Focusing on the Individual Worker

Amidst our concern for group identification with company goals, we should recognize that "internalization" is basically an individual matter with American workers.

What has been produced in America is a heterogeneous working population whose diversity and complexity expose as naive and foolish our neat categorizations and definitions, especially those emanating from our own personal system of values. Who can proclaim the American work ethic (or, more accurately, work ethics)? Who can predict, with confidence, that American workers will march in lock step to management's drum in exchange for a bit of participation? Or plunge unreservedly into a group venture to gain recognition for the group?

The best answer we can give is that some will and some will not, which leads to the larger question: How should we proceed in such an uncertain venture? Our manner should be modest, of course, but there are a few proposals that appear to be useful in the effort to elicit the commitment of American workers.

Perhaps the most effective means for ensuring identity of interests lies in providing to employees rewards of value to them individually for the kind of performance of value to the company. This endeavor, in view of the differences in the motivational makeup of individual employees, would require that a wide range of rewards be made available—that rewards, in short, be maximized so that each employee could find rewards of enough value to him to elicit from him, contingently, correspondingly valuable services to the company. Group incentives and rewards can be helpful in group activities, but the differences in motivational pattern among American workers will inevitably necessitate rewards of considerable variety, some of them monetary, that are geared in significant degree to individual performance.

It should be noted that most of the factors identified by Buchanan (1974) as being related to commitment—notably initial job challenge, self-image, personal importance, and realization of expectations—appear to have a heavy personal and individual reference.

While American managers should take account of group influence as an important element in the internalization process, the major appeal of company goals to the independently oriented American workers would seem to lie in the employees' perception of the degree to which the goals serve their individual interests. We should stress, therefore, the broad use of rewards to meet individual needs under the assumption, amply justified, we believe, that the individual American is the key to the identity of company and employee goals in the United States.

An accompanying requirement would be a variety of jobs differentiated by nature of tasks, skill level, and mode of performance (whether performed individually or jointly). We should avoid establishing jobs on the basis of minute distinctions but should take care to provide enough separate jobs to permit the utilization in significant degree (there are practical limits) of the talents and interests of individual employees. We must continue to recognize individual differences. If there is one fact American psychologists have established beyond question, it is the fact that individuals differ in aptitudes, abilities, interests, and temperament. The origin of individual differences is under dispute, to be sure; the geneticists and environmentalists will be debating this issue indefinitely. But the presence of individual differences is indisputable—and should be a pervasive influence on our personnel policies and practices. A major concern of psychologists historically has been the measurement of individual differences. And a major concern of industrial psychologists has been to attempt to match employees to job requirements through measurement of employee characteristics. It would be foolish indeed to abandon job distinctions and abolish the bell-shaped curve in order to emulate the Japanese. Differential placement in terms of beginning job assignments and promotions would still appear to be the way to proceed befitting the American situation, although the enlarging of some jobs to provide the desired variety in job choices would seem to be the indicated course in many American companies. In addition, whatever the structure of the job, it should be so defined as to make clear to the employee what is expected of him.

In ultimate sense, commitment is arguably to self. An employee is concerned with gaining satisfactions or rewards of importance to him. If a company provides the setting and conditions for his realization of these desired advantages, commitment to the company is more likely to occur, especially if the company vigorously executes the organizational means (training as the prime example) for employee attainment of rewards.

Personal experience would suggest to us, however, that some rewards are more important than others in keeping the employee strongly and positively involved in his work role. For many employees, the rewards that have the most powerful influence on commitment, it can be hypothesized, are those that augment pride and self-esteem—those specifically associated with achievement, skill, and performance successes. These experiences carry intrinsic satisfaction and can increase self-esteem, but pride would demand that they also result in recognition and commensurate compensation.

The organization, in its instrumental role in making such rewards possible, can elicit commitment. But one element of Buchanan's definition of commitment (1974, 533) refers to an employee's attachment to the organization "for its own sake, apart from its purely instrumental worth." This attachment is probably most accurately designated, as Buchanan indeed labeled it, as loyalty.

One might conjecture that in order to command loyalty an organization would have to have exemplary characteristics and a record of achievement that could endow an employee with a sense of pride in membership independent of (or perhaps supplementary to) any advantages he might gain through membership.

5

Social Pressures for Job Maintenance

There is another consideration in addition to the issue of the cost to companies and employees that appears to dictate enhanced efforts to stabilize a workforce. Maintenance of employment is receiving increased attention as a social issue. Support is growing among legislators, unions, communities, and religious leaders for job maintenance. The employment-at-will doctrine is coming under closer scrutiny, and means are being sought to regulate plant closings and mass layoffs and to cushion their effects on employees. The movement has not progressed very far in regard to some issues, but there are stirrings.

EMPLOYMENT-AT-WILL

Consider the basic matter of an employer's right to discharge employees. The common law doctrine of employment-at-will, which has supplied a legal underpinning for discharges over the years, still provides employers with a substantial legal basis for discharging employees; but exceptions are now being recognized in many states (Steiber 1984). A major exception is that an employer may not fire an employee for reasons contravening fundamental principles of public policy—for the employee's refusal to commit an unlawful act, or his performance of important public obligations, or his exercise of a statutory right. Other exceptions involve (1) an implied promise of job tenure (in employee handbooks, personnel manuals, or statements made in employment interviews) for employees who perform satisfactorily and (2) an obligation (required in a few states) that the employer deal fairly and in good faith with the employee.

The courts have tended to take a rather narrow view of the exceptions, although the judiciary has been increasingly active in modifying the terminable-at-will employment contract especially in the case of unorganized workers, apparently in recognition of their lesser protection against unjust discharge (Youngblood and Tidwell 1981, 33).

A remedy against arbitrary discharge is a union collective bargaining agreement containing a grievance and arbitration procedure. Where a union is absent, action by the employer to provide due process, including impartial arbitration, can provide a remedy, although this remedy depends on the volition of the employer.

A legal remedy remains: the explicit striking down of the employment-at-will doctrine by state legislatures. There have been recent legislative proposals to protect employees against unjust discharge, notably in Michigan and California (Steiber 1985). A Michigan bill, introduced in 1983, would provide for notification to an employee of reasons for discharge, mediation by the Michigan Employment Relations Commission, and the employee's right of appeal to final and binding arbitration if mediation fails. The bill would exempt employers who had grievance procedures that provided for impartial final and binding arbitration. The original California bill, introduced in 1984 (two additional bills were introduced in 1985), contained many provisions similar to those in the Michigan legislation.

Speculating on the future, St. Antoine (1985) indeed sees legislative action as the next recourse. He states, "The courts, at least in the more progressive states, have gone as far with unjust discharge actions as they are going to go. They will entertain suits alleging serious violations of accepted public policy. They will hold employers to their unretracted word not to fire except for good reason. But ordinarily they will not impose an affirmative obligation on employers to prove just cause to support a discharge. They will not subject nonunion firms, as a matter of common law, to the same requirement exacted contractually from nearly every employer party to a collective bargaining agreement. The next move is therefore up to the legislatures"(556).

Opposition comes understandably from employers who feel they are giving up a right. And the union reaction tends to be ambivalent (556), again understandably, because unions are concerned about weakening a "drawing card"—the remedy they provide through collective bargaining agreements.

Although the traditional right of an employer to terminate the employment of workers is still largely in place and opposition to restraints is heavy, one can expect that the issue will receive increasing attention in the state legislatures.

A reportedly effective approach to resolving disputes over discharges has been tried in South Carolina by the Division of Labor Management Services of the state Department of Labor (Bierman, Ullman, and Youngblood 1985). Representatives of this agency serve as mediators (conciliators) in a process which, in contrast to arbitration, is quick, inexpensive, and less formal and legalistic.

LAYOFFS AND PLANT CLOSINGS

In regard to layoffs of employees, although managements in the United States still have the power and legal sanction to resort to layoffs in confronting economic hardships and in making technological changes for improvement of efficiency, mass layoffs in such circumstances are apparently encountering increasing challenges from workers, their representatives, and the government (Survey in *Management Review* 1982).

Provisions for protecting the interests of employees on layoff have gone much further in Western Europe and Japan than in the United States. The approach to the problem in Western Europe and Japan involves (1) submission in advance of plans for workforce reductions to workers' representatives and public authorities, and consultation with the former; (2) efforts to avert or minimize reductions with public assistance (subsidies for short-time work, for example); and (3) mitigating the adverse effects of layoffs (with measures aimed at income protection and employee mobility). These approaches involve legislation and collective agreements.

The United States has moved more slowly to set conditions applying to mass layoffs, but signs of such movement are beginning to appear. A member of Congress proposed to the House of Representatives in 1984 the use of a short-term compensation approach by which the workforce would remain intact during a recessionary period but the work week would be reduced proportionately and each worker would receive a supplemental share of unemployment benefits. (This proposal was made in connection with the issue of affirmative action versus seniority in layoffs, but its wider application is obvious.) Senator Gary Hart has suggested reforms of unemployment insurance programs, including the payment of partial unemployment benefits to employees whose work hours are temporarily reduced to avoid layoff (1983, 101).

A major occasion for mass layoffs has been, of course, the closing of plants. An increasing number of restrictions and regulations concerning plant closings have been written into legislative acts and labor contracts (Folbre, Leighton, and Roderick 1984). In 1980–1981, of 1,550 collective bargaining agreements examined by the U. S. Bureau of Labor Statistics, 10% required advance notice of plant shutdowns or relocations. In early 1984 advance notice of plant closings was in effect in Wisconsin and Maine; Maine also required that firms closing plants with more than 100 employees must provide severance pay to workers with at least three years of seniority. Early notification concerning plant closings was provided in 11 bills introduced in state legislatures in 1981.

Legislation lessening the impact of plant closings on workers by means of retraining or assistance programs was passed in Connecticut and California in 1982, and Connecticut in 1983 passed a bill requiring employers of 100 or more laid-off employees to continue to pay health insurance premiums for terminated employees.

Studies of effects of plant-closing regulations in Maine in the 1971–1981 period suggest that advance notification significantly lowers the unemployment resulting from a closing, although compliance with advance notice and severance pay requirements was found to be relatively poor (Folbre, Leighton, and Roderick 1984, 189–196).

Craft (1984) assesses the efforts, direct and indirect, to control plant closings through the three major means employed (legislation, collective bargaining, and community action) and speculates on future prospects. Concerning legislation, he notes that of the three governmental jurisdictions covered by plant-closing legislation as of early 1984 (Maine, Wisconsin, and the municipality of Philadelphia), minimal procedural requirements (for example, advance notice of 60 days) apply to all, and rights to severance pay are provided in one (Maine). The weight of the evidence from the limited experience in these jurisdictions suggests a limited impact, if any, on shutdown decisions. In regard to collective bargaining, he notes that methods of control are not widespread in labor–management agreements and only 10 to 12% of them contain provisions for advance notice of plant relocation or closing. Community action includes pressure from community action groups and actions by city governments; the more common approach by the latter is to offer inducements to keep a plant open.

As to the future, Craft expresses doubt that there will be a federal plant-closing law or many additional state laws, or that the union contract provisions will extend much beyond current coverage. He suggests that community action may play a larger role in certain limited areas and may be influential in certain circumstances (involving an organization's wish to preserve its image and avoid controversy and its dependence on community customers).

The federal government has passed legislation to help workers whose jobs are lost or are threatened. The Federal Trade Act of 1974 contains provisions for assisting employee groups whose plants and jobs are adversely affected by imports; and the Dislocated Worker Program (1983, Title III of the Job Training Partnership Act) protects ''structurally displaced'' workers in mass layoffs and plant closings resulting from technological changes and world competition. And in 1978 Executive Order 12073 was issued to encourage procurement in labor-surplus areas.

A number of states have adopted legislation permitting partial unemployment insurance payments in work-sharing programs, thus encouraging work sharing as an alternative to layoffs.

Social pressures for a high employment level will predictably increase as a result of the issuance of the U. S. bishops' pastoral on Catholic social teaching and the American economy, the first draft of which was released late in 1984. The view taken in the first draft that work is a fundamental right (and duty) of every person places unemployment in a moral context. Work rights, as a practical matter, would require translation into job rights. And, on alleged moral grounds, advocacy will build for the creation of more jobs by the private sector and the government and for a national commitment to the goal of full employment (to a reduction in unemployment to the minimum level represented by ''frictional'' unemployment).

It should be understood that the drive for fuller employment, under whatever auspices, involves not only the provision of employment but its continuance also. In this latter aspect, as well, the government can be expected to play a larger role, even if a modest one, by placing greater restraints on plant closings and large-scale layoffs. The effect of the bishops' pastoral is to give a moral dimension to such decisions. Corporate executives, the message seems to say, cannot regard layoffs as strictly economic matters; the consequences to employees are such as to raise moral questions which should be taken into account in layoff decisions. Employment in this light represents the assumption of a substantial degree of responsibility for the welfare of the individual employee.

An enlightened personnel policy is necessarily concerned not only with hiring and retaining employees but with developing them as well. It is pertinent in this regard to note that the pastoral draft, referring to one aspect of the "three-fold moral significance" of work, views work as embodying "the distinctive human capacity for self-realization and self-expression." There is no realistic expectation that such ultimate condition can be realized by every employee in a job. But employers are well advised to provide for whatever skill and personal development is practical for the individual employee.

UNION JOB SECURITY MEASURES

Whatever their efforts to influence plant-closing decisions, unions are showing an increasing concern for job security, and through agreements with managements and their own efforts have sought to minimize layoffs and ameliorate their effects on members. Pressures from unions for job security assurances are likely to increase.

Unions have traditionally negotiated contract agreements governing layoffs and spelling out the role of seniority in layoff decisions. Abraham and Medoff (1984), in a survey of 200 firms, found that senior workers were better protected against permanent layoff in union firms than in nonunion firms, although long service was an advantage in both cases (leading to added protection against job loss in 97% of contract-covered groups and 86% of noncovered groups). But, importantly, there was a difference in the strength of the added protection. It was found to be considerably stronger in the average union group than in the average nonunion group.

Unions recognize that they are in "a new ball game." They are confronting not so much the "normal" problems of business fluctuations involving layoffs and recalls as major changes in the economy that have a more drastic effect on employment. As a publication of the Human Resources Development Institute of the American Federation of Labor and Congress of Industrial Organizations (AFL–CIO) puts it, "Foreign imports, declining consumption, high industrial investment costs, and changing technologies all have eroded employment in manufacturing industries where these workers would ordinarily look for jobs at comparable wages and skill levels. The growth occupations of today and tomorrow are likely to require skills and technical experience the typical displaced worker does not possess"(1982, 1).

Consequently, new responses are required, responses giving major emphasis to job security measures. In many cases agreements on job protection have been reached with employers. A Work in America Institute Policy Study (1984) lists 16 collective bargaining agreements in basic industries that have been signed in recent years. In most of these cases, the union made concessions in regard to wages, benefits, cost-of-living adjustments, and work rules in return for greater assurance of job security and avoidance of a shutdown or relocation of a plant. (It should be noted that the 1985 Chrysler–UAW agreement, signed in 1986, provided for restitution of $2,120 in earnings given up earlier by concession when Chrysler was in financial difficulties.)

Job security was the major focus of contract negotiations between the UAW and GM in 1984, and what emerged was a pioneering agreement referred to in the contract as the Job Opportunity Bank-Security (JOBS) Program. (See Appendix to this chapter for wording of contract clauses.) Under this program, employees with one or more years of seniority are protected against certain events that would otherwise result in permanent layoff: introduction of technology, outsourcing, negotiated productivity improvements, and specified kinds of transfer of work and of consolidation of production.

If a designated event occurred, the eligible employee would not be laid off but would be placed in an Employee Development Bank, and by the decision of the local JOBS Committee would be placed in a training program, used as a replacement to facilitate the training of another employee, or placed in a job opening or given a job assignment under specified conditions. The local JOBS Committee, which would administer the program, would include management and union representatives.

The program is funded by the corporation, whose total financial liability will not exceed $1 billion during the term of the understanding.

A job security agreement with similar provisions was negotiated by the UAW with Ford Motor Company and Chrysler Corporation.

Job security was also the main concern of the UAW in its 1984 negotiations with International Harvester Company and the consequent agreement ratified in 1985. The program resulting from these negotiations is called the Job Content Preservation Program and takes a different approach. Jobs are protected under this program by committing the company to a guaranteed level of straight-time hours in the product it sells.

The program works in this manner for each segment of the company's business:

Straight-time hours per unit of production/sales will be calculated for the 12-month base period ending March 31, 1985.

The job content levels thus arrived at (hours per unit of production/sales) become a target for each six-month measurement period that follows.

The job content level is multiplied by the actual volume of business occurring during the measurement period, thus giving a "total hours worked target."

This target, adjusted for productivity changes, is then compared with the actual number of total straight-time hours worked for the same six-month period.

If the total of actual hours falls below the total of targeted hours, the company incurs a contingent obligation to be reduced or eliminated during the next succeeding six-month period. Reduction is to be accompanied by one or more of these ways:

Working proportionately more straight-time hours than needed to meet the next six-month target levels.

Instituting training–retraining programs for active and laid-off workers.

Providing additional funding for SUB and other benefit programs for laid-off workers.

Insourcing work previously outsourced or performed by suppliers.

If, after these actions, actual hours are still below the targeted level, the shortfall becomes a fixed obligation, which, along with means of preventing future shortfalls, will be addressed by joint agreement with such steps as instituting mandatory company-wide half or full paid days off or funding jointly determined training and other programs for laid-off or active members.

To cover shortfalls in hours, the company has pledged up to 2 million hours or $30 million.

The inclusion of job security clauses of such a comprehensive nature in union contracts has not yet spread very widely. By early 1986, such clauses had been negotiated primarily by the UAW in the GM, Ford, Chrysler, and International Harvester contracts. But job security is obviously an increasing concern of employees, and we can anticipate that it will find its way progressively into contract negotiations involving other unions and other industries.

To confront the problems of actual layoffs, unions (along with companies, communities, and governmental agencies) have been active in establishing and conducting outplacement and retraining programs (see Chapter 7).

A unique new approach to job security, the concept of an "investment guarantee," was taken by the UAW and Ford at Ford's Rouge Steel subsidiary in 1983 (Friedman 1985, 557). In return for union economic concessions the company needed for investments to ensure the continued viability of the facility, the union received a written commitment by the company to make the investments for necessary modernization. Under the agreement, the union could revoke its concessions if it believed responsible progress on modernization investments was not being made by the company.

The question of union clout arises in regard to union advocacy of job security measures. It is popularly believed that union membership has diminished substantially and union influence along with it. Yet, according to an estimate of union membership among eligible American workers for the 1973–1981 period, while membership dropped from 23.6% in 1973 to 21.2% in 1981, it remained "fairly constant" over the decade (Kokkelenberg and Sockell 1985, 502–503, 540). Membership by sex in 1981 was male 26.3%, female 14.7%; by race, white 20.5%, black 27.5%, other 20.9%. There were demographic trends. The percentage of unionization among the more highly educated workers increased from 1973 to 1981; the percentages for women and blacks increased from 1973 to 1979, but this trend was reversed slightly over the years 1980 and 1981.

Although the decline has been gradual and by relatively small decrements, it has apparently persisted into the early 1980's. In recent estimates, the percentage of union membership in 1984 was put at 16.1% of the civilian labor force and 19.5% of the non-agricultural labor force, down from 16.6 and 20.7 in 1983 (Hirsch and Addison 1986, 47). It was speculated that the decline since the mid–1950's "is in large part a consequence of significant employment shifts into industries and regions where unionism is less prevalent, of a declining share of production jobs, of increased foreign competition, of increases in female labor force participation, of a younger and more mobile labor force, and of changing attitudes and a legal environment decreasingly conducive to union organizing" (Hirsch and Addison 1986, 72). In gauging contemporary union stature, however, it is worth noting that in a period when total union membership in the country was reportedly declining, the UAW negotiated with auto manufacturers job security agreements of historic significance.

A related question arises as to whether unions, in the light of seniority provisions, stand in the way of employment growth for minorities and women. Leonard (1985), in a study of 1,273 California manufacturing plants in the 1974–1980 period, found that unions have not generally been a hindrance.

APPENDIX

GM–UAW Memorandum of Understanding: Job Opportunity Bank-Security (JOBS) Program. Source: Agreement Between General Motors Corporation and the UAW September 21, 1984, effective October 14, 1984, pp. 185–195.

As an outgrowth of these negotiations the Corporation and the Union expressed a mutual commitment that General Motors employees receive a full measure of job security, and mutual recognition that this measure of job security can only be realized within a work environment which promotes operational effectiveness.

The willingness of the parties to reach these understandings has led to the creation of the JOBS Program, through which the Corporation and the Union jointly intend to enhance job security and operational effectiveness.

The cornerstone of the JOBS Program is a commitment that: No employee with one or more years of seniority will be laid off as a result of the introduction of technology, outsourcing or negotiated productivity improvements as defined in this Memorandum of Understanding.

I. SCOPE OF THE PROGRAM—The Corporation and the Union agree that:
   (A) Job security will be provided for an eligible employee in the event technology is introduced which would otherwise result in the permanent layoff of an employee. Technology for the purposes of this document only is defined as any change in product, methods, processes or the means of manufacturing introduced by management at a location which reduces the job content of existing work at that location.
   (B) Job security will be provided for an eligible employee in the event of the outsourcing of a product manufactured in or work performed at a location which

would otherwise result in the permanent layoff of an employee at that location. Outsourcing as used herein means the Corporation's sourcing to non–General Motors Companies in the U.S. or Canada, or to any facility outside the U.S. or Canada. Location as used in this Paragraph means the GM–UAW location from which the product is outsourced and the location(s) that directly supplies parts or components to the GM–UAW location for the product that is outsourced.

(C) Job security will be provided for an eligible employee in the event of negotiated productivity improvements that would otherwise result in the permanent layoff of an employee.

(D) Job security will be provided for an eligible employee in the event of:

(1) a Paragraph (96) transfer of work; or

(2) a decision to consolidate into a GM plant the production of a given component previously assigned at that plant and one or more other GM plants; which would otherwise result in the permanent layoff of an employee to the extent that the work has less job content at the plant to which it is assigned than it had at the plant(s) from which it was removed.

(E) This program is not provided for an employee impacted by changes in either retail or non-allied commercial customer preference, volume related reasons attributable to market conditions, other reasons beyond the control of the Corporation, the sale of a part of the Corporation's operations as an ongoing business, or the cessation of business at a Corporation facility that does not involve outsourcing. This program does not apply to an employee laid off after having been reassigned or recalled from layoff to fill an opening known in advance to be temporary (in this regard the JOBS Committee will be notified of such openings), or to employees laid off for a period of model change or plant rearrangement until they otherwise would have been recalled. An employee impacted by any of the above reasons is, if otherwise eligible, covered by the appropriate Supplemental Agreements which are attached to the National Agreement as Exhibits.

(F) The number of employees protected by this JOBS Program will be the equivalent of the employees with one or more years seniority who would otherwise have been laid-off as a direct result of the events described in Paragraphs I(A), I(B), I(C) and I(D), exclusive of the impact of a concurrent volume increase.

II. JOB SECURITY AND OPERATIONAL EFFECTIVENESS—In recognition of the fact that job security can only result from joint efforts to improve operational effectiveness, the Corporation and the Union agree that:

(A) For a period commencing with the effective date of this Memorandum of Understanding and expiring with the expiration of the National Agreement next following the 1984 National Agreement, no employee with one or more years seniority will be laid off as a result of the events described in Paragraphs I(A), I(B), I(C) or I(D) that occur on or after the effective date of this Memorandum of Understanding.

(B) An employee whose regular job is eliminated due to the events described in Paragraphs I(A), I(B), I(C), or I(D) will be placed pursuant to the applicable provisions of the National Agreement and the Local Seniority Agreement.

(C) The number of employees protected from layoff due to the JOBS Program will be that determined in Paragraph I(F). Each protected employee will be identified by application of the Local Seniority Agreement provisions as if such job security were not provided.

(D) An employee protected by this Program will be placed in an Employee Development Bank. The parties recognize that the scope of this program requires flexibility with regard to the assignment of Bank employees and the selection of employees for training. In this regard, the Local JOBS Committee will insure that assignments are made which meet plant needs, minimize work force disruption and enhance the personal growth and development of employees. After a decision by the Local JOBS Committee an employee in the Bank may be (1) placed in a training program, (2) used as a replacement to facilitate the training of another employee, (3) placed in a job opening at another GM plant provided there is no employee on layoff from that plant with a seniority recall or Paragraph (64) (e) rehire right or an Area Hire applicant who has not been offered a job at that plant, (4) given a job assignment within or outside the bargaining unit which may be non-traditional, (5) placed in an existing opening or (6) given other assignments consistent with the purposes of this Memorandum of Understanding.

(E) Efforts of the local parties to improve operational effectiveness will be encouraged and supported by the national parties including, as may be appropriate, approval of requests to waive, modify or change the National Agreement.

III. ADMINISTRATION OF THE JOBS PROGRAM [Contains provisions for membership and duties of the local committee and higher administrative committees—area and national—involved in the program.]

IV. FUNDING—The Corporation and International Union agree that: Notwithstanding the commitments set forth in this Memorandum of Understanding, the Corporation's total financial liability for the cost of the JOBS Program, to be calculated as agreed between the parties, shall not exceed $1,000,000,000 during the term of this Memorandum of Understanding. In the event this liability is reached, all existing Employee Development and Training Banks will be discontinued. Thereafter, to the extent that layoffs of such employees are required, the provisions of the Local Seniority Agreements will apply and eligible employees will receive benefit treatment in accordance with the Supplemental Agreements attached to the GM–UAW National Agreement then in effect.

V. EFFECTIVE DATE—TERMINATION DATE—The Corporation and International Union agree that:

(A) This Memorandum of Understanding will become effective at each bargaining unit covered by the 1984 GM–UAW National Agreement one hundred and eighty (180) days following the effective date of this Agreement.

(B) This Memorandum of Understanding shall expire with the expiration of the National Agreement next following the 1984 National Agreement.

6

Addressing Involuntary Turnover: Steps to Curb Layoffs

A number of investigators have explored the subject of job security, looking into the policies and strategies employed by companies to avoid or minimize layoffs.

APPROACHES TO EMPLOYMENT SECURITY

Feuer (1985, 24–31) discusses a number of approaches that have been tried:

Recalling work from nonregular employees (outside vendors, subcontractors, and temporary employees when their contracts expire). This approach assumes that the organization runs "lean" with a core of regular employees and uses outside arrangements and temporary employees for certain work which can be recalled in times of decline.

Manufacturing for inventory.

Reassigning employees for lower-priority work such as cleaning and repairing equipment.

Retraining workers for new specialties; replacing obsolete skills with new skills.

Creating a flexible workforce through cross-training.

Effecting voluntary reductions through such means as time off without pay, unpaid educational leaves, work sharing, voluntary terminations, and early retirement.

Intensifying sales and marketing efforts (perhaps using, in this effort, employees whose workloads are down).

Gutchess (1985, 3–10) lists six job security strategies and illustrates their use by citing cases involving specific companies:

Guarantees and other no-layoff policies.

Employment-buffering strategies to preserve lean staff of core personnel: a regularly scheduled use of overtime; hiring (and dismissal) of temporary staff; internal job assign-

---

* Approaches to employment security related to the particular companies discussed in this chapter are of course subject to changes in policy.

ment shifts; subcontracting work with the option of recalling it in declining times; above-average or below-average inventory building; and rescheduling of deliveries.

Voluntary workforce reductions: work sharing (reduction of work hours and pay); lending out temporarily surplus workers (in the company or to other employers); voluntary early retirement.

Worker-oriented adjustment strategies: responding to shifts in the market (through new products, redefinition of markets, profitability efforts), but if workers must be displaced, using retraining programs and outplacement programs as adjustment techniques.

Easing the adjustment to technological changes: management–union programs for retraining employees in new technology.

Job replacement strategies: helping new businesses to get started, through company funding and expertness, in communities where plants are closed (or through joint ventures of government, employer, union, and community).

A policy study by the Work in America Institute (1984) makes an important distinction between managing employment security in the case of temporary declines and managing employment security in the case of permanent declines.

For responding to temporary declines so as to avoid layoffs, the study discusses (89–104) such approaches as restriction of hiring; sustaining the workload through recalling work from "nonprotected" workers (on temporary contracts or employed by subcontractors) for assignment to "protected" employees, increasing demand through intensified sales efforts, assigning lower-priority work (manufacturing for inventory, maintenance, consulting, helping dealers); reducing payroll costs through such means as wage-rate reductions (in some cases with negotiated trade-offs) and work sharing; and placing employees in training and development activities, including training for flexible assignments.

Actions discussed as responses, short of dismissals, to permanent decline of workloads include (107–117) the development of additional workload by recalling work from temporary employees, subcontractors, or vendors and by developing new products, creating subsidiaries, and subcontracting for other companies; reducing wage costs by restricting hiring, sharing work, early retirement, and phased retirement; and reducing unit labor costs by negotiating pay and benefit reductions and by productivity programs.

Lehr and Middlebrooks (1984, 53) refer to three means of reducing labor costs without dropping employees from the workforce: reclassification of employees (demotion or downgrading of job responsibilities); transfer of employees (requiring effective training and employee evaluations for success); and work sharing through proportional reduction of hours.

Motorola presents a prime example of the use of work sharing and buffering to avoid layoffs (Burge 1986, 135–145). The company sets labor-staffing levels below maximum capacity and, to meet fluctuating labor requirements, uses a buffering system, as a formal operating procedure, that includes such steps as freezing of hiring, recall of work from outside vendors, termination of resident contract workers, and transfer of work between divisions and facilities.

Work sharing involves a reduction of work hours (say from 40 to 32 per week) for employees as an alternative to layoffs. This plan is more effective and acceptable when combined with unemployment insurance payments as partial compensation for reduced hours. Motorola pioneered in the movement for enactment of shared work compensation (or short-time compensation) laws, providing for such payments, which in 1985 were in effect in California, Arizona, Florida, Illinois, Oregon, Washington, and Maryland.

The provisions work like this. A company reduces its production, say, by 20%, but instead of laying off a fifth of its workforce, it reduces work hours by 20% and places its full workforce on a per-week schedule reduced from 40 hours to 32. All employees receive their wages for four days and an unemployment insurance payment equal to a certain amount of the total unemployment insurance benefits they would have received if they had been unemployed for a full week. The California law, adopted first in 1978, provides for paying the worker in the participating firm, in the circumstances cited above, 20% of his regular full-week unemployment benefits. These partial benefits may be paid for up to 20 weeks a year, and the employee would still be eligible for his regular unemployment compensation benefits if later laid off (but not to exceed, in combination with the partial benefits, the regular unemployment insurance payment total per year the employee is entitled to).

A 1984 study of the costs and benefits of work sharing during 1982 and 1983 in six Motorola production departments indicated that work sharing will result in a net saving for any layoff of less than six months and will probably result in a net saving in most layoffs of less than one year (Burge 1986, 145).

A rather unique form of work sharing was used by United Airlines (by agreement with the Association of Flight Attendants) in 1980 as an alternative to layoffs of senior flight attendants (Job Sharing 1982). The participants chose their own partners in a job-sharing program involving "partnership time off." They accrued vacation and sick time at a half-time rate, but the airline continued, as before, to pay for health and life insurance and pensions.

The use of a core group of employees and buffering techniques is a key aspect of Dana Corporation's efforts to avoid layoffs. Part-time people are hired for peak periods; and, especially in nonproduction areas, outside contractors are used. Employment preference is given to Dana people when openings occur in any facility.

Hewlett-Packard (HP), well known for progressive personnel policies, does not take the buffering approach to a period of decline but instead has sought to hold onto its workforce through reduction in production expenses. One such means—a limited amount of time off without pay—might be considered a work-sharing procedure, but it is perhaps more properly understood as a manifestation of a sharing relationship the company has sought to establish with its employees.

HP's corporate objectives include this statement on job security (Hewlett-Packard 1983, 4): "Job security is an important HP objective. Over the years, the company has achieved a steady growth in employment by consistently developing good new products, and by avoiding the type of contract business that requires hiring many people, then terminating them when the contract expires. The company wants HP people to have stable, long-term careers—dependent, of course, upon satisfactory job performance.''

In keeping with its corporate goal regarding employees, the company has deliberately taken steps through the years to avoid layoffs. In its situation in 1985 when it was experiencing the effects of a general slowdown in the electronics industry, HP put limitations on travel, company expenses, and the hiring of new employees. And it did not resort to layoffs; instead, most employees, including top executives, took two days off per month without pay (representing a 10% pay cut) in order to reduce operating expenses.

HP's stated goal is to help its people share in the company's success, as evidenced by programs like the profit-sharing plan. But it is also part of HP's overall philosophy of operation to share equally in the down times.

It is evident that many managements are rethinking their human relations policies to confront periods of decline that involve a condition of contraction requiring a reduction in force. Ferris, Schellenberg, and Zammuto (1984, 386) suggest that the appropriate human resources strategy in such case is ''domain consolidation'' and the primary human resource issue is ''consolidating competencies.'' (Other human resources strategies are proposed for confronting other conditions of decline.) The objective of the organization's response is to reduce personnel without disrupting operations, and mechanisms should be devised for that purpose. Namely, it is proposed that the performance appraisal system be refined for accurate identification of good and poor performers as a basis for decisions on reduction of labor force; that the reward system be redesigned to enable the organization to reward valued personnel while conserving resources; and that, as the situation stabilizes, renewed emphasis be placed on training involving quality-of-work-life programs and additional skill training.

DISTINCTIONS AMONG SITUATIONS AND AMONG RESPONSES

A company experiences varying situations and will usually make corresponding distinctions among its responses. In general terms, the response to decline may involve an avoidance of layoffs, short-term layoffs with retention of job rights, extended layoffs with no expectation of recall, and outright job loss. Each general response will carry specific strategies and programs.

Temporary declines involving lowered need for personnel are routinely addressed by companies through hiring restrictions; reduction of force through normal attrition; work sharing in terms of reduced work schedules; assignments of lower-priority work to employees who are temporarily surplus in their regular work; training and cross-training of affected employees as a holding device; and the building of inventory to policy or prudential limits. Where the company policy is to maintain a core group of employees, buffering personnel procedures of the type discussed may be invoked effectively.

When a situation appears permanent and means elimination of jobs (the operation continuing), some of the same company responses are useful: restricting hiring in the remaining jobs, training employees for remaining jobs, and transferring them to those jobs. But when employees are still in surplus, early retirement or phased retirement (part-time work as a transitional phase, for example) is an indicated action for older employees. Voluntary retirement, with monetary inducements, may be offered to employees. Retraining for placement elsewhere and outplacement assistance are possible courses of action when retirement is not indicated. Productivity improvement programs may also be in order to protect remaining jobs, programs that may require negotiations with the union and the trade-off of pay and benefit reductions for better assurance of continued employment.

A midwestern company with a deservedly good reputation for employee relations resorts to layoff only if confident, on the basis of a study of market share and market trends, that the downturn will last several months. If the production rate reduction is determined to be short term, the company moves available employees into nonproduction work until demand increases. When a layoff is unavoidable, the company has placement centers to assist employees with job search and to give employees access to programs of help in confronting financial and family pressures. In a recent layoff, an early retirement package was offered to employees.

To make its operation less subject to the volatility of the market, this company is making efforts to increase productivity. It is also entering new businesses that can employ people made available from the productivity improvements.

Aware that layoffs can affect "stayers," the company responds to this aspect of layoffs with heightened communication on the reasons for layoff and with training programs aimed at increasing productivity and market share and reducing the need for layoffs.

A major American corporation, in making distinctions between situations, considers workforce surpluses to be of three types: business swing excesses, permanent excesses, and general company excesses. It has options for addressing each kind.

Business swing excesses result from temporary situations and are predicted to last less than six months. The options include:

Replacing contractors and temporary employees on the site with permanent employees.

Expanding the opportunities for excused absences without pay.

Encouraging employees to take their vacations.

Temporarily adopting a reduced work schedule (four days rather than five days per week, for example).

Putting employees on a schedule of alternate work weeks in those places where employees are eligible for unemployment compensation for the weeks off under this schedule.

Allowing employees to take voluntary leaves of absence for up to six months so that a job may continue for another employee who would otherwise be terminated for lack of work. Those taking voluntary leave receive no pay but gain service credit.

If excesses persist and layoff is required, the junior employees are laid off but with severance pay of one week's pay per year of service. Health care coverage is continued for them for up to 12 months, and life insurance coverage is continued for one year or 2 months per year of service, whichever is the longer period. Recall rights are retained for one to three years.

Permanent excesses result from full or partial shutdown of a facility or other situations where recall or restaffing is unlikely. Options to deal with these kinds of excesses are admittedly more limited, but such provisions as these are used:

Giving as much advance notice as possible, usually several months.

Applying a voluntary termination incentive policy under which volunteers, who must continue a job for another employee who would otherwise be excess, are given one week's pay per year of service in addition to any voluntary pension rights they have. Recall rights are forfeited.

Providing assistance to nonexempt employees involuntarily terminated for lack of work in permanent excess situations. For those who qualify for it, the assistance includes:

Job interview assistance of up to two days off with pay for job interviews.

Outplacement assistance (usually provided in shutdown situations).

Change of resident allowance for nonexempt employees with a minimum of ten years of service. The employee must be reemployed by a corporation plant in another location within one year of termination and must relocate his residence within six months of reemployment. The monetary allowance is $1,500 plus three cents per mile moved (total amount not to exceed $4,000).

Employees involuntarily terminated for lack of work receive the same severance pay and extended health care and life insurance benefits as those described above for employees made excess by business swing situations.

An example of a general company excess situation is an overstaffing on the basis of growth in business that occurred less rapidly than anticipated. To improve its competitive position in this case, the corporation offered early retirement opportunity under an incentive calculated on years of service and age. The plan did not apply to upper management.

The corporation's policy on job security states that prospects for continuing employment increase with length of service for those employees whose performance is satisfactory. As indicated above, the approach to excesses is to attempt to resolve the situation without involuntary terminations, but where the corporation must lay off it provides employees with severance pay, continued benefits, and assistance in locating new jobs.

A termination allowance plan, paid for by the company, is a major feature of the Eastman Kodak Company's management of layoffs. The policy on stability of employment, as given in the employee handbook *You and Kodak* (1985, 4), states: "Continual attention is given to efforts which contribute to stable employment. In the event business conditions result in a change in personnel needs, the company will give consideration to retraining individuals or reassigning to areas of need. However, if a reduction in personnel becomes necessary, consideration will be given to such factors as performance, length of service, and overall record." The termination allowance plan (130–133) provides, for eligible laid-off employees, a continuation of pay for a limited period of time, based on length of service.

To qualify for payment under the plan, an employee must be a regular employee and his employment must terminate as the result of a layoff for a period expected to exceed 30 days. He must also work until a termination date acceptable to the company.

Employees involved in three types of layoff qualify for benefits:

1. Decrease in workforce as a result of a slack-work situation caused by completion of or changes to production schedules or by consolidation of work functions. But an employee will not qualify for payments if he refuses a reasonably equivalent job (within 10% of his current base wage rate) in the same geographic area.
2. Relocation. Employees are not disqualified by refusal to relocate to a reasonably equivalent job in a different geographical area. But if an employee agrees to relocate and then refuses, he will not qualify.
3. Inability to meet job requirements despite a good-faith effort.

Under the termination allowance, the employee's pay continues for a specified number of weeks after termination. The number of weeks is based on the number of full years of continuous service, up to a maximum of 52 weeks for 30 or more years of service. The employee may choose to receive 100% of his weekly allowance each week or to spread out the payments by opting to receive 50% or 25% of the weekly allowance each week. In the case of extended schedules, payments may not continue beyond 104 weeks; if the allowance is not all paid out by then (as happens with employees with more than 17 years of service), the remainder will then be paid in a lump sum. If an employee is entitled to any other benefits and allowances, they are paid according to the rules which apply to that specific benefit or allowance.

In regard to benefits, life and health insurance coverage will be continued for two months after the month of termination, and the employee will receive payment for the value of his account in the savings and investment plan and in the tax credit stock ownership plan and also will receive tuition aid payments previously approved.

Merck & Company, Inc., does not have a formal policy concerning maintenance of job stability, but its attempts to manage toward that end have had considerable success. Its approach makes certain distinctions. Layoffs—meaning the termination of employees who continue to have some job rights and some expectation of recall—only occur among the Merck production and maintenance employees. In the case of all other employees, the company would be dealing with permanent reductions in the workforce. In regard to this group, Merck has not had a layoff in the basic portion of its business for at least 15 years. In regard to production and maintenance employees, it is the nature of the operations in the pharmaceutical portion of the business to have highs and lows of business and thus to require layoffs. (In the unionized plants, provisions for amelioration and recall are set forth in the collective bargaining agreement.) With a view to establishing a more stable work environment for these classes of employees, the company is looking at mechanisms such as operating with a lean workforce and using temporary employees in peak periods and contractors to do certain unskilled work which the regular workforce would assume in slack periods; and it is testing these kinds of approaches in a small plant. But Merck does not guarantee employment; its position is that the best guarantee of job security is a successful and productive company.

DIFFICULTIES WITH APPROACHES

Obviously, the management of layoffs is a difficult task, and solutions that work in some settings will not work or are inappropriate in others.

Inventory Building

Building inventories is a remedy requiring judicious and discriminatory application. In a highly competitive industry or in a company where cash flow is a problem, this approach can be dangerous. As executives in such enterprises are quick to point out, taking great risks by continuing full-scale operations in periods of slack sales can have disastrous results that could undermine a company's solvency and eliminate the very bases on which job assurance is possible.

An executive in the highly competitive textile industry gives this kind of explanation regarding the role of inventories in decisions regarding operations levels in his company:

Managers resort typically to accounting safeguards against potentially damaging decisions concerning the level of operations, the primary touchstone being the level of inventories. Maximum inventory levels are commonly set, above which the operating manager by policy restriction may not build. Managers know the cost of carrying inventories and the number of times their average monthly inventory must "turn over" within a year to provide them with adequate cash-flow. These accounting concepts are an essential part of the standard repertoire of managerial knowledge. When the inventory exceeds the designated limit, the manager sets about adjusting his operation downward and with it his manpower requirements.

Obviously, the acceptable level of inventory cannot be set without reference to sales forecasts, and a typical arrangement is to forecast annually but to update the forecast figures monthly and to review the situation critically at quarterly intervals.

In product lines which change little in style or pattern and which experience a stable sale, a substantial inventory may be carried with relatively small risk. But tolerable inventory levels will be lower for style-oriented product lines which are subject to short-cycle shifts in consumer preference. A single plant may produce both types of products, in which case management will set differing inventory limits—lower for short-lived items than for "core" items.

Adjustments in inventory limits will be made for those items having seasonal sales. Since manufacturing is not an instantaneous process, it will be spread over a period of time and inventories will thus be built up in preparation for the seasonal demand. Obviously, marketing forecasts for this kind of item are of paramount importance.

The response of managers in this company to production cutbacks it considers necessary is to take into account the costs associated with a reduced schedule of production (overhead costs continue) and to seek to achieve the maximum efficiency possible within the unfavorable situation and at the same time seek to minimize the adverse impact on employees. A reduced work schedule is considered early as an alternative to layoffs. There are numerous scheduling choices. A work week reduced, say, to three or four days will have the effect of spreading the work among employees. But when the work week schedule is cut back appreciably—and especially when it dwindles to three days per week— the danger is substantially increased that workers, especially experienced workers, will seek employment elsewhere because of the sharp drop in earnings; thus, voluntary turnover is induced and key personnel are lost to the company, perhaps permanently. A manager may find advantages, in terms both of operational efficiencies and of sustained employee earnings and employee retention, if he schedules his full complement for five-day weeks for four weeks running and stands the plant every fifth week (for which employees would receive unemployment compensation in this company's location).

In unionized plants, the contract will typically specify, as in this company, the provisions for reducing work hours and the point at which the reduction will trigger a layoff.

In those plants which, by the nature of the product, only produce items ordered and sold, inventory building is, of course, an impractical alternative to layoffs. A structural steel plant is an example. The response to temporary business decline in this plant, as an executive explained, is a work-sharing arrangement (involving some lower-priority work assignments) which will enable the plant to retain a corps of skilled employees. He would hold onto a minimum of 40% of the employees "at all costs" because the problem of training replacements in this high-skilled operation when business improved was considered virtually insurmountable. In terms of marketing, an intensified effort is indicated in periods of decline, and decisions may have to be made as to the temporary acceptability of "cheap work" (including contracts taken below cost) in light of the company's long-range marketing objectives.

Use of Core (Regular) Employees and Temporaries

An objection commonly voiced against the use of a core group of regular employees and buffering techniques to protect them is that the invoking of buffering techniques in periods of decline simply shifts the burden of layoffs. Someone ultimately loses work. An accompanying criticism is that the division of employees into regular or core employees who are to be protected and other workers (inside the company or ouside it) who are expendable is, in effect, to establish a primary and subordinate class of workers, a two-caste system. This model appears to be more acceptable in Japan than in the United States where equality of treatment and opportunity is an essential value of our democratic society.

It should be noted that Motorola, unlike companies that use nonrenewable contracts, provides a means by which its contract employees can attain regular employee status provided a continuous need exists for such workers (Burge 1986, 136). While in the status of contract workers, they will have received the prevailing wage scale, and the experience and training gained in such status are considered valuable to the company.

Another major American corporation which uses temporary and regular employees provides this procedure by which a temporary hourly paid employee can attain regular employee status: He becomes a regular employee if he works 170 days in a calendar year. This company's business is somewhat seasonal, but the company has enjoyed steady growth. All of its new hourly paid employees are hired as temporary employees. They have the same wage scale as regular employees but not the same benefits. They are covered by special provisions for benefits if they work 80 hours per month or more; these benefits include medical and life insurance but exclude pensions. Certain aspects of the union contract apply to the temporaries. Grievances and pay and disciplinary provisions apply; but the temporary employees have a different basis for holidays and special vacation arrangements, and seniority does not apply. In addition, they are not promoted.

This system is used under union contractual agreement. Indeed, it evolved from a union request for relief against overtime requirements. Temporary employees were brought in. Under the established system, temporaries continue to work on weekends but may also fill in for absentees and be assigned to fill special requirements for additional employees. Some of the temporary employees also hold jobs outside the company.

Because of continuing heavy demand for its product, the company has not resorted to layoff of regular employees; it has no outplacement service. However, by agreement with the union, it does provide, in event of layoffs, supplemental unemployment pay for regular employees with three years or more of seniority. Payments may be made for up to 26 weeks in a 52-week period.

The effects of pulling in contracted work on employees of subcontractors can be somewhat lessened by such measures as dispersing subcontractors geographically; limiting the amount of work contracted with any one; encouraging sub-contractors to take job security steps, including their own buffering; and giving advance notice to subcontractors (Work in America Institute Policy Study 1984, 78). But some of the effects will nevertheless dribble down inevitably. As a model for the economy as a whole, the core group-buffering system may depend for its effectiveness on a sufficient supply of workers who want or will accept temporary or part-time work.

Unfortunately, we know little about the attitudes and aspirations of workers who take temporary employment. We do know that unemployed adults over-whelmingly seek full-time work; Bureau of Labor Statistics figures show these percentages seeking full-time and part-time work among unemployed people in 1982 (*Workers without jobs* 1983, 29):

	Full-time	Part-time
Total unemployed	84%	16%
Adult men	95	5
Adult women	84	16
Teenagers	58	42

We know some of the characteristics of the part-time workers (Nardone 1986, 14–16). Especially among the men, they tend to be younger workers (16 to 24) and older (65 and over). Women make up two-thirds of the total part-time workers. Of the part-time women workers, most are married; in contrast, most of the part-time male workers are single. The proportion of whites employed part-time is slightly higher than the proportion of blacks (18 vs. 16%). Part-time workers are likely to hold jobs in the retail trade and service industries. There were 13.5 million "voluntary part-time" workers (part-time for noneconomic reasons) in 1985. An additional 5.6 million workers were part-time for economic reasons (on slack time or unable to find full-time work) and were included in the full-time labor force.

Use of Temporary Help Services

We also know that the "temporary help service industry" is growing rapidly, and a recent study by Mangum, Mayall, and Nelson (1985) has thrown consid-erable light on the characteristics of that industry. The number of establishments providing such service is over 5,000 nation-wide, and the total employment figure for the industry in 1979 was 436,445 (601). The service of providing temporary employees is not yet a major force in the labor market, but these are substantial figures and are likely to increase. Indeed, the total of workers reached 735,000 in 1985, still less than one percent of total non-agricultural employment but growing (Carey and Hazelbaker 1986, 37).

The advantage to employers in using the services is that they provide a ready source of help when production demands increase without imposing on the company the same costs (in benefits primarily) and commitment that occur with regular or "permanent" employees. Thus, a company can provide job security for a core group of employees with assurance that a buffering peripheral group will absorb the ups and downs.

The increasing use of temporary employees through these agencies raises public policy issues. We tend to applaud the company that gives job security assurances to its core employees, but consideration must also be given to the needs of the peripheral employees. In some instances their route to permanent status is through temporary status, but this is not an assured process and is not the goal of most temporary help service organizations.

The question of commitment is a pertinent one. While companies make significant efforts to increase the commitment of their employees to the company and make reciprocal commitment to employees in terms of equitable pay, benefits, job security, career advancement opportunities, and other rewards, the increasing use of temporary workers diminishes the role of commitment in the employer–employee relationship. The company in effect evades a commitment to these employees, and the temporary employees, on their part, cannot be quite sure where their commitment—if any develops—is supposed to lie. With a temporary employer? With the service agency?

Some benefits may be provided by the temporary employer or the agency, but these are likely to be limited (retirement provisions are likely to suffer most, along with safety) and hardly sufficient to inspire loyal attachment. Indeed, many of the satisfactions that, through substantial research over the years, we have found to be sought by employees are likely to be unavailable to temporary workers. It is difficult to accept the thesis that a large majority of temporary workers prefer temporary work and "peripheral" status and are not seeking permanent employment and its associated rewards.

The companies that use the services of the agencies may find compelling economic advantage in doing so. Factors such as firm size, stability of production, and the kinds of occupations and skills appear to influence the use.

But, from the employees' point of view, is this the way to go? It is doubtful that workers with high need for achievement and those with high need for affiliation—segments of the population representing a high percentage of the whole—would find satisfaction in temporary employment. If they do not, the consequences may have social significance. A larger percentage of the labor force would be expecting to find life satisfactions in nonoccupational sources, an expectation that society may be hard put to fulfill.

Employees who reconcile themselves to temporary status are likely to be primarily persons whose personal circumstances—perhaps temporary circumstances—compel such choice. The size and dependability of the labor pool represented by this group are suspect. For this reason, along with the potential for performance problems among those who find inadequate satisfaction in temporary work, the further question needs to be raised: Is this the way to go for employers?

We have arrived, after a long struggle with the issue, at somewhat valid means of motivating ''employees'' (a term traditionally applied to people hired by an employer for an indefinite period). Employers who now rely heavily on temporary employees are moving into a realm of employee relations that is largely uncharted. Experiential indications provide some guidance, and we may try to extrapolate results from earlier industrial research; but research has not yet been focused on the motivation of temporary workers specifically, and the experiential indications await codification.

Another alternative to the direct hiring of employees by an organization is to ''lease'' employees, an approach of possible cost advantage to small businesses or professional practitioners and one made attractive by the ''Safe Harbor'' provisions of the Tax Equity and Fiscal Responsibility Act of 1982 (Jagels 1985). The employee-leasing industry, distinct from temporary employment agencies, has increased its total of leased employees from an estimated 7,200 to more than 68,000 in the 21-month period from early 1984 to late 1985. The leasing company is the employer, handles the administrative work, and provides employee benefits. The client retains the right to supervise the leased employees and to direct their activities. Employees might be expected to find difficulty functioning under the divided jurisdiction, but ''information from within the employee leasing industry indicates leased employees become loyal supporters of the employee leasing concept once they understand their role and the benefits received because of the concept'' (Jagels 1985, 23). One can question whether understanding is enough to bring job satisfaction to people who are leased. Our experience with the concept has been insufficient to give us conclusive answers. But before we go much further with it, a more extensive examination of the motivational ramifications is in order. In the midst of our soul searching over the issue of what employees really represent in an organization, the status of being leased has some unpleasant connotations.

The author's experience with specialized personnel who reported functionally to a staff superior and administratively to a line superior does not justify expectations of good results from organizational arrangements involving divided jurisdiction.

Adopting Foreign Models

The fit or adaptability of foreign models is a problem in the case of job replacement strategies by means of which the company, government, and unions jointly finance and operate an agency to establish new businesses in locations where plants have closed. Such projects have been carried out in Western Europe (with the American exception of the Downriver Community Conference in the Detroit area) (Gutchess 1985, 10–11). It must be realized that Western European governments have a substantial role in the conduct of business and in employment practices; indeed, nationalized or government-subsidized industries are commonly found there. In addition, with certain differences between countries, collective bargaining involves large segments of workers and confederations of employers and tends to be politicized and confrontational. Governments in Western Europe obviously take a more direct hand in such matters as plant closings and layoffs, as earlier indicated. To adopt European solutions would require political structures and actions largely unacceptable in American society. But cooperative "native" models are feasible here. A project illustrative of an American approach is being undertaken by Fieldcrest Cannon, Inc. in Eden, N. C., where the closing of two Fieldcrest plants resulted in a loss of several hundred jobs. The company is developing a favorably located tract of its land as an industrial park for the purpose of attracting, with city and county collaboration, other employers to the community.

CONFRONTING CAUSES OF DECLINE

While it is prudent for a company to develop strategies for dealing with business decline and associated layoffs, the more fundamental objective is to address causes of decline and attempt to arrest developments at their source, before they require the application of after-the-fact strategies.

Temporary declines can often be avoided by competent market research which stays abreast of consumer needs and preferences and directs the manufacturing operations into changes in product specifications. When signs point to a possible drop in demand, an intensified research effort, along with an intensified sales effort, may help to head off the potential decline.

Bringing predictability and reliability to the market is a difficult chore, but there are marketing strategies that can reduce sharp fluctuations and help stabilize the work load (Work in America Institute Policy Study 1984, 80–81). These include short-range and long-range sales forecasts, frequently updated, as a basis for scheduling production and planning inventories. Distribution systems may also be changed. Other strategies (81–86) include launching new products with deliberate speed permitting the ironing out of bugs, relying on multiple markets, and maintaining paced growth that is sustainable and nondestabilizing. With these strategies it may be possible to avoid major declines resulting in large-scale losses of jobs.

Of course, whatever economic actions a company takes to compete more effectively and control costs can contribute to job security. In addition to revising market strategies, it can, for example, reduce product lines, retrench, improve technology and production efficiency, and improve financial decisions (Ferris, Schellenberg, and Zammuto 1984, 382).

Harrigan (1980) discusses "endgame" strategies for confronting declining demand: increase investment in the industry to attain market dominance, hold investment level, shrink selectively, "milk" the investment (to retrieve the value of earlier investments), divest now (14–19, 45–49). Variables seen as influencing the formulation of strategy are market characteristics, structural traits of the industry, needs of the company external to the endgame industry, and competitive strengths of the firm within the industry (20–43).

Although many of the suggested strategies are intended to curtail declines, some of them, when based on sound predictions, may serve to prevent declines.

Since a major cause of business decline and job loss is the effect of environmental changes (including technological developments), some greater awareness of what is going on in the world might help a company to meet impending contingencies that have a potential for impacting on the business. A means of detecting environmental changes in their incipient stages and evaluating their potential impact on the company would be highly useful. Large corporations have the resources and personnel to do this sort of monitoring, but it appears to be infrequently done as an organized, continuous function. And smaller companies are likely to restrict the scope of their surveillance and to depend on scattered staff specialists to call attention to outside developments likely to affect the company.

Monitoring on an international scale is surely indicated since any company of significant size is affected to an appreciable extent by foreign as well as domestic developments and movements. These include developments, here and abroad, involving governmental legislation, regulations, and policies; international relations; climatic changes; natural resource discoveries and other developments related to raw materials sources and availability; ecology; population growth; social movements; technological breakthroughs; product utility and acceptance; production technology; markets and distribution; manufacturing costs; and employee relations. Comprehensive monitoring and the related evaluation of impact and recommendations for addressing it would require experts in a wide range of basic disciplines such as political science, psychology, sociology, natural resources, geography, history, meteorology, geology, physics, chemistry, biology, and engineering.

This is not to suggest that international corporations do not monitor environmental changes; they are geographically positioned to detect signs of change and are doubtlessly vigilant to developments. It may be advisable, however, if it is not already done, to conduct the function of environmental monitoring (including interpretation of indications and recommendations for corporate response) in a systematic and coordinated way and with an adequate staff.

A company need not have a college faculty at hand. Governmental agencies, trade associations, and research foundations provide much of the needed information. (Smaller companies especially must rely on these sources.) In addition, for most companies the fields in which pertinent developments may occur will be limited and therefore the monitoring function can be kept within encompassable bounds. But enough expertness should be present in a company to detect developments, from whatever source of information, that are germane to the company's business, to collect data, and to read into them whatever meaning they have for the future of the organization.

Of course, a monitoring system, formal or informal, must provide a means by which information and recommendations reach the executive level where decisions on response can be made—and an assurance that the report will receive an adequate hearing. Staff specialists who are aware of developments in their own fields that might impact significantly on the company's operations are often frustrated by difficulties in reaching decision makers with their "discoveries." Memoranda are not a good answer since this sort of information requires clarification and consideration of applications, processes that necessitate discussion. If the information must find its way through various hierarchical levels, its message tends to be perverted or lost. In order to give adequate consideration to the data, assuming they reach him, the executive at the decision-making level should be a broad-gauged individual who himself stays abreast of environmental developments generally and is somewhat knowledgeable in a number of fields of study.

It is often through the effects of international trade developments and global competition that temporary layoffs in the United States become permanent and jobs are lost. Knowledge of the developments would be helpful, but no amount of monitoring of trade practices and of governmental policies of foreign countries will erase the competitive disadvantage they may place the American manufacturer in. When reducing costs through efficiency measures (and sometimes union concessions regarding wages and benefits) is unavailing, decline appears inevitable, with its economic, social, and personal costs. While free trade is a meritorious objective as a universal practice, it can hardly be defended as in the interest of the country when a trading partner engages in import restrictions and subsidizes manufacturing directly or indirectly.

If plant closings and mass layoffs occur, the impact on workers alone is a staggering consequence which, as its dimensions grow, will inevitably demand a political response. Doctrinaire insistence on free trade, whatever its desirability in the absolute and its ultimate promise of economic good, will not "sell" among jobless Americans who see "unfair foreign competition" as the cause of their plight.

Under the Trade Adjustment Assistance provisions of the Federal Trade Act, the government does provide benefits to workers displaced as the result of imports. But, as pointed out in the Work in America Institute Policy Study (1984, 146–147), the benefits have been used more to supplement unemployment insurance payments than to retrain affected employees and relocate them in jobs.

An executive of a large corporation with widespread facilities and international sales foresees an era of world-wide "structural" changes involving financing, technology, and governmental deregulation. One might speculate on a resulting scenario. The economy, in effect, would be without borders and the competition would be global; barriers to trade and technology transfer would be down and subsidized manufacturing would cease; and the advantages in the world-wide competition would go to those companies which managed most efficiently on even terms. The personnel, in a version of this scenario, would be in significant part professionals who would give their primary loyalty to their professions and would be, in effect, transferable. The attraction to an individual company would be chiefly monetary, and pensions would be transferable. The scenario would not only involve a remaking of the world economy, which indeed is in process, but a remaking of man himself. He would, in effect, become a rootless wanderer forfeiting attachments, as salary inducements and professional advancement called him, to working associates, company, friends, and community. In view of the increasing number of college graduates in the American workforce, one might anticipate a greater mobility if mobility is related to educational level. But the educated person and the professional still have human needs, which this scenario is unlikely to fulfill. Professionals may see professional and economic advantages in moving, but social adjustments for families are a problem (Brett 1982).

Whatever the projected scenarios for the future, they do not provide answers to current problems of decline, nor do they invalidate the current personnel response that attempts to tighten the bond of commitment between organization and employees.

THE ISSUE OF TECHNOLOGY

A largely unquantified factor in the employment equation at this point is the effect of advancing technology, especially of automation. It is obvious that the nature of job tasks performed by employees in manufacturing operations is changed by technology. The "manual" operations will be performed increasingly by machines, and employees will engage more heavily in monitoring and troubleshooting duties. Employee responses to job situations will tend to be more procedural than motor-manipulative in nature.

Manufacturing tasks assigned to employees are certainly changing. The crucial question is whether there will be enough demand for human performance to keep employment levels from dropping significantly. Technology resulting in new products and new industries will obviously produce jobs. But the effect on employment of technology which assumes a greater share of the processing tasks in an established manufacturing operation is a different issue of concern. Perhaps this latter kind of technological advance will have spreading effects beyond a particular company or industry, and the ultimate results may be an increase in total employment. Economists can provide models showing conditions under which such development might or might not occur. But employees in a particular company (and the union representing them) are concerned with what happens, more immediately, to them. If the technology leaves enough "indirect" labor (maintenance and adjusting, monitoring and troubleshooting, programming robotic equipment, etc.) to employee performance to absorb a high proportion of current employees, programs providing for retraining and transfer of employees make eminent sense. But however felicitous the distribution of tasks between men and machines, continued employment of affected employees is likely to require expanded placement opportunities involving other plants of the company and possibly other employers.

On a strictly economic basis, a hard look at the capital investment required by an automated system is in order, along with a realistic consideration of the capacities and dependability of the system. While a blind opposition to technological changes is woefully short sighted, an effort to create a virtually workerless plant is similarly unwise. A balanced concept of what machines can do best and what people can do best is likely to lead to the most cost-effective system. This concept will shift as machine design becomes more sophisticated, but to try to program equipment to make every response a worker is capable of is a vain pursuit. The skill in human performance of manufacturing tasks has never been fully understood or appreciated. The accuracy and speed of motions, the quick perceptions of feedback and adjustments to it, and the ingenuity shown in anticipating and meeting contingencies and operating under unusual conditions are indications of the impressive performance capacities of human beings. Machines may replace their motor responses and, to some extent, their detection and processing of feedback information. In this latter regard, the author was once involved in a project to automate a hemming operation to replace "hand sewing" and learned quite early that the tactile and kinesthetic feedback by which the skilled hemmers controlled the flow of the unstable and often uneven and biased material into the sewing head could not be adequately substituted for by mechanical contrivance. Technological refinements were possible but were considered prohibitively costly and still of questionable reliability. This is not to suggest that such difficulties with an automatic process cannot be solved, but that elements of human skill should not be underestimated and lightly discarded. Further, if machines can indeed master responses and feedback as well, there are still tasks requiring human performance for successful execution. There is room for human beings.

Peter Unterweger of the United Auto Workers Research Department (1985) suggests that technology should utilize the skills and knowledge of the workforce and free people to do what they do best. He adds, "There is still another reason for opting against the model that would deskill production work and ultimately eliminate it. Doing so would create a technocracy that is out of touch with the actual process of production. It is questionable whether the complicated process of parts production and assembly will ever be reduced to the kind of science that will allow effective previsualization and predetermination of the entire process. Thus, there will continue to be a role for people with hands-on experience of the manufacturing and assembly technologies in the development of new products and processes, and in the management of the unforeseeable, but inevitable crises that arise in production processes. The deskilling of production work and its attempted elimination destroys the system that prepares workers for these functions. The workerless factory may turn out to be the ultimate in inflexibility" (573).

The effects of robotics are easy to overstate and dire predictions easy to make unless we take into account the total number of jobs and employees in the United

States. The proportion of the total American working population displaced by robotic equipment has been minor to date. Applications have been made primarily in the automotive and electrical industries. To be sure, applications are expanding. And the research is continuing; improvements are being sought in visual and tactile sensing, and responses to sound are being investigated. We may see a significant occupational impact if the capabilities of robots are enhanced and their associated costs reduced through mass production (Silvestri, Lukasiewicz, and Einstein 1984, 45). The purchase, installation, and maintenance costs are a constraining factor; in regard to capabilities, a major problem is visual capability. The process of robotic development appears to be a somewhat measured one and hardly justifies a panicky response. We have time to work out accommodations if we organize to do it.

An historical perspective tends to temper alarmism over our growing technology. Studies over the years by the Bureau of Labor Statistics on the employment effects of new technology have suggested these conclusions, in the words of Dr. Janet L. Norwood, Commissioner of Labor Statistics: "First, the gloomy predictions of a world of machines to replace most workers have not yet come to pass. Second, new technology has found its way into almost all types of business over the past several decades, and yet more workers are employed today in the United States than ever before in our history. Government policy-makers must pay attention to the possible disruptive effects of the application of new technology and foster retraining and other programs to cope with the problems which many workers will face. But the scenario of a technology-created huge labor surplus seems unlikely to occur in the foreseeable future"(1985, 13–14).

A similarly restrained view is taken by Fey (1986) in regard to the effects of robotics on employees. Noting that robots had arrived in American industry without catastrophic consequences, she examines some of the "realities of life with robots": robots are not replacing whole shifts of workers; they are just a tool; they are maintained by regular plant personnel; employees trained in them are usually selected by job category and seniority (49–51).

Currently we know enough about individual motivation and group functioning to devise a sociotechnical work structure that would strike a workable balance between automated activities and human activities and provide for employee satisfactions. Sweden (Volvo and Saab) has attempted to establish such structures. The task in the United States is not to copy such models slavishly but to devise structures that fit the American workers and serve the economic interests of American industry.

Certainly, the issue of the optimal social and economic amalgam of human skill and automation will have to be confronted. There is no lack of awareness of the elements of the problem, and certain industries and unions have taken a cooperative stance. The problem will not be solved once and for all. But the combined efforts of industry, unions, and government can provide for a rational and accommodative development.

We can be sure of this: For the health of the American society, the imperative is that its people have meaningful and rewarding work to do.

Training the Affected Workers

Apprehension about the effects of robotic technology appears to be felt primarily by low-skill workers. A review of industrial robotic literature (Chao and Kozlowski 1986) found a less favorable reaction to robot implementation among low-skill workers than among high-skill workers; the former perceived robots largely as a threat to their job security in contrast to high-skill workers who saw opportunities to expand their skills.

The lessons learned from introduction of earlier technological changes are useful in implementing robotic technology. Providing realistic information that may help modify erroneous employee perceptions is an essential early step. Where there are correct expectations of favorable effects, realistic information can fortify the expectations; where unfavorable effects are incorrectly anticipated, the information can help employees move to a constructive view. Problems are more acute when unfavorable results are correctly anticipated and when the employee expects favorable consequences that cannot be realized. In both these cases, realistic information is still in order, but information that gives due emphasis to whatever positive aspects are validly present even though the general effect is largely unfavorable. If certain advantages are to be made available to employees in the way of reassignment, transfer, retraining, job-search assistance, termination allowance, etc., these provisions should be made clear (but not overstated). And, of course, the outcomes which the company promises must occur in fact if a positive change in employee attitudes is to be sustained. Evidence of personnel planning and other company activities that demonstrate concern for the welfare of affected employees can influence attitudes favorably. A vigorous retraining program has a particularly strong appeal.

It is especially important to assure low-skill employees as well as high-skill employees that the company will make a strong effort to train them. In the reconstruction of jobs associated with technological changes, a company is well advised to design jobs of varying levels of skill so as to provide opportunities for employees of varying degrees of trainability.

Employee perceptions have a wide causative base, including past experience as well as present events and related explanations. It is reassuring to employees to have witnessed and participated in strong ongoing training programs in a plant; their expectations of training help in times of technological dislocation is likely to be enhanced thereby.

To give minimum training assistance to employees, whether of high or low skill, when their jobs are substantially changed would be a grave mistake since it would force them to rely on the transfer of largely inappropriate skills. Fortunately, we are in position at the present state of our knowledge of training to:

1. Utilize certain procedures that have served us well in the past, such as the

breaking down of a job into learning units; scheduling and sequencing units to minimize interference and maximize retention; sufficient practice to ensure overlearning; direct coaching for the purpose of cuing, feedback, and reinforcement; and follow-up for reinforcement and further correction. Our awareness, though somewhat belated, of the perceptual aspects of performance in traditional jobs should serve us well in the training of employees in technical jobs having enhanced perceptual requirements.

2. Gear our approach to the learning difficulties of individual employees in every case and avoid a premature negative judgment of the trainability of slow learners if found among low-skill employees. Generally, the effort to train slow learners would require the use of smaller learning units; more cuing, feedback, and reinforcement; more practice; a longer period of follow-up for analysis and correction of performance difficulties; and greater help to the employees in bringing the parts together for mastery of the full job. In some tasks we can reduce the burden on learning through the use of performance aids such as printed procedures and checklists.

We have also acquired some proficiency in the use of advanced training techniques involving, as primary examples, audio-visual and display techniques and computer-based programs. By these means we are better able to address the cognitive aspects of learning which are so prominent in technically advanced jobs. Through group presentations we can efficiently provide explanations and illustrations of how the new equipment works and demonstrations and explanations of required operator actions. Mock-ups and vestibule equipment can be used advantageously to give employees preliminary practice in certain cases. All in all, we can give the kind of introduction needed (1) to reduce employee apprehension, detrimental to learning, that arises from the novel and often intimidating characteristics of the new equipment and (2) to prime the employee for confronting the learning challenge of performing actual job tasks in the job setting.

There is a compelling need, whatever the start, for "hands-on" experience on the production floor. But that experience should be organized and directed to produce learning efficiently and ensure safety. Guidance by a coach should be a major element in the on-job training effort.

For all learners on all kinds of jobs, the experience of success is important to learning. It is especially important in complex jobs and with slow learners. Unless efficacy expectations are enhanced by early experiences of success (and related reinforcement), confidence in meeting later learning requirements and mastering the full job may not develop, with adverse effects on the learning process. Our training should be aimed at eliciting successes early and progressively.

Of course, some employees may fail. Conclusive signs of ineffective learning under a maximum training effort should not be ignored. But the extra training effort is justified at times of technological change. An employee's learning failure should not be attributable to poor training.

Experiences with Instituting Automation

Ford and Honeywell have developed exemplary programs of robotics training (Fey 1986, 51, 56). In Ford's four-day introductory program at Dearborn, instruction is given in a learning laboratory through the use of computers and video-disc machines and through simulated experience in manipulation of a computer-controlled electric robot. Further instruction, with heavy emphasis on safety, is given on the plant floor. Honeywell directly addresses the problem of giving robotic training to technically naive employees in that part of its program that teaches workers in the semiskilled job of molding-machine operator to use robots to unload the machines. The program in its classroom phase ensures that the employees understand the molding machine (through a return to basics) and the communication links—electrical voltages—between the molding machine and the robots. With this foundation in understanding, facilitated by a slide-tape show and a clear technical narration, the training group then proceeds to the factory floor for on-the-job practice. But a deliberate training progression, from the simple to the more complex, is observed. The computer aspect of the robot, for which the employees lack background, especially requires training help for mastery. But Honeywell's experience indicates that employees do get the "hang" of computer commands.

Advanced technology, it should be noted, may not utilize robots significantly. O'Toole's report (1985, 187–198) on Deere and Company's large new automated plant in Waterloo, Iowa, indicates that robots do "dirty, unsafe work" there but are not considered appropriate for most of the operations performed in this "flexible" manufacturing system. An effort has been made in this plant to strike a balance between technology and people. Machines do, indeed, perform all the labor but not all of the "work"; "brain work" is done by employees. Technology and human motivation are regarded by management as the two key variables in corporate performance.

Concerning the introduction of automation into office jobs, a number of lessons have been suggested by Harris (1985, 156–158), among them: small start and gradual process; continuation of training and education, one aspect of which is to "relate the new technology and skills to alterations in corporate culture" (158); and flexibility about "differences in people's pace of adjustment to the changes, in their learning capacities, and in their creative use of automated equipment" (158).

Since technological changes in manufacturing and their incremental installation have long been a way of life for operating managers, the managers may underestimate the importance of the issue of compatibility with values in the organizational cultures when they attempt to institute truly substantial technological changes. In planning for technological changes, a company should give attention to corporate values and the possible effect on them of the new technology (Hutchinson and Gilbert 1985).

The psychological adjustment required of still-employed workers by major technological changes and robotic installations in the workplace has not been very extensively investigated, but the presence of so-called "technostress" and "robo-shock" has been observed. Obviously, the question of job satisfaction needs reexploring in the light of the new work environment, job activities, and pay basis. Opportunities for social contact with fellow employees will diminish as a source of satisfaction, and the man-robot interaction represents an uncharted realm of human functioning (although not beyond the imagining of science fiction writers.)

Among the proposals that Harris (1985, 189–190) makes to managers for installations of robotics, based on insights from cases, are several that appear specifically aimed at easing the problem of psychological adjustment. "Seek to develop a user friendly attitude toward the robot: Involve workers in the planning process, let them have contests to name the mechanical device, conduct initiation parties for the new robot, emphasize its positive applications, inform employees' families about the development" (189). Provide communication that among many aspects, prepares employees for the change in the pattern of social interactions. Train employees in the new work culture as well as in the technical aspects of robotic operations.

THE ROLE OF GOVERNMENT

Any discussion addressing the problem of curbing involuntary turnover would be incomplete without a final reference to the role of government. As indicated earlier, restrictions on plant closing have been somewhat slow in evolving. Yet the federal government has passed such legislation as the Job Training Partnership Act and Trade Adjustment Assistance (though questions can be raised about the effective use of the latter); and the number of states providing for short-time compensation attached to work-sharing plans has been increasing. There are definite signs that further trade legislation calling for "fair" competitive practices but short of protectionism is in prospect. We can also expect that the federal government will move further to encourage business development in depressed areas and to assist laid-off workers to relocate.

It is safe to predict that additional legislative action will occur. The pace of the legislation and its provisions are likely to be moderate, unless the incidence of large-scale layoffs increases. But whatever the future holds in regard to employment, social concern for job security appears to be now firmly in place, and legislators are not likely to be unmindful of this development or unresponsive to it.

The Work in America Institute makes a number of recommendations on the supportive role government could play (1984, 144–158). Among the proposals is the inclusion of job security provisions in congressional actions on tax policy, trade assistance (import protection or export subsidies), awarding of major governmental contracts, and allowance for accelerated depreciation.

While the government certainly has a role to play in job security and workforce stabilization, it is still not likely to be the major one. The primary agents will be the companies themselves. Job maintenance is unlikely to be mandated by legislation to a substantial degree, although some actions aimed at greater employee protection can be anticipated. If further significant movement is to occur, it will be largely on the basis of company convictions (arising from realistic evidence) that greater job security for employees is an expression of both sound economic policy, of benefit to the company, and of the company's social responsibility—and that these two objectives are not incompatible.

CHANGE IN COMPANY VIEWS OF EMPLOYEE SECURITY

It is evident that progressive companies are shifting their thinking from the concept of job security narrowly viewed as long-term retention in a relatively unvarying job, to the concept of employment security involving continued employment but requiring a wider range of competences and the continuing development of new skills. Very heavy emphasis is therefore placed on training. It is "cross training" in existing jobs that will enable employees to continue to function effectively when minor changes are made in product mix or processing methods and employees must be shifted among job assignments. And it is preparatory training in new technology that will enable employees to adjust to whatever major changes in processing and product a company may make in order to hold or strengthen its competitive position. In both cases, efficiency of operations among changed circumstances is better assured and the company is in better position to retain its employees.

A fundamental characteristic of a stable workforce currently is its adaptability to changing requirements in performance and learning. Cultivation of such a workforce is now seen by many companies as necessary for meeting the competitive challenges of a changing world.

7

Addressing Involuntary Turnover: Outplacement

When workforce reductions occur—which realistically can be expected at times despite a company's efforts to retain its employees—employers are increasingly coming to accept some measure of responsibility for assisting terminated employees to adjust to their status and to search for new jobs. Employees may lack the psychological toughness, the resources, and the know-how to carry out this process efficiently or successfully on their own. The help commonly given by companies has taken on the designation of "outplacement." Outplacement services are given primarily to salaried personnel and in increasing numbers; but their application to hourly paid employees is growing.

OUTPLACEMENT SERVICES AND PROCEDURES

Outplacement procedures can be planned and executed by the organization itself or with the service of a consulting firm. Outplacement consultants also conduct seminars to train company personnel in how to proceed. Foxman and Polsky (1984), in their discussion of selecting an outplacement firm, suggest a list of services a good outplacement firm should provide: alleviation of separation trauma, career exploration, resume preparation, communicating with the individual's contacts, audiotaped role-playing sessions (for teaching telephone techniques), videotaped role-playing sessions (for interview practice), and outgoing advice and counsel. Adequate facilities are required if the services are to be effective. These include office facilities, research resources, secretarial equipment and services, and audio-visual equipment. And, of course, trained personnel are needed to conduct the program.

In some companies, the outplacement function is split between company personnel and the consulting firm; the company itself may conduct a program for hourly paid employees and use a consultant for salaried employees. Or the company may give services to hourly paid employees, supervisors, and middle

management but employ a consultant in the termination of highest-level managerial personnel. Consultants may set up shop at or near the company site, or
terminated employees may be sent to the consultants' headquarters. In the interest
of immediacy of help, important in confronting job loss, the on-site arrangement
is probably preferable.

The "boom" in outplacement programs is evident in the proliferation of
outplacement firms. The Directory of Outplacement Firms (1982) lists 54 firms
that provide services compensated only by employers and 28 firms that also offer
services to individuals.

It is clear that outplacement firms should be concerned—as many are—not
only with assisting an employee to institute a job search but with uncoupling
him as felicitously as possible from his old job (Sweet 1975). There is life for
the employee after job loss, and it is not suspended during the period between
the termination notice and the job search—between termination and outplacement. He faces immediate problems after termination, such commonplace matters
as informing his spouse and family and confronting friends and fellow workers
or professional associates. Delay in providing help can be psychologically risky.
Indeed, a comprehensive outplacement service will back into the termination
process itself, where the trauma is created, at least to the extent of giving guidance
to company personnel who carry out the termination procedure. The termination
is stressful enough; botching the process can compound the ill effects.

A straightforward statement of the case appears advisable, and an avoidance
of personal criticism. If the termination is the result of "impersonal" decisions
to cut or restructure staff or eliminate jobs, a clear statement to that effect might
lessen the blow to the employee's self-esteem. He should have an opportunity
to express himself and vent his feelings. Timing of the termination is considered
significant; right before a weekend is not seen as a propitious time, especially
if the outplacement process and particularly its beginning attempt to reduce
trauma are delayed.

The problem of helping the employee cope with the emotional trauma caused
by his separation apparently must be faced early if practical help in job hunting
is to be acceptable and effective. This aspect of the program especially requires
professional personnel, and it is comforting to know that a foremost consulting
firm has 12 certified psychologists on its staff. Unfortunately, this part of the
program is likely to be the weakest link, especially in company-conducted programs that have a limited professional staff to call upon. This is not to advocate
the hiring of consultants but to emphasize the importance of trained personnel
in an outplacement program, whoever the conductor.

Outplacement services by consulting firms do not come cheaply. In a random
sampling of ten such firms taken from the 1982 directory, the fees ranged from
12 to 16% of compensation (total yearly salaries). Most firms—six of the ten—
charged 15%. Minimum fees were specified in most cases, and several firms
added a charge ($750 or $1,000) for administrative expenses.

Dislocated Worker Program

Title III of the Job Training Partnership Act of 1983 provides for a Dislocated Worker Program which gives assistance to workers who have lost their jobs or are in danger of losing them because of plant closings and massive layoffs caused by competition and technological changes (Cook and Turnage 1985). The legislation requires that 70% of Title III funds go to training, but other services (financial, counseling, job search) may be provided to help the displaced workers gain employment. The states have almost complete jurisdiction over the use of Title III funds and administer the program.

The program as carried out in a community can be illustrated by reviewing the activities of a Displaced Worker Program representative attached to a local State Employment Security Commission office.

For those eligible for the program because of plant closings or elimination of jobs, the representative conducts a two-hour workshop, for groups, on job-seeking skills and a one-hour counseling session with each worker. From the counseling and related identification of qualifications and interests (which may involve testing), the displaced employee could be placed in one of these programs:

1. A two-year (or less) occupational training program at a two-year college, in this case a community college. The program pays for tuition, books and supplies, and insurance.
2. On-job training up to a year in a company which gives assurance of employment at the end of the training. The program reimburses the company for half the hourly wage paid during training.

In the case of displaced employees who take the course of directly seeking employment, the representative assists in the job search. He also follows up those in training to assist in job placement. The resources of the Employment Security Commission office are used in the job placement endeavor.

As the representative observed, the goal is to place employees within 90 days but is modified in terms of the particular program undertaken. The representative may have additional interviewing contacts with the worker in the job-seeking period. The services may be given at a facility established by the company terminating the employees and may be synchronized with the outplacement procedure of that organization. A relatively high percentage of the displaced personnel choose the training options. As might be expected, the percentage is higher for those whose jobs are unique to the particular plant than for those whose job skills are marketable in the community.

Trade Act of 1974

Under the "adjustment assistance" provisions of the Trade Act of 1974, help is provided to American work groups who suffer total or partial separation from their jobs (or whose jobs are threatened) by an increase of imports.

The purpose of the Trade Act is broad: "To promote the development of an open, nondiscriminatory, and fair world economic system, to stimulate fair and free competition between the United States and foreign nations, to foster the economic growth of, and full employment in, the United States and for other purposes."

The adjustment assistance benefits provided under the original 1974 legislation in regard to its employment intent include the following:

1. A trade readjustment allowance of 70% of the worker's weekly wage (reduced by 50% of the amount of the remuneration for services performed during each week, also by the amount of unemployment insurance received) for a period up to 52 weeks. Payments may be made for up to 26 additional weeks in special circumstances involving completion of training of older workers. Special provisions apply to eligible workers undergoing approved training.

2. Training and related services. The Secretary of Labor will attempt to secure, for eligible workers, counseling, testing, and placement services provided under other federal law and, when appropriate, procure such services through agreement with cooperating state agencies. In regard to training, if it is determined that there is no suitable employment for the adversely affected worker but that such employment would be available if the worker received appropriate training, the Secretary shall provide or assure such training on the job. In addition, he may authorize supplemental assistance for transportation and subsistence expenses if the training facility is beyond commuting distance. Subsistence allowance: up to $15 per day. Travel allowance: up to 12 cents per mile.

3. Job search and relocation allowance. An eligible worker totally separated from his job (and who cannot reasonably be expected to secure employment in his commuting area) may be granted 80% of his necessary job search expenses, up to $500. If a worker has obtained employment (expected to be long term) in an area in which he wants to relocate, he may receive a relocation allowance that includes 80% of reasonable and necessary expenses for moving his family and household and a lump sum equivalent to three times his average weekly wage (up to $500).

EXAMPLES OF OUTPLACEMENT PROGRAMS

The following descriptions, along with critical comments, are given of actual separation and outplacement programs. These programs involved relatively large numbers of involuntarily terminated employees.

Program 1: For Hourly Paid Employees

In example 1, hourly paid employees were laid off, with little likelihood of recall, when the operational level was reduced in response to lower product demand.

The company established and ran the program itself, setting up and staffing an off-the-premise office for the operation. The local Employment Security Commission office cooperated in the program, making a staff member available to assist.

The services provided by the company in the outplacement office included help with filling out resumes and applications, typing these forms, providing free telephoning for contacting prospective employers or following other leads, and supplying informational material concerning job openings. The employees were given copies of their own resumes for their use, and the company compiled a book of resumes and distributed copies of it to a large number of companies within a 100-mile distance of the plant, directly contacting the employment manager or the facility manager of these companies in making the distribution. The company helped employees set up interviews in the sense of identifying interested employers, but the further initiative was left up to the employees.

The program was voluntary. Sixty-five percent of the laid-off employees responded positively to the letter of invitation to participate in the program. Time spent in the outplacement office varied; it was not unusual for an employee to spend up to five hours there. The company stressed its role as a helper in the job search but made clear that responsibility for ultimate placement was the employee's and that the company was not establishing a job referral and placement system. Once a prospective employer expressed an interest in a distributed resume, it was up to the employee to pursue the matter. Or if the employee found leads of his own, it was his function to follow them, but with the help of the typing and telephoning services available to him in the outplacement office if he chose to use them.

Of the employees participating in the program, 66% were placed in jobs and another 7% in training under the Job Training Partnership Act Program.

Major problems of outplacement anticipated by the company in this program were (1) acceptance by the employees of lower-paying jobs since its own wage scale was high and (2) the appeal to other, lower-paying employers in the area of applicants accustomed to high earnings. It was found that most employees in the program were willing to take jobs paying less money and were interested in stable employment. And there were no complaints from other companies on the score of earnings expectations of the applicants; some of them made more than one request that applicants be referred to them.

The company regarded the program as a success and ascribed the success in part to the positive attitude toward it which developed among laid-off employees and the public at large. Employee frustration was present, along with skepticism about the program, but there was also a genuine desire for help. Skepticism diminished in the light of the company's obviously substantial effort.

One could characterize this program generally as being heavy in practical help to the laid-off employee in his search for a job. It did not directly address the problem of ''separation trauma'' experienced by employees; nor did it provide vocational or career counseling, although it did explore employee experience and interests as it assisted with the preparation of resumes. In addition, the long-range results remain to be determined, particularly the degree of satisfaction and persistence of the placed employees in their lower-paying jobs.

Program 2: For Hourly Paid Employees

In example 2, a company discontinued major items in a product line because of reduced demand and closed the old plant that manufactured the product. A significant percentage of employees were transferred with retained seniority to another and newer plant in the same town where the remaining product items were to be made ("moved with the machinery," as some employees described it). The others—a majority—were given preferential hiring in the company's other plants, some of which were located in the same town and others scattered in the state and outside it. Production of the line items scheduled to be dropped was to continue for about six months, at which time the old plant was to be closed.

A week after the original announcement to employees and the public concerning the closing of the plant and the provisions for employees, the plant manager and two personnel staff members met with employee groups in each department and on every shift. The plant manager presided at the meetings, and the personnel people provided information on unemployment compensation, vacation pay, benefits, and other matters of rights and procedures associated with the layoff. The personnel representatives then conducted interviews in the plant with each of the employees over the next three-week period.

In the interview, the employee and personnel representative jointly explored the employee's job experience and skills and other qualifications and the employee's preferences as to type of job, shift, and plant location. The intent was to develop an informational base for placement of the employee within the company. The employee was also referred to the displaced workers' program and to the Employment Security Commission office for information and help in regard to other job opportunities and training.

From the information secured in the interviews, supplemented by information from supervisors on employee skills and by the employee's service record, the employment office compiled a placement file for each employee. This file served as a vehicle for referring employees to company plants where openings occurred. For placement outside the company, the Employment Security Commission office provided the service.

A month after the plant had closed, about 40% of the employees had been placed in other company plants. Fewer than 1% of these elected to accept employment in out-of-town plants, these in the plant nearest to town.

In the interviews, many employees expressed anger, found fault with the company, and expressed the view that the company was obligated to "take care" of them. These sentiments persisted in a number of cases. And rigid demands as to earnings, shift, and location continued in many cases and did not seem to moderate substantially while unemployment compensation was being received.

The interviewers were not regarded altogether as providing help objectively, but were seen by some employees as representing the organization that "caused the trouble."

In an early reaction, a large number of the employees indicated an interest in taking training under the Job Training Partnership Act, but most of them dropped this option later.

A basic approach of the program was to help the employee find a job, particularly within the company, but to lead him to assume a large share of the job-finding responsibility himself. This approach was considered to have moderate but not substantial success. It is possible that the long period between the beginning announcement and the actual closing of the plant worked, unexpectedly, to the program's disadvantage. It would permit time, the thought was, for the employees to adjust to their situation and to pursue other employment. But the continuation of adverse attitudes suggests that many employees did not move to positive personal efforts to solve their problems or to the frame of mind needed for such efforts. They seemed to reinforce each other in a negative stance. Perhaps the period was too long. An alternative hypothesis is that constructive action during a long period requires that the employee be helped early in the game to cope with his emotional responses. Although this program provided practical help, it did not address the problem of the employees' psychological adjustment at the crucial time when the problem arose.

Although the employee must ultimately shoulder the burden to ameliorate his own condition, as the program recognized, the program appears to have thrust the burden on him without sufficient regard for his readiness to take it.

There may be merit in the view that the displaced employee's attitudes and frame of mind may be favorably influenced by moving him, as the prime actor, into the practical business of seeking a new job. But there are questions concerning the timing of the movement and the help that should precede and accompany it; and the larger question of a company's degree of responsibility in the whole matter and particularly for providing more than "practical" help.

This case also raises a question concerning the mobility of laid-off employees. Employees in this instance were simply not willing to move any significant distance from home base.

Program 3: For Salaried Employees

In example 3, a retrenchment program involved the dismissal of salaried employees in middle-management staff positions and plant supervisory positions. The outplacement program was carried out by the company itself and was the responsibility of a personnel staff member experienced in counseling.

Notification of dismissal was given to the affected employees by the managers of the particular staff department or manufacturing plant. They followed a set of guidelines ("do's and don'ts") issued by the outplacement manager.

The terminated employees then met with the outplacement manager in groups for a session of three hours devoted to the task of reducing negative attitudes, instituting a positive view of future prospects, and beginning the process of job search.

The employees were invited to explore and express their feelings; they were asked to identify the feelings and consequences associated with the job loss (and related losses), but were directed toward means of rebuilding self-esteem and finding support. After expressing and discussing feelings, they were asked to take stock of themselves (their experience, skills, abilities, interests, needs), to set employment objectives, and to develop a job-hunting strategy. They were given an assignment to write a resume and to develop a set of index cards of prospective employers (companies, agencies, institutions). There was evidence that the employees received psychological support from each other in the group session.

Thereafter, the process became an individual matter with the outplacement manager providing guidance and the organization providing office space, resume typing, telephone privileges, and sources of placement information (newspaper advertisements, directories of manufacturing firms, etc.). On a voluntary basis, employees remained in contact with the outplacement manager and continued to use the outplacement facilities. This process went on for as long as four months in some cases. Coaching in interviewing was provided as requested, but no career counseling, as such, was given.

This program gave attention to the early reduction of emotional trauma and the restoring of self-confidence. Many of the personnel in the program appeared to take a rather positive view in the early going. They seemed to recognize that the industry in general had to retrench, but were raising the question: Why me? They tended to assure themselves, through the program, that personal deficiencies were not the answer. But self-doubt was found to reemerge in some cases as time went on without success in the search for a new position. The question arises: Was the early effort by the outplacement manager to help the employees confront the stress of job loss, though it appeared to have salutary effects, strong enough to sustain the employees in their continuing efforts to find work, especially when the process was prolonged? Were further such efforts indicated?

Certain individuals were found to adhere rigidly to unrealistic requirements as to job location, type and level of job, and salary. The three-hour session, though skillfully conducted, did not manage to instill pliability in their job search; nor, in some cases, did later events avail.

About two-thirds of the terminated employees found positions with the company itself or with other firms. Mobility was an insurmountable problem with some employees, but most were willing to move for an attractive position. In general, the program was considered a success, but it raised several questions in addition to the issue of the adequacy of the attitude-altering efforts.

Follow-up was recognized as a weakness in the program. There were no provisions for extending the contact or for systematically tracking the entry of personnel into new jobs or the status of those who had dropped out of the program or failed, despite it, to find a job or establish a business. Training in interviewing, it was felt, could have been carried further and applied to more people. The larger question could be raised: How far should the outplacement function move into the new hiring process? Is it sufficient to assist the employee to reach the entrance door and not to prepare him to go through it or actively help him through it? Since terminated personnel in a case like this one occupied key positions in the organization and helped to keep it functioning satisfactorily in better times, perhaps pointing them in the direction of a new job may not represent a sufficient obligation, even allowing for the salving gesture of giving a separation bonus.

In such a case an organization is well advised to address the possible adverse effect on those who remain—the collaborators and buddies of those who left—and on whom the effectiveness and recovery of the organization now heavily depend.

Program 4: For Professional Employees

In this example, a high-technology company reduced its force of scientific and technical personnel, employing a consulting firm to conduct the outplacement program.

The account below was given, in response to questions, by a research scientist who was terminated in the third of a series of cutbacks involving a significant number of employees.

How was the program conducted?

The very morning of being informed of the layoff, I was taken by my boss to a comfortable meeting room in the personnel building where there were a dozen others of my rank who also had been laid off that morning. In this room was a representative of the company who was handling the outplacement program. As we entered, we were asked by the representative how we felt, and there was a discussion among the group of the feelings we were experiencing. This lasted less than an hour, after which we were escorted back to our work locations so that we could clean out our desks. It turned out that for the next four days of meetings, our group was kept together and led in the training sessions by the same leader present with us the first day.

For the next four days we were in training sessions held during the same work hours as our job, 8:30 a.m. to 5:00 p.m. These sessions were held in a building off site which the company had rented. During these sessions, we were instructed in resume writing, job search methods, and interview technique. The interview training was the most valuable, and in the course of instruction we were shown a videotape of mock "bad" and "good" interviews, and several volunteers were led and analyzed in practice interviews by our instructor.

For a following period of several months, we were provided unlimited long-distance telephone access at the outplacement center, and the secretaries on site acted for us as an answering service. These secretaries had also typed our resumes and provided us with clean photocopies thereof. No charge was made to the employee for any of the services I have mentioned.

What were the strengths of the program?

The leader of my group was able to create in each group member a feeling of confidence in the prospect of securing a new job. We felt that after the training sessions we were much more capable of "selling" ourselves than we had been, and in particular more capable than the average person who would be competing for a job against us.

Other, more tangible strengths of the program certainly included the secretarial services and telephone access.

What were the weaknesses of the program?

I was able to find a job soon after the outplacement program. Many others were not able to find new employment after several months, and it would have been helpful to have some sort of a follow-up program to maintain their levels of confidence. (This might even have been provided; I'm not sure it wasn't.)

*Did the consultant do anything beyond the discussion of feelings
to reduce the emotional response?*

He assured us that we would be busy for the rest of the week. He didn't explain exactly what we'd be doing, but said we'd find out the next day. But just the mention, that our immediate futures had been planned for, created a note of healthy expectation.

We just sat around the conference table. He sat at the head. There wasn't the impression that we would be there very long. In fact, I now recall that each of us was called out after a bit to have our exit interviews with the personnel people, in order to choose retirement money distribution options and sign nondisclosure documents. After this we were taken back to our desks for the last time.

*How did he create the feeling of confidence in the job-securing
prospect that you mentioned?*

He convinced us by example and anecdote that certain interview behaviors can affect the chances of being hired. (Examples: style of dress, posture, fielding of the "impossible" questions, for example, "What are your weaknesses?") Now that we had been shown the "correct" behaviors and responses (which we tailored to our own job specialties), now that we were becoming versed in them (and most of us were quite sloppy in every regard at the beginning), we felt much more capable. Part of the feeling of confidence came also because we were in a group and were able to witness each other's weaknesses and improvement.

What were the effects on those who stayed?

I was with the company during two earlier rounds of reduction in force. In the first, special incentives were provided for early retirement. At this time it was already widely rumored that more severe layoff actions were on the way. With the arrival of the incentive program, cynicism among my co-workers blossomed and evidenced itself in hall jokes and a general attitude of "waiting," which in my own case had the curious effect not of reducing productivity but of lessening deadline tension. Time tables seemed up in the air. But it did seem as if a lot of time was taken in pondering and discussing the health of the company.

Several months later there came another reduction-in-force action where a couple hundred employees were forced to leave. Following this action, rumors of more layoffs persisted, and the general effect on worker attitude was a lack of confidence in the future of the company. Many became convinced the company was headed for bankruptcy in a year or two. I know of one worker who simply quit producing reports, quit going to meetings, since he was planning to leave the company anyway, but felt he wouldn't be fired until the lay off and then could participate in the lay off program. (He was right.) Another worker suffered a fatal coronary at work during this period of lay off rumors. This report naturally worsened employee attitude, which now took the line of how cruel the company was. Rumors came that people rather high in management were losing faith in the company and searching for jobs elsewhere. Several employees in my group, myself included, began to make inquiries for jobs elsewhere. A few months later came the lay off wave in which I was included.

It might be conjectured that the relatively low level of anxiety and relatively high level of confidence expressed by this respondent were due in part to the fact that these employees were highly trained professionals for the most part and appeared to have little doubt about the salability of their skills.

Program 5: The UAW–Ford Program at San Jose

This example is based on the published report (Hansen 1985) of a noteworthy program developed by Ford Motor Company and the UAW to assist employees who lost jobs when Ford closed its San Jose, California, assembly plant. The closing was announced in November 1982 and was to be effective in May 1983.

Heavy emphasis was placed on training in this program. The Employee Development and Training Committee, a joint union–management committee which had been created earlier as part of the 1982 contract agreement to address employee-training matters, moved in collaboration with state and public agencies to devise and carry out a program specifically for confronting the San Jose problem. The program included these features:

Orientation and benefits information: Employees were informed in meetings concerning the plant closing, benefits, the outplacement program, and procedures for participating in the program. Each employee was also informed concerning his specific benefit situation.

Assessment and testing: Employees wishing to participate in remedial education courses and targeted vocational retraining programs were required to take tests for evaluation of educational and training needs. Counselors from the California Employment and Development Department explained the results to employees and channeled them into appropriate directions (among adult basic education, vocational training, and job search).

Adult basic education: Courses were given by the Milpitas Adult Education office in academic subjects and in general educational development. These were taught in the plant after work.

Vocational exploration courses: These were courses for exploration of skilled trades lasting from two days to two weeks and given by experienced Ford personnel in the plant during assembly-line downtime. Employees who on the basis of this short exploration became interested in pursuing a trade could enter formal training courses.

Seminars: Outside providers gave a variety of in-plant seminars, some with a vocational orientation but others addressing matters of personal concern (financial counseling, loan seminar).

Targeted vocational retraining: Workers were enrolled in more than 30 targeted retraining courses in skilled trades and technical occupations. The courses were given by selected area educational and technical training institutions. This part of the program was a major aspect of the total undertaking and was paid for through the Employee Development and Training Program fund (the so-called "nickel fund"—five cents per hour worked—made available by the company in the 1982 contractual agreement), Title III of the Job Training Partnership Act, the Trade Adjustment Act, and the California Employment and Training Panel.

Prepaid tuition assistance: A tuition assistance program for employees, provided for in the 1982 contract, was applied to laid off San Jose workers. Tuition and fees up to $1,000 per year at an approved educational institution could be granted.

On-the-job training: An on-the-job training program was funded through a grant from the California Employment and Training Panel. Under this program a team of developers—experienced Ford production personnel—were hired, occupations and training sites were determined, employees were selected and placed in on-job training slots, and trainee progress was monitored.

Job search training and job placement: Job search training workshops of two days were conducted by California Employment Development Department staff members for employees ready to begin a job search. But the Employee Job Development and Training Program Committee was also active in placement endeavors; area employers were contacted and, as plant closure approached, the activities were formalized, an expanded job placement center was opened, and a "job club" was formed.

Preferential placement: Ford assisted qualified employees to transfer to other company locations where openings existed, in terms of the preferential placement provisions of the 1982 national agreement with the UAW.

As measured by the heavy participation of employees in the program and the large number of workers placed, this program could be considered effective, indeed exemplary. Its success can probably be ascribed in large part to the substantial dimensions of the undertaking in terms of program components and the number of organizations and agencies involved in the effort. In addition, program parts had "teeth" in them to ensure placement; the institutions given targeted vocational retraining contracts had to place a substantial number of trained employees in jobs in order to receive payment, and the companies selected for on-job training programs had to commit themselves to hire the trainees.

But Ford and the UAW had the unique advantage of already having a joint company–union training committee and available training funds as the result of earlier contract agreements. These could be targeted on the San Jose layoffs. Furthermore, other contract provisions, involving tuition assistance and preferential placement, were at hand to be applied to San Jose employees in constructing a comprehensive reemployment program.

As indicated earlier, a concern of outplacement program managers is the adequacy of the help given for countering the emotional effects of job loss. It would appear that psychological counseling for this specific purpose may not have been needed as much in this layoff as in others because of the heavy commitment of resources and personnel, obvious from the start, to help the employee prepare for and acquire new jobs in this case. The six months between announcement of the closing and the closing were marked by a number of ongoing activities. Employees apparently felt confident—and remained confident as the program went forward with their participation—that a maximum effort was being made in their behalf and that the chance of a favorable outcome was good. In addition, aspects of this program, such as the evaluation of qualifications and the vocational exploratory courses, gave the program characteristics of career development and doubtlessly, for some employees, imparted a positive tone to an otherwise troubling circumstance. And the organization of a job club apparently provided a means of mutual support.

Evidence that the employees coped comparatively well with the traumatic effects of the San Jose layoffs under this program is seen in a lower incidence of social pathologies than experienced in similar plant closings.

Other UAW–Ford Programs

The joint UAW–Ford effort to assist displaced workers has expanded significantly in the last few years (Goldberg 1985). A program similar to the San Jose program, with local variations, was instituted in Sheffield, Alabama, when a Ford casting plant closed there in 1983. There, as in San Jose, a joint labor–management committee in collaboration with state and community agencies and the UAW–Ford National Center provided broad services to displaced workers. Under the guidance of local committees and National Center personnel, discrete services pertinent to the local situation were given to displaced Ford employees in many locations. And, beginning in March 1984 at Fraser, Michigan, the establishment of regional Career Service and Reemployment Centers was undertaken. Three centers were established in southeastern Michigan, one in Indianapolis, Indiana, and one in Lima, Ohio (another in Ohio was being planned). These centers give a wide range of counseling, educational, and placement assistance services.

It is noteworthy, in the light of relocation difficulties noted generally with displaced employees, that in the Michigan area a Family Relocation Service Center was established to provide adjunct services before and after relocation to families that move. The services include family and individual counseling, placement assistance for family members, relocation planning, financial assistance referral, and community information.

AFL–CIO Program

The AFL–CIO itself has taken steps to help union members affected by plant closings and resultant layoffs (Human Resources Development Institute 1982). The Human Resources Development Institute, the employment and training agency of the AFL–CIO, has developed and administered a two-phase program to address the displaced workers' immediate and long-range needs. Immediate assistance is given primarily through a worker assistance workshop which addresses the topics of union benefits, tips on getting a job, coping with job loss, and claiming unemployment compensation. In the second phase, following the workshop, the program gives further services to facilitate reemployment such as job search assistance, retraining, and other special services (providing help and referrals to employees who have financial and personal problems or need stress-related counseling, for example).

In this program, the Human Resources Development Institute works in cooperation with representatives of the AFL–CIO Department of Community Services, with community agencies, and the state Employment Service and utilizes applicable governmental programs (Job Training Partnership, Trade Adjustment Assistance).

THE LESSONS OF EXPERIENCE

The need for advance planning, a comprehensive program, and collaborative efforts of union, company, and community (such as demonstrated in the UAW–Ford programs) in the event of plant closings is a lesson painfully learned in the experience with steel plant shutdowns in Youngstown, Ohio, in the early 1980's. An evaluative study by Buss and Redburn (1983) indicated difficulties and failures in programs at Youngstown to reduce the stress to employees and to increase their competence and coping skills. It found existing human services to be inappropriate and unable to overcome the obstacles of lack of knowledge and understanding (at local and higher levels) and to modify the structure of programs sufficiently to recognize and address the particular needs of the recently unemployed workers (128–131). The investigators propose social policies for mass unemployment that would include developmental and maintenance programs as well as crisis intervention programs. The proposals include employment policy and specify what the private sector can do (prepare for plant close, early warning, reemployment and training responsibilities, and dissemination of information);

they also specify the role of the community (133–148). An effective human service response, the authors conclude, would be one that "recognizes the distinctive needs produced by sudden, massive layoffs of experienced workers; devises new outreach techniques to provide early identification and intervention to prevent severe personal crisis; and consistent with local priorities and funding limits, develops innovative service programs that lie outside the normal responsibilities (although not the capacities) of local service providers and require a reorientation of staff and administrative procedures"(153).

Experience generally with outplacement programs points rather convincingly to the need for a highly supportive and sustained approach, including help to the employee in adjusting emotionally to his situation; highly visible practical steps to place him, including realistic training geared to actual job placement; relocation assistance; and follow-up of his situation for a reasonable time. But outplacement is best viewed by those administering it not as an isolated technique but as a multifaceted part of the general effort to keep the individual employed and occupationally developing. And if outplacement is carried out effectively, the affected employee, despite the negative aspects of his situation, may come to the relatively constructive view that outplacement is a transitional episode in his progressive work experience (an interim period in his occupational career, as many professional-level employees seem to perceive it). The requisite condition is that outplacement come to mean placement.

For the individuals suffering job loss, reemployment success may be related to expectations of successful job search, as indicated in a study of terminated hospital workers by Kanfer and Hulin (1985). The expectations associated with reemployment success, it was found, were expectations on the part of employees that they would master the behaviors required in the job search itself. The obvious lesson for outplacement officers is to emphasize the development of competence in job-search activities among terminated employees.

8

Labor Sources: The Labor Force and the Unemployed

Effective personnel policies and personnel planning would seem to depend heavily on accurate knowledge of labor sources. A corporation may seek to stabilize its workforce in order to retain high-producing work groups, preserve job skills of individual employees, or enhance the organizational commitment of its employees, but another fundamental choice must be made. If the corporation concludes that it can continuously fill its workforce requirements by finding adequate applicants, in terms of numbers and qualifications, in the labor market, it may see no compelling reason to take deliberate steps to stabilize its workforce. But if it perceives uncertainties and inadequacies in the outside labor source, it will see strong advantages in stabilization. The crucial question: How deep, dependable, and enduring are the labor sources?

The obvious requirement is to examine the labor force and the unemployed segment of it to ascertain characteristics, developments, and projections. Otherwise, personnel policy decisions in regard to recruitment, selection, promotion, layoffs, benefits, and related personnel matters would be made somewhat in the blind; and an important ingredient would be missing for the kind of personnel planning that would ensure the presence of employee competences to meet corporate objectives.

We shall examine progressively the general population, the labor force, and the unemployed population. The governmental estimates or projections cited are "middle" or "moderate" ones.

THE POPULATION

According to the middle estimates of the U. S. Bureau of the Census (Series P–25, No. 952, 1984), the U. S. population total will reach 268 million in the year 2000 from 232.1 million in 1982. In terms of percentages, the rate of growth during the 1980's will be 0.92 per year (the lowest decade growth since the

1930's). The population will grow even more slowly after 1995, and by 2050 the growth will virtually stop.

Average percentage of growth for the rest of the century:

1980– 1985	0.94
1985– 1990	0.90
1990– 1995	0.78
1995– 2000	0.64

The middle growth projection of the population age 16 and over is an average rate of 0.9% between 1982 and 1995. Within that period the annual growth rate will drop from 1.1% annually in the 1982–1988 period to 0.8% annually between 1988 and 1995 (Andreassen, Saunders, and Su 1984, 10).

Age

One of the most notable characteristics of the population is its overall aging. In 1982 the median age was 30.6 years, an all-time high, but it is projected to go considerably higher—to 33.0 years by 1990 and 36.3 by 2000 and even higher in the next century. A principal factor in the upward shift is the aging of the "baby boomers"; they will all be over age 35 by the year 2000.

The elderly population (65 and over) will increase steadily from the 1982 level of 26.8 million to about 33.9 million in 1995; the growth will slow down at the turn of the century as the small "cohorts" of the depression then reach their late 60's; and after 2005 the elderly population will climb to 64.6 million in 2030 as the baby boomers reach the elderly age. The 85-and-over population, part of the elderly group, will grow even faster than the 65-and-over group as a whole.

Percentage of elderly in total population:

1985	12.0
1990	12.7
1995	13.1
2000	13.0
—	—
2030	21.2

Race

The white population will grow from the 1982 level of 198.5 million to 222.7 million in 2000. The population of blacks and other races will experience a higher rate of increase, going from 33.6 million in 1982 to 45.3 million in 2000. The proportion of the population that includes blacks and other minority races will reach 16.9 in 2000 from 14.5 in 1982 and a projected 15.6 in 1990.

Percentage increase in population by race:

	White	Black and Other
1990	0.75	1.83
2000	0.55	1.53

In 1984 the black population grew more than twice as rapidly as the white (1.5 to 0.7%), but rates for both races have dropped appreciably since 1960 (Series P–25, No. 971, 1985). The higher growth rate for black and other races is attributed to a higher fertility rate of both blacks and other races and the high volume of immigration of other races.

Dependency

The significant change in the dependency ratio (number of children and elderly for every 100 people in the working age of 18 to 64) is the rise in the expected elderly dependency ratio. The dependency ratio of the youthful population is expected to decline to 36.2 in 2010 and then to stabilize. The ratio for elderly dependency will rise slowly until 2019 but will then increase sharply and, after 2030, will exceed the youthful dependency ratio.

Dependency ratios:

	Under Age 18	Age 65 and over
1985	42.7	19.4
1990	41.9	20.6
1995	42.3	21.4
2000	40.7	21.1

Geographic Distribution

The movement of population to the south and west continued in the early 1980's; these regions accounted for 91.2% of the 9.6 million growth in the 1980–1984 period (Series P–25, No. 970, 1985). California led the growth, followed by Texas and Florida.

A notable fact, however, is that several of the midwestern states turned their situations around in the 1983–1984 period. Ohio, Indiana, Michigan, and Iowa gained population after experiencing losses in 1981 and 1982, and Illinois recorded growth for the second straight year.

In addition, the northeast, after a decade of no growth, experienced moderate growth in the 1980–1984 period.

The elderly population increased in this period in every state; Florida had the highest proportion of elderly. School-age population is the most rapidly declining age group, dropping in 40 states and the District of Columbia (prominently in the District, Connecticut, and Massachusetts) in the 1980–1984 period.

Immigration

The Bureau of the Census reported an estimated total of 2.2 immigrants per 1,000 population in 1984 (Series P–25, No. 971, 1985). This rate represented a slight reduction from the 2.3 rate in 1983 and a substantial reduction from the 3.5 rate in 1980, the peak year for immigration since the Great Depression. The net civilian immigration in 1980 was nearly 800,000. The Bureau's middle population projection from 1990 to 2080 assumes a yearly net immigration total of 450,000, leading to an essentially zero-growth population after 2050 (Series P–25, No. 952, 1984).

LABOR FORCE

In its "middle" scenario, the Bureau of Labor Statistics projects a labor force of 125 million in 1990 and 131.4 million in 1995, a growth rate of 1.6% per year in the 1982–1990 period, and a lower rate of 1.0% during the 1990–1995 period (Fullerton and Tschetter 1984). Slow growth actually began in the late 1970's after a peak period—at 3.0%—in 1976–1979.

Age

The median age of the labor force will rise slightly over the next 10 to 15 years, going from 34.8 in 1982 to 37.3 in 1995.

Although the population of persons aged 55 and over is projected to increase, the participation rate of this group is expected to continue declining. Persons in the prime working age (25 to 54) will increase in number, accounting for 73% of the 1995 labor force (up from 61% in 1970 and 64% in 1982). Younger workers (age 16 to 24), who accounted for a large share of the labor force growth in the 1970's, will decline in number.

Median age of labor force (Fullerton and Tschetter 1984, 4):

	1982	1990	1995
All participants	34.8	35.9	37.3
Men	35.3	36.4	37.8
Women	34.2	35.3	36.8
White	35.0	36.1	37.5
Black and other minorities	32.8	34.8	36.3

Labor force growth by age group (Fullerton and Tschetter 1984, 2):

	1970–1982	1982–1990	1990–1995
Age 16 and over	2.4	1.6	1.0
16 to 24	2.7	− 1.3	− .8
25 to 54	2.3	2.9	1.6
55 and over	.3	− .7	− .2

Women and Minorities

Almost two-thirds of the projected growth in the 1980's and 1990's will occur among women, and almost one-fourth will occur among blacks and other minority groups.

Women (not including teenagers) represented 40% of the labor force in 1984, a substantial increase over the 34% in 1968; the projection for 1990 is 43% (Collins 1985). Yet there is doubt that the participation rate of women will continue indefinitely to show substantial increases. The rate is "beginning to approach some sort of natural limit" (Collins 1985, 3). The increase was 3.4% in 1968–1973 and 4.2% in 1973–1979, but the growth rate decelerated in 1979–1984 to 3.0%, and a smaller increase is projected in 1984–1990.

The growth rate of the black labor force is expected to be nearly double the white rate, a development reflecting the younger age structure of the black population. The minority groups (black and other) will account for 28% of additions to the labor force in 1990–1995, in contrast to 21% in the 1982–1990 period.

Labor force growth rates (Fullerton and Tschetter 1984, 4):

	1982–1990	1990–1995
Total	1.6	1.0
Women	2.3	1.4
Black and other minorities	2.6	2.0
Black	2.3	1.8

Economic Dependency

The economic dependency ratio (the number of persons not in the labor force divided by the number in the labor force) was high in the 1960's but dropped sharply in the 1970's as large numbers of baby-boom members and women entered the labor force. The decline should continue but at a moderate pace in the 1980's and 1990's, attributable to continued increase in women's participation rate. By about 1986 the number of people in the labor force should exceed the number not in the labor force.

The general indications from data on dependency rates for age groups are that there will be fewer children per labor force participant but more older persons.

There has been a significant increase in the number of wives working (Devens, Leon, and Sprinkle 1985, 11). Forty-four percent of all married-couple families had both a wife and a husband employed in 1984 in contrast to 39% in 1977. The proportion of employed persons who are the sole support of their families has been moving downward, reaching 24% in the last quarter of 1984, a decline of four percentage points over a seven-year period.

The high incidence of employment of both husband and wife may have personal and social consequences which we have not fully anticipated. Research studies, though not without contradictory findings, have indicated generally that wives' employment is related positively to the mental health of wives but negatively to the mental health of husbands. A study by Staines, Pottick, and Fudge (1986) found a lower level of job and life satisfaction among husbands of working wives than among husbands of housewives. A suggested explanation supported by the data: Husbands of working wives feel less adequate as family breadwinners.

As might be expected, a smaller proportion of married women are in the labor market than unmarried women, and married women with pre–school-age children are less likely to participate in the labor force than married women with older children. But the impressive facts are that the participation of mothers is so high and that the largest increase in labor force participation has occurred among married women with preschool children (participating at a 55% rate, representing almost a ten-point increase in five years.)

Education

The number of college graduates in the labor force increased greatly in the early 1980's (Young 1985) and now represents about one-fourth of all adult workers. The increase from 1983 to 1984 was 1 million, following two yearly increases of similar size. Primarily because of the high participation rate (87.8%) of black women graduates, the proportion of black college graduates who were in the labor force as of March 1984 continued to exceed the proportion of white graduates.

Summary

The major labor force projections for the next decade are these: The labor force will grow more slowly; women and minority groups will account for large proportions of the growth; the younger (16–24) will decline in numbers; the prime-age members (25–54) will grow 1.0% faster than the total labor force; and the older (55 and over), despite a population increase, will decline in labor force numbers because of a continuing drop in participation (Fullerton and Tschetter 1984, 4, 8). In addition, the labor force continues to have an increasing proportion of college graduates. The participation rates for major population groups (1982 and projections for 1990 and 1995) are shown in Table 3.

Table 3
Civilian Labor Force, by Sex, Age, and Race, 1970–1982, and Middle Growth Projections to 1995

	Participation Rate		
	1982	1990	1995
Total, age 16 or over	64.0	66.9	67.8
Men	76.6	76.5	76.1
16 to 24	72.6	74.7	74.5
25 to 54	94.0	93.8	93.5
55 and over	43.8	37.4	35.3
Women	52.6	58.3	60.3
16 to 24	62.0	69.1	71.6
25 to 54	66.3	75.6	78.7
55 and over	22.7	20.5	19.9
White (total)	64.3	67.3	68.1
Men	77.4	77.4	77.0
Women	52.4	58.1	60.0
Black and Other Minorities	61.6	64.8	65.7
Men	71.0	71.0	70.6
Women	53.9	59.7	61.7
Black, Age 16 and Over	61.0	64.5	65.4
Men	70.1	70.4	70.5
Women	53.7	59.0	61.2

Adapted from Fullerton, Howard N., Jr., and John Tschetter, "The 1995 Labor Force: a Second Look," Employment Projections for 1995, Bureau of Labor Statistics, Bulletin 2197 (1984), tables 1 and 2, p. 3.

UNEMPLOYMENT AND THE UNEMPLOYED

The national unemployment rate was slightly above 7% for most of 1985. In August it fell to 7% after remaining at 7.3% for the previous six months. In September and October the rate stayed at 7.1%, in November was at 7%, and in December dipped to 6.9%. In the first six months of 1986, the rates were 6.7%, 7.3%, 7.2%, 7.1%, 7.3% and 7.1%.

The projections of unemployment rates for the next few years vary from economist to economist, but most of the forecasts seem to fall into the range from 6.0% on the most optimistic side to 7.3% on the least. The Bureau of Labor Statistics, in its middle or moderate projection, sees a 6.3% rate by 1990 and 6.0% by 1995 (Andreassen, Saunders, and Su 1984, 13; Personick 1984, 23). A projection by the Conference Board is for 6.0% in 1990 (Collins 1985, 4). The Commerce Department in a December 31, 1985, news story predicted a drop in the unemployment rate to 6.7% in 1986 and a steady decline to 5.6% by 1991. John Hagens of Chase Econometrics, in a statement reported by Associated Press on December 31, 1985, saw unemployment neither declining nor increasing in the new year. Hymans and Crary (1985) of the Department of Economics of the University of Michigan forecast that the employment rate would stabilize at about 7.2% for most of 1986. *Fortune* in its October 14, 1985, edition indicated that it expected the rate to "rise a little." It was 7.1% in September. David Burson of Wharton Econometrics, according to a newspaper report of November 2, 1985, predicted that unemployment would rise to about 7.3% in the first half of 1986.

It is not within the professional province of managers and human resources personnel to forecast unemployment rates. Their indicated course is to strike a balance among the projections of competent forecasters who have credentials in economics. They can reasonably expect, on that basis, to be faced with about a 7% unemployment rate (or a little less) in 1986. They should also be aware of major indications affecting the unemployment rate and be alert to changes in these factors.

It is advisable, for example, to recognize a relationship between population growth, labor force growth, and unemployment—and to stay abreast of population and participation trends. Table 4 shows the participation rate, employment–population ratio, and unemployment rates for various segments of the population in the last quarter of 1984. Comparative projections of rates of population growth, labor force growth, and employment growth for the next decade (Bureau of the Census and Bureau of Labor Statistics data) are given below:

	Total Population	Population 16 & over	Labor Force	Employment
1980–85	.94			
1982–88		1.1		
1982–90			1.6	1.8

	Total Population	Population 16 & over	Labor Force	Employment
1985–90	.90			
1988–95		0.8		
1990–95	.78		1.0	1.5

Table 4
Labor Force Indicators, 4th Quarter, 1984

	Participa-tion Rate	Employment-Pop. Ratio	Unemploy-ment Rate
Civilian labor force (total)	64.5	59.8	7.2
Men, 20 years and over	78.3	73.4	6.2
Women, 20 years and over	53.9	50.4	6.6
Both sexes, 16 to 19 years	53.8	43.9	18.4
White	64.7	60.7	6.2
Black	63.0	53.4	15.1
Hispanic origin	65.1	58.4	10.3

Adapted from Table 1, Selected labor force indicators, seasonally adjusted averages, 1982–84, in Devens, Richard M., Jr., Carol Boyd Leon, and Debbie Sprinkle, "Employment and Unemployment in 1984: A Second Year of Strong Growth in Jobs," *Monthly Labor Review*, Vol. 108, No. 2 (1985), p. 4.

It will be noted that the rate of employment growth in the next decade is expected to exceed the rate of labor force growth. In addition, the economy will not have as many new workers to absorb as in the 1968–1979 period when the labor force increased at a 2.7% annual rate. Still, significant growth in the economy will be required to support an increasing employment rate and to prevent a rise in the unemployment rate. In this regard, the major indicator available to managers is the gross national product (GNP).

The GNP grew at a rate of 2.2% in the year 1985, a considerable drop from the 6.6% rate achieved in 1984. Predictions for 1986 vary widely, from over 5% at the most optimistic to below 1% at the most pessimistic. The administration predicted 4% (later 3.2%); other economists predictions, appear to fall, at an average, at slightly over 3%. Three percent, it is popularly held, will be needed to keep unemployment from increasing. As the economy headed into 1986, the first-quarter rate was 3.8%, and second quarter, 0.6%.

Of course, there are numerous factors impacting on the GNP, but predictions concerning them and their effects are best left to the economists. It is probably advisable also for managers and human resources practitioners to allow the issue of the inflation–unemployment relationship to remain in the hands of the economists. At the heart of this relationship is the concept of the natural rate of unemployment, which may be defined in broad terms as the inflation-safe unemployment rate. There is uncertainty as to what that rate is now. Current research appears to peg it at 6 to 6–1/2% (Hymans and Crary 1985, 59). But estimates seem to have risen progressively from 3% in the early 1950's to 4% in the 1960's, to 5% in the early 1970's, and then to 6% (Gordon 1985, 263). The rise in the noninflationary unemployment rate appears to have occurred, as some economists view it, because of demographic changes in the labor force (higher proportions of women and youths) and expanded income maintenance programs (unemployment benefits and public welfare payments) (Greenwald 1982, 732, 881).

As a further complication, the presence of an inverse relationship between the inflation rate and the unemployment rate has come into question. In the "stagflation" period of the 1970's, the country experienced rises in the inflation and unemployment rates at the same time; and a long-term trade-off between inflation and unemployment lost credibility. Yet it must be recognized that the economy was not operating under ordinary conditions in the 1970's; a massive increase occurred in the labor force, particularly among young workers. And the increase in the unemployment rate should not obscure an impressive record of job creation (Schwarz and Volgy 1985, 103).

In the short run, a trade-off between unemployment and inflation appears feasible; that is, we can achieve temporary reductions in unemployment with higher inflation, or fight inflation with temporary increases in unemployment (Baumol and Blinder 1982, 316–317).

The direction of the relationship between inflation and unemployment appears to depend on whether the shift is in the aggregate supply curve or the aggregate demand curve. In the first condition, with adverse shifts in the aggregate supply curve, inflation and unemployment can be expected to rise together. But if the government, in its monetary and fiscal policies, stimulates demand to reduce unemployment, inflation will rise; and if governmental policy restricts demand to address inflation, unemployment will rise. In this situation, a trade-off can occur (Baumol and Blinder 1982, 315).

The natural rate of unemployment, though referred to as the full employment rate, obviously does not represent full employment in the popular sense. In the most favorable employment circumstances, there will be people between jobs or otherwise temporarily out of work, people who would be classified among the "frictionally" unemployed and who would create a minimal—though relatively sizable—unemployment rate.

Classifying the unemployed involves troublesome definitions. Structural unemployment may be defined as unemployment resulting from a mismatch of unemployed and job vacancies; the unemployed are in the wrong place or do not have the right skills, and therefore the unemployment cannot be eliminated by expanding "aggregate demand." Frictional unemployment may be considered search unemployment, unemployment which exists in the same local labor market and occupations in which vacancies exist but where time is required to bring people and jobs together. Structural unemployment may be thought of as a severe form of frictional unemployment. And "speculative" unemployment (when real wages fall and employees withhold hours) and "precautionary" unemployment (waiting for a better job offer) may be considered forms of frictional unemployment.

For the operating manager and personnel practitioner, there are more helpful formulations of structural and frictional unemployment, by means of which they can begin to characterize people in unemployed status. In the structurally unemployed category—people who have lost jobs because of changes in the economic environment—are persons put out of work by changes of technology or consumer tastes that adversely affect established manufacturing, by relocation of factories, by cuts or shifts in defense spending, etc. In an age of swiftly advancing technology, changing products, and changing markets, the number of structurally unemployed can be expected to be high. In the frictionally unemployed category are people who will return to jobs soon, are between jobs, or are looking for their first job.

Another system of grouping unemployed workers, related to the structural and frictional categories, is by broad reason for unemployment, including new entrants, reentrants, job leavers, job losers (permanently separated), and job losers (on layoff). Job losers (temporary and permanent separations) tend to account for less than half of all unemployed in nonrecession periods but for a substantially larger proportion during downturns. This point is illustrated below in the percentages of total unemployed in each grouping for selected quarters in 1979 and the recessionary period of 1980–1982 (*Workers without jobs* 1983, 57). The volume of job leaving also appears related to the state of the economy.

	1979 2nd quarter	1980 3rd quarter	1982 4th quarter
New entrants	14%	11%	11%
Reentrants	30	25	21
Job leavers	15	12	7
Job losers (permanent separation)	28	31	41
Job losers (layoff)	13	21	21

While exceptions are likely to be numerous, it is reasonable to assume that most employees in the first three groupings and some in the layoff group can probably be considered as frictionally unemployed, and that most of the job losers who are permanently separated or on long layoff can probably be classified as structurally unemployed.

Statistics for 1984, at a time when the general unemployment rate was 7.5%, identified those components of the labor force that then experienced the highest unemployment rates for the separate unemployment reasons: job losers (layoff and other)—blacks (8.3%); job leavers—teenagers (1.4%); reentrants—teenagers (4.7%) and blacks (4.5%); new entrants—teenagers (9.4%).

If, in combination, the unemployed categories were to add up to the projected 7% unemployment rate, what does the rate mean in terms of adequacy, availability, and qualifications of the labor supply? This is the question practitioners must raise. Does the rate represent "excess" unemployment if it stands at a percentage point (or fraction) above the natural unemployment rate?

The natural unemployment (or full employment) rate may be considered to be the rate representing frictional unemployment only. Achievement of this "full employment" rate, so defined, still may leave us with problems since among the group will be new labor force entrants seeking their first job. The primary matters of concern with the frictionally unemployed, therefore, seem to boil down to the questions of the number and qualifications of new job seekers.

Of the frictionally unemployed groups, a large pocket of unutilized people exists among such persons. They comprise a significant proportion of the 7%. But the percentage of teenagers in this group is diminishing. Kasper (1984) has pointed out that although teenagers comprise the majority of unemployed new entrants to the labor force, the fraction has declined (from over 85% two decades ago to less than 75% in 1983). The number of unemployed new entrants over 20 years of age has grown, a development probably associated with increased enrollment in higher education and the increase in job seekers among adult women. In the period 1958–1983, the proportion of unemployed who were new entrants has been steadily rising. In 1983 nearly one out of every eight (slightly over 1 million) of the unemployed were new entrants looking for their first job. Persons in this category are having more difficulty locating jobs than before, for reasons apparently not adequately determined by the research.

There are, however, rather convincing indications that the minimum wage has had the effect of limiting employment opportunities for unskilled workers.

In any event, the new job seekers will continue to be a significant percentage of the unemployed, but will be a slightly older population group than in the past. As the median age of the labor force rises in the 1980's and 1990's, the new job seekers are indeed likely to be more mature and better educated, a favorable development in light of the findings that school dropouts have the highest unemployment rates among younger workers and that, among adult workers, joblessness declines with higher educational attainment (*Workers without jobs* 1983, 10–13). On the other hand, the new entrants will be occupationally naive and will need substantial job training, especially if the jobs contain technical elements. And teenagers, though a substantial labor source now, are not being replenished in the labor market at the earlier rate.

In the case of the structurally unemployed, the employment criteria of availability and pertinent qualifications come into question. These workers are not likely to have the right skills on the basis of prior training and job experience or to be in the right geographic place to move into existing job openings. The issues of mobility and training, then, are highly pertinent.

Mobility of Unemployed Workers

In regard to mobility, our expectations should be realistic. Unemployed workers do not tend to move very readily from one location to another and particularly when the move involves a considerable distance. Reasons for reluctance to move are important and numerous; they include community ties, home ownership, employment of other family members in the locality, and insufficient information about job opportunities elsewhere.

The reluctance to move is evident in the statistic that in 1979–1983 only 680,000 (13%) of the 5.1 million displaced after at least three years on the job moved to a different city (Flaim and Sehgal 1985, 8). And a sizable percentage of those who do relocate are likely to return. The data on household moves in the United States and experience with interplant transfers (Bendick 1984, 48, 51) suggest that relocation is unlikely to be an option acceptable to more than 20% of workers.

Where are they to go? The relative unemployment rates among geographic regions are suggestive. In 1984 unemployment was highest in the East-North-Central area and the East-South. It was lowest (20% or more below the U. S. average) in New Hampshire, Vermont, Massachusetts, Connecticut, Rhode Island, Maryland, Virginia, Georgia, North Dakota, South Dakota, Nebraska, Kansas, Colorado, Texas, Arizona, and Hawaii (Shank 1985, 19). But all regions benefited from the 1983–1984 recovery. And new configurations will occur.

Many of the states with the highest unemployment rate in 1984 were heavy in old goods-producing industries and were hard hit by the 1981–1982 recession. The New England experience is a lesson in recovery. The development of a high-technology industry there was instrumental in a striking reversal in employment between the mid–1970's and 1984.

But the statistics show an apparently strong employee reluctance to move very far. Although unemployed workers are more likely to move than employed workers, in the year preceding March 1983 only a third as many unemployed workers moved between states as moved within the same county (U. S. Bureau of the Census, Series P–20, No. 393, 1984).

The records for the 1979–1983 period reveal that unemployed men were more likely to move than women and that very few older workers relocated (only 6% of those 55 and over) (Flaim and Sehgal 1985, 8). There is evidence that moving can pay off; of those who moved, a higher percentage were reemployed in January 1984 than nonmovers (75% in comparison with 60%). A difference was noted in favor of the movers even in the case of old workers. Of the movers, proportionately more men were reemployed than women (77 vs. 60%).

The expectation that early notification of impending plant closings would result in employees leaving jobs before being laid off was not borne out; most workers remained on the job even with advance notice. But of those displaced workers of 1979–1983 who left the job before being laid off, more were employed in January 1984 than those who stayed on (79 to 60%) (Flaim and Sehgal 1985, 8).

Moving to a new location was not a popular option, even under a funded program, for displaced Detroit automobile workers in the Downriver Community Conference Economic Readjustment Program, one of a series of pilot studies funded by the U. S. Department of Labor in 1980–1983. Only 8% of the program enrollees relocated outside the area although resources were made available for job search and relocation; and 20% of these returned later (Flaim and Sehgal 1985, 4). The earnings of participants who were reemployed under this program were, on average, more than 30% lower than their prelayoff earnings.

Earlier funded relocation projects in the late 1960's (Schnitzer 1970) were regarded as having generally favorable results, although the results varied from program to program, and the author can attest to a rather futile effort, in his own experience, to relocate unemployed workers. But we can learn something from the early experience; it pointed to certain requirements which can serve to guide us if similar funded programs are undertaken in the future.

In the early program, 37 projects were funded in 28 states in the period from March 1965 to the end of 1968 and were operated by state employment services or private contractors. A total of 12,234 workers received relocation assistance; direct financial assistance in 1968 averaged $380 per relocated worker. Followups two months (in some cases, four months) after relocation indicated that an average of 20% of the workers had returned home and another 20% had changed jobs. It appeared likely that, for most projects, about 30% of the relocated workers were in the original job in which placed (in the "demand area") a year after relocation (Schnitzer 1970, 185–186).

Schnitzer summed up the results and related indications in this way:

The results of the relocation projects tend to confirm orthodox economic theory. Workers respond to expected earning differentials, and distance adds a barrier to mobility both by raising the cost of moving and by reducing the labor market information available to workers. Personal characteristics, such as age, education, and race, are significant with respect to workers' initial motivations to move and their ability to respond to opportunities. Single persons are more willing to relocate than married persons, yet their rate of return to the home area is much higher than the rate for married persons. Older persons, i. e., those 45 and over, and the hardcore unemployed are the most difficult to relocate. A low level of educational attainment also tends to mitigate against successful relocation. Extensive supportive services appear to be a necessary desideratum for the unskilled, the long-term unemployed, and the rural worker with little or no history of employment (180).

The foremost obstacle to effective relocation was the housing problem. It was also evident that more extensive supportive services were needed for unskilled rural workers than for semiskilled or skilled industrial workers.

An alternative to relocating employees is to locate industry in areas where unemployment is high through governmental inducements such as tax incentives, grants, or loans. Schnitzer concluded in 1970 that there was no convincing evidence "that this type of approach would be more than moderately successful," noting that though the use of tax incentives for this purpose has merit on value grounds, "it is more difficult to justify this approach on the basis of efficiency" (175).

The idea of establishing enterprise zones has a somewhat strong political advocacy. And Executive Order 12073 in 1978 encouraged government procurement in labor-surplus areas.

It is too facile an answer to propose the establishment of high-technology industries in order to revive economically depressed areas. The prospects are remote if high technology is narrowly conceived as including primarily the production of computers and semiconductors. However heavy the demand, it will hardly support an indefinite number of Silicon Valleys. But prospects widen somewhat if the view of advanced-technology industries is broadened to include also pharmaceuticals, health care, scientific instruments, publishing, communications systems, and the whole gamut of knowledge-intensive manufacturing. Beyond the appreciation of expanded possibilities, certain ingredients for successful results apparently must be present. A lesson from the recent New England economic revitalization is that these major factors are needed: risk capital, skilled labor, aggressive entrepreneurship, and the presence of preeminent universities (Howell 1985, 23). It would seem that a number of depressed areas have a leg up on requirements. The nearby presence of outstanding research institutions is particularly true of the east-north-central region where unemployment is high. And if employees laid off from basic industries lack required new skills, they are demonstrably capable of learning; the necessary condition is that insightful training be given.

The answers are not all in on the approach of locating industries. It is likely to have continuing political backing. And if, as appears probable, labor mobility continues to be a formidable problem, a national policy encouraging strategic location of plants in depressed areas might be pursued further—but with careful advance planning of the installations including, importantly, provisions for pertinent training.

It would be unwise, though, to discontinue programs for relocation of employees despite the difficulty. One should avoid overblown expectations, but it is reasonable to expect that improved programs will increase the success rate. National policy should include an upgrading of such programs, taking into account the need for training and the lessons learned through earlier experience in regard to the need for supportive services and housing—and the effects of earnings losses, particularly for persons displaced from jobs in high-paying industries.

Training Needs of Unemployed Workers

Training as a means of endowing unemployed persons with new and more pertinent skills is now a considerable enterprise nationally, engaged in by the federal government (through Title III of the Job Training Partnership Act and the Trade Adjustment Assistance Program) and by state and city agencies, labor unions, and employers. The organizational framework and funding arrangements for such training are in place—or moving into place.

The magnitude of the retraining requirement is evident in the fact that job growth is shifting heavily to the service-producing sector of the economy (Personick 1984). In the 1982–1995 period, job gains in manufacturing are expected to account for almost one of six new jobs—some upturn occurred in the last quarter of 1985 and, as the automobile industry rebounded, earlier in the year— but the service-producing industries (transportation, communications, public utilities, trade, finance, real estate, other services, and government) are projected to produce three of four new jobs. Indeed, such segments of the service industry as medical care, business services, professional services, hotels, personal services, and nonprofit organizations in combination are projected to account for one of three new jobs, twice the rate of manufacturing industry.

The projected annual rates of employment gain (moderate forecast of the Bureau of Labor Statistics) for the 1982–1995 period for the private economy sectors:

Mining	1.2
Construction	2.9
Manufacturing	1.5
Durable	1.9
Nondurable	1.0
Transportation & public utilities	1.4
Trade	1.8
Finance, insurance, and real estate	2.1
Services	2.5
Private households	1.5

The fastest-growing industries in terms of employment changes are projected to be medical and dental instruments, business services, iron and ferroalloy ores mining, computers and peripheral equipment, radio and television broadcasting, other medical services, plastic products, scientific and controlling instruments, electronic components, and new construction.

A major training problem arising from this significant shift in the nature of economic enterprises involves the transfer of employee skills. As employees from declining industries join companies engaged in different operations, the new occupations are likely to be so dissimilar from the old as to eliminate any substantial transfer of old skills. But old habits die hard. The retraining will require careful assessment of the transferability of skills, as a precaution against interference of old habits, and strong training, including an emphasis on overlearning, to stabilize the new job habits.

Effective training will require the use of both learning and motivational techniques. It should involve direct coaching that utilizes cuing and feedback and is geared to the progressive stages of the individual's development of skill and his particular learning problems. For motivational purposes associated with the learning, improving performance should be reinforced; performance successes should be progressively induced and recognized and the person's efficacy expectations and self-confidence thus enhanced. The motivational component of learning may be crucial to the effectiveness of the training since the motivation and self-esteem of the unemployed worker may be at a low ebb generally. Finally, through the example of the instructor and reinforcement consistently contingent on performance, the individual should be led to adopt high standards of performance and to require such performance of himself as a basis for self-reinforcement. The achievement of a high level of skill in a new occupation is an intrinsic satisfaction of value as a sustaining force in the employee's continuing effort. Our objective should be to bring the employee to that level as soon as possible. The effect may be not only to replace his skill but to restore his self-esteem as well.

A primary requirement is that the training heavily emphasize the development of job skills and avoid overplaying the strictly orientational aspects. This means moving the person into the performance of job duties without undue delay and doing so under the guidance of a worker–instructor who knows the job. Of course, the job skills acquired should be in demand in actual jobs. Further, the training should be tied to actual job placement. That is, the person completing the training should be assured of employment in the particular job. Otherwise the training experience may be a mere exercise and just another source of frustration.

Further Characteristics of the Unemployed

We know many things about the unemployed population. Black men, teenagers (especially black teenagers), and older workers have a disproportionately high representation. As general characteristics, the unemployed tend to be young, blue-collar, minority workers. A substantial number of school dropouts are among the young unemployed. The unemployed are increasingly likely to be single and from families maintained by a woman (usually a single parent). In terms of occupational groups, blue-collar workers classified as "operatives" and nonfarm laborers (in the least-skilled blue-collar occupations) had the highest jobless rates in 1982 (*Workers without jobs*, 1983).

Blacks and Hispanics are underrepresented in skilled industrial occupations and in managerial and professional specialty jobs. Women are underrepresented in skilled production jobs and in managerial jobs. White women, however, are relatively well represented in professional specialty occupations.

Unemployed persons are disproportionately present, as indicated earlier, in geographic areas where old basic industries in the goods-producing sector of the economy are depressed. These groups are the victims primarily of structural unemployment, and many of the workers can be absorbed if the economy grows and the problems of training and of bringing jobs and people together can be ameliorated.

A notable geographic shift in unemployment occurred between the mid–1970's and 1983–1984 (Shank 1985). In 1976 the highest jobless rates (more than 9%) occurred in the New England, Mid-Atlantic, and Pacific divisions; and low rates (5 to 6%) occurred in the West-North-Central and West-South-Central divisions. In 1984 when unemployment rates were highest in the East-South and East-North-Central divisions and neighboring states, New England's jobless rate became the lowest among the nine geographic divisions. The rates of unemployment also dropped in the Pacific and Mid-Atlantic divisions, moving both divisions from a high jobless rate ranking to an average ranking.

The employment–population ratio of the foreign born, as of April 1983, was 60.7 for those who had arrived in the United States in 1960–1979 and 49.6 for those who arrived in 1980–1981, in comparison with a 57.6 ratio in 1983 for native born (Sehgal 1985).

The number of long-term unemployed in the unemployed ranks declined in the period from the last quarter of 1983 to the last quarter of 1984 (Devens, Leon, and Sprinkle 1985, 5). The total of people jobless for six months or more decreased by three quarters of a million over the year, and the average duration of unemployment fell 2.9 weeks to end the year at 17.1 weeks. Still, at year-end there were 1.4 million persons who had been unemployed for a half-year or more. And prolonged unemployment was particularly a problem of men 55 years old and older.

Flaim (1979, 21–22) reviewed the studies on the effects on the unemployment rate of such legislative and social changes as expansion of unemployment insurance, multiworker families, and job-seeking requirements of welfare programs. The unemployment insurance program, the studies found, induces some unemployment through longer duration or greater frequency of jobless periods. Data indicate that during periods of high unemployment in the 1960's and 1970's unemployment tended to be slightly longer for unemployed husbands with a working wife than for other unemployed husbands; but quantification of the impact of other workers in the family awaits further studies with broader controls. The question regarding welfare recipients is whether the unemployed rate is overstated when recipients of food stamps and mothers receiving aid under the Aid to Families with Dependent Children Program are required to seek work in order to qualify for benefits. The evidence appears to show a mild effect on the unemployment rate.

In addition to the "officially" unemployed, there is another segment of the working age population who are out of work. These are the "discouraged" workers who are not in the labor market (and not in the unemployment statistics) because they are not looking for work (Devens, Leon, and Sprinkle 1985, 11). They totaled 1,303,000 in the last quarter of 1984. As their reason for not seeking work, most of them cited market factors rather than personal factors (such as age, low education, lack of skill). At the end of 1984, 935,000 were not in the labor force because of market conditions, 368,000 because of personal factors. The composition of this group shows about 60% women, a rather constant proportion. Blacks represented more than 35% of the total in the last quarter of 1984. The total number declined by about 130,000 in 1984. (A drop of 100,000 in the last quarter of 1985 reduced the total to 1.1 million.)

Minor alleviation of a potentially tight labor market might occur if a substantial percentage of the discouraged workers entered the labor force. If job market conditions improved, some who were discouraged because of job market factors might seek work. It would appear, however, that a somewhat irreducible number would remain out of the labor force because of personal factors (the number has fluctuated between 286,000 and 423,000 in the quarters of the 1980–1984 period). In any event, discouraged workers represent a minor fraction of the working age population and are not a deep or reliable source of employees.

A significant though not large percentage of the unemployed workers—a percentage that probably peaks when times are good—leave jobs voluntarily. The percentage was 8.9 at the end of 1983 and 10.3 at the end of 1984 (Devens, Leon, and Sprinkle 1985, 5). Many of these can probably be classified as frictionally unemployed workers who will soon return to employment. They would appear on the whole to be rather good prospects for employment if an employer could arrange to catch them during a "window" of availability. They are not a large pool but are likely to be the targets of competitive recruitment when the economy is strong.

A development which must be taken into account as affecting the adequacy of future labor resources is the accelerated rate of departure of older workers from the workforce (Wolozin 1985). There has been an accompanying increase in the ratio of retired workers to active workers. The workforce between ages 16 and 44, which has experienced heavy growth in recent years, is projected to peak at 90 million by 1990 and then to start to decline.

If an expanding labor force is needed for continuing economic growth, the expansion may have to be found in middle-aged and older workers, but the participation rate of these groups has been falling, attributable in part to the national trend toward early retirement. Whereas in 1948 half of the men aged 65 or over worked, in 1983 the number was only one in five. A decline, though not precipitous, has also occurred among women workers in this age group over the recent decade.

The economic rationale which appears to underpin corporate adherence to the "retirement ideology" and policies encouraging early retirement is that older workers are less productive than younger, a thesis which a number of studies do not support (Wolozin 1985, 482–483).

As the baby-boom generation grows old and the tendency toward early retirement continues, there are grounds to argue that the labor force trend may be toward shortages by the end of the century, particularly in skilled workers.

The statistics given in this chapter arise, of course, from specific periods of time. Still, they are of more than transient importance. They tell us where employment matters stand in the mid–1980's, and equally significantly they indicate developments and trends that inevitably will project their influence into the future. Without knowledge and understanding of this kind of data, we would be hard put to solve our contemporary human resources problems; moreover, we would severely limit our ability to anticipate the evolving events of the next decade and to prepare to address them.

9

Personnel Procedures for Stabilizing Workforce

There are a number of supportable propositions that can serve to guide a company executive or plant manager in his decisions and efforts concerning workforce stabilization.

1. That, as a basic proposition, stabilization is a desirable objective, that high rates of turnover, voluntary and involuntary, are unacceptable in terms of economic, human, and social costs. This is not to argue that layoffs are never justified; economic necessity may compel them at times. But the related recommendation is that a company take a comprehensive view of layoff consequences and of alternatives before arriving at a decision to lay off employees.

That the labor pool at 7% unemployment, though it appears large in terms of absolute numbers, does not give absolute assurance as to adequacy when we take into account:

2. The availability of labor: Mobility is likely to remain a problem, although efforts by government, unions, communities, and companies to bring workers and jobs together may intensify.

The suitability of skills: Workers in the structurally unemployed group (especially those experienced in "old" technologies) will have inappropriate skills; and workers in the frictionally unemployed groups (especially workers just entering into the labor force) may have inadequate skills or no appreciable occupational skills. Training efforts on the part of government, unions, companies, and communities are likely to accelerate. The problem of training may prove to be more amenable to solution than the problem of mobility, but individual companies will bear the primary responsibility for training or retraining employees in pertinent skills.

3. That the available supply of temporary workers is likely to dwindle if the economy remains strong (or moderately so, as generally anticipated) and that a

widespread and continuing reliance on a large buffer force of temporary employees may be ill founded.

4. That temporary work may present serious problems among American workers in regard to motivation and the satisfying of needs.

The use of temporary employees (provided by outside agencies, given temporary contracts by the company, or hired directly by the company as temporaries) as a buffering device would better satisfy critics of the approach if the temporaries represented a small percentage of the workforce, the staffing of regular employees were based on a reasoned and researched projection of production requirements, and the number of regulars were pegged at a level not drastically below the "full" projected need. In addition, the approach would have greater motivational appeal to many temporaries and receive better acceptance if a pathway, without excessive obstructions, were provided to the status of regular employee. Such arrangements are present in plans cited earlier.

The treatment of core employees by employers tends to be exemplary. But the possibility of heavy pressures for production exists. An executive, commenting on the guaranteed employment offered to core employees by a competing firm, was highly critical of the workloads and production incentive program of the competitor; indeed, he viewed the system as exploitative—as a means of "getting more out of the employees."

The method of avoiding layoffs which appears to have a high degree of acceptability among employers and employees alike is work sharing, especially when it is accompanied by partial payment of unemployment compensation. Such payment provisions are likely to spread to additional states, and work sharing is likely to be adopted as an alternative to layoffs by an increasing number of companies.

Assuming that layoffs can be minimized and greater stability of employment achieved in that part of turnover represented by involuntary terminations, turnover control and the general stability of the workforce are then reduced largely to the problem of combating voluntary terminations (quits and resignations). Various means of addressing voluntary turnover were discussed earlier, but a procedural framework is required to deal with the basic processes of selection, placement, promotion, and development of employees so as better to ensure that employees, with better expectations of steady employment, will opt to stay with the company.

The proposition guiding us is that workers will choose the employment option that, in addition to other—and often related—satisfactions, will provide suitable placement, adequate training, and opportunities for promotion, that will, in effect, provide for the development of employees as a major objective. At the same time, we as managers will view these procedures, in our personnel planning, as a means of guaranteeing that the organization has within its workforce the competences required for the attainment of corporate economic goals and the carrying out of strategic plans.

PERSONNEL PLANNING

It is obvious, in view of the labor market situation and other personnel factors influencing corporate functioning, that personnel planning is taking on increasing importance.

The basic point of view concerning employees is likely to govern the amount and kind of personnel planning done. If workers are considered a commodity, little planning is likely to take place. A company will lay off workers as an immediate response to declines in production demands and will hire (or rehire) employees as the demands go up, much as it would decrease or increase the ordering of materials and supplies. It will be dependent on the local labor market for immediate adjustments to changing situations. Those companies that regard labor essentially as a cost of manufacturing are likely to be similarly restricted in their personnel planning. A company using a standard cost system, for example, will set up cost allowances in regard to labor, materials, etc., for the budgeted output at each processing center. Personnel requirements are thus tightly tied down, and the purpose of training is to ensure that standard outputs, as established by industrial engineering techniques and pegged to standard costs, are attained. The system is not designed for long-range personnel planning, indeed, is intended to eliminate "excess" staffing.

Those who consider employees as a "human resource" are more inclined to plan if they take as an objective the development of that resource and do not equate it, as the commodity and cost approaches tend to, with physical and economic resources. Perhaps the point of view most conducive to personnel planning is that the employees are "parties" in the enterprise, that they represent, in effect, the organization itself, and that their competence in total is the organization's competence.

The performance of the company obviously cannot be divorced from the performance of its employees. And in order for an organization to implement its business plans and to make strategic moves, it must take into account the personnel requirements in terms of numbers, kinds of skills, and levels of competence.

The object of personnel planning is to have the necessary people in place, possessing the necessary competence, for effective execution of the company's business plans. If the personnel conditions are not propitious for implementation of these plans—the right people unavailable or performance goals unattainable—the plans may require revision. Mills's model of the human resources-planning process (1985, 104) provides a feedback loop for this purpose. As he states, "Many companies would have spared themselves embarrassing marketplace failures if they had first recognized that the human resource implications of their strategic plans were unrealizable" (105).

The author can cite a striking example of poor personnel planning in a company which was pridefully "running lean" with a trimmed-down managerial and supervisory force and at the same time was planning an expansion involving the construction and start-up of a new plant. Its planning for hourly paid employees in regard to staffing and training was adequate, but it relied, for technical and administrative leadership, primarily on the transfer or temporary assignments of personnel from its existing line and staff groups. There were just not enough qualified managerial people available in the organization to meet the new need and still maintain managerial strength in existing facilities. The expansion floundered.

Mills suggests that personnel planning go beyond personnel and skills forecasts to "morale management"—the planning of activities to elicit high performance from individual employees and groups (1985, 105).

COMMITMENT AND COMPETENCE

Companies wishing to engage in this kind of personnel planning are well advised to review the issue of organizational commitment. Amidst the academic hypothesizing concerning factors in commitment, it is useful to examine the indications arising, as in the author's case, from long experience in middle-management positions affording a clear view of the workings of an organization and the employees' role in them. Such experience raises serious questions concerning autonomy as a hypothesized condition for organizational commitment. Autonomy may lead to commitment to just a segment of the organization and to arbitrary decisions and a self-centered operation which defies integration into the organization's full mission. Some executives cannot "handle" autonomy. A case in point is a product executive who, given more-or-less carte blanche to revive an inefficient facility, insisted on a solo performance and rejected the help of experts available to him in the organization. He developed no staff of his own but relied on his own inexpert knowledge of many facets of the operation. Of course, autonomy can be better used. But the point is that the response to it will vary widely, resulting in possibly destructive as well as constructive consequences to the organization, and in minimum commitment to the organization as well as greater.

It is more likely that a condition for commitment among most managers is not independence but the opportunity for individual achievement, with provisions for reinforcement, amidst the interdependent and interactive process which makes the organization go. The requirement seems to include responsibility for a function but in a setting in which consultation and communication are present and influence is wielded in the relationship with higher levels and in the relationship laterally with other managers and staff members. This sort of personal contribution imbedded in an effective network of supportive interdependent relationships cannot be dictated or achieved by procedures. Policy statements and statements of corporate goals may help, but it occurs primarily as a result of organizational climate, precedents, and example.

And it may be a principal producer of commitment if the personal achievement is good. The individual may then have a sense not only of functioning in the core of the organization but, with his individual performance, of functioning as one of the prime movers, as an indispensable cog in the performance of the total organization. This is, in essence, a deeper kind of participation than we can contrive with fragmentary and superficial techniques aimed at increasing "participation." In this ideal state, the manager is immersed in the organization as a unique and significant contributor to its welfare. He is not simply an appendage to be removed at someone's will. He is the thing itself; he is, in a real sense, the organization. And his loss is an organizational loss.

It is more difficult for hourly paid employees to reach this high degree of commitment. They may feel removed from the "power wielders" in the organization and may consider their individual efforts to have very limited effect on organizational success. But the truly competent employee is likely to feel that he represents something of value to the organization. If he is not indispensable, he is at least unique, and his loss would be felt; the company would be less well off without him. In certain jobs and at certain levels of skill, he indeed approaches indispensability. Dependence on a company may compel commitment in some cultures, but for American workers, interdependence would appear to be the desired state of employer–employee relations.

The author can vividly recall the lesson taught him by skilled employees in key positions (weavers and fixers) in a textile plant whom he interviewed in a program aimed at demonstrating to them, through profit-and-loss information, that they were "participants" in the mill's economic results. They already knew that, but they defined participation as doing the job well. "You do your job and we'll do ours, and everything will then be all right," they replied. And with this simple formula they expressed their commitment to the organization.

The suggestion has been made in the research literature that lengthened tenure may result in increased commitment in the circumstance, among several, in which employees acquire a skill pertinent to the plant but not marketable outside it (Mowday, Porter, and Steers 1982, 65–66). One can speculate that whatever commitment occurs in this circumstance may arise not from the employee's feeling that he is dependent on the company but from his feeling that the company is dependent on him and his competence in a unique skill.

Since competence, along with its many advantages to the individual in terms of associated rewards and personal development, appears to be an ingredient essential to organizational commitment—with predictable effects on turnover— we should set about the business of making employees competent. Procedures for selecting and promoting employees are required for this purpose.

"CLASSICAL" TEST VALIDATION PROCEDURES

Job suitability, an indispensable factor in the development of competences, has long been estimated by means of employment tests.

The classical route to the determination of the tests' acceptability as a selection device was to conduct criterion-related validation studies which attempt to establish the statistical relationship between test scores and job performance. The techniques for making such studies were taught in early industrial psychology classes (World War II and post–World War II eras) and continue to be taught to a considerable extent. The application of the procedures, straightforward enough on paper, to the practical problems of validating tests in an industrial setting is a formidable task, as practitioners soon discover.

There is, to begin with, the problem of the sample of employees to be used in the study. It is a rare manufacturing plant that has enough employees in specific job classifications to comprise a sample large enough to permit statistically meaningful results. Sample composition is a complication: How should we deal with minority members? In addition, there is a choice to be made (involving samples and other considerations) between a "concurrent" validity study and a predictive study ("longitudinal" or "follow-up" study). If we choose concurrent validity, administering tests to current employees and correlating test scores of current employees with measures of their job performance, it is usually found that so many other factors influence the performance of members of this group of survivors that the effect of tested abilities may be somewhat obscured. Further, there is usually a narrow distribution of performance measurement "scores" since all sample members (trainees are necessarily excluded) are performing more or less satisfactorily, else they would not have been retained in the job. Thus, the possibility of the emergence of a significant relationship between test scores and the performance measure is reduced. If we conducted a predictive study, we would use, as our sample, individuals entering a classification and correlate their measures of later performance, when stability of performance was attained, against the test scores (which would not, of course, have been used in the selection). In such case we have extreme problems of sample size since we would have to wait until an adequate number of tested employees reached a stable level of job performance, which is likely to be a very long wait in even large job classifications. In addition, to secure an adequate number of cases, since large enough numbers do not march along together from the same hiring period, we must take our cases from varied times, picking up a few at a time as employees reach a reliable state of performance. The complication is that many factors and conditions bearing on performance will change over time and the sample members will be differentially exposed to them.

In a criterion-related study of any sort, the difficulty of finding satisfactory criteria of job performance against which to correlate test scores is a major problem. The criteria should represent important aspects of performance, be relatively objective (the use of ratings is highly suspect), and be a statistically reliable measure. In addition, the performance criteria should be true measures of the performance of the individual employee and should not represent an outcome that is produced by the joint effort of several employees.

The correlation coefficient that emerges from the study should, of course, be statistically significant—at least at the .05 level of confidence—in order for the test to be acceptable as a selection device. Beyond this point it is necessary to engage in another statistical procedure for the setting of a "cutting score" on the test, the level that separates acceptable from unacceptable candidates.

Finally, it is wise to cross-validate, that is, to go through the same procedure again with a new sample to confirm our findings.

All in all, it is a long and demanding process and not conducive to easy optimism; but, fortunately, not impossible of achievement in the main.

REEXAMINATION OF VALIDATION

Criterion-related validation techniques are embedded in the Uniform Guidelines on Employee Selection Procedures adopted in 1978 by the four concerned governmental agencies [Equal Employment Opportunity Commission (EEOC), Civil Service Commission, Department of Justice, and the Labor Department's Office of Federal Contract Compliance Programs]. Earlier guidelines had been issued by the EEOC in 1966, but they did not represent a unified governmental position concurred in by the other concerned agencies. Indeed, the differences between the EEOC and the other agencies resulted in two different sets of guidelines by the end of 1976. The Uniform Guidelines that emerged in 1978 were intended to resolve differences and give employers a clear indication of how to proceed.

In addition to criterion-related validation, the Uniform Guidelines discussed two other validation procedures: content validation and construct validation. The three procedures were presented as alternative methods to pursue.

The Uniform Guidelines appeared to have professional sanction. They stated in Section 5C: "The provisions of these guidelines relating to validation of selection procedures are intended to be consistent with generally accepted professional standards for evaluating standardized tests and other selection procedures, such as those described in the Standards for Educational and Psychological Tests prepared by a joint committee of the American Psychological Association, the American Educational Research Association, and the National Council on Measurement in Education (American Psychological Association, Washington, D. C., 1974) (hereinafter "APA Standards") and standard textbooks and journals in the field of personnel selection."

On March 2, 1979, the government issued an explanatory supplement, consisting of 90 questions and answers, which as stated in the introduction was intended "to interpret and clarify, but not to modify, the provisions of the Uniform Guidelines." In October 1979 the APA, acting through its Committee on Psychological Tests and Assessment, raised additional questions concerning three areas of possible inconsistency between the government's Uniform Guidelines and the APA Standards. The concerns (as stated in the guideline supplement that followed in May of 1980) were "(1) that the Guidelines might call for 'a more rigid demand for a search for alternatives than we would deem consistent with acceptable professional practices'; (2) that, with respect to criteria for criterion-related validity studies, the Guidelines failed adequately to recognize that 'a total absence of bias can never be assured' and that the standards of the profession required only that 'there has been a competent professional handling of the problem'; and (3) for criterion-related validation studies 'in some circum- stances there may exist just one or two critical job duties, and that in such cases sole reliance on such a single selection prodecure relevant to the critical duties would be entirely appropriate'.'' The answers given in the 1980 explanatory supplement stated that a ''reasonable'' investigation of alternatives was called for; that significant differences between groups on criterion measures do ''not necessarily'' mean that the criterion measures are biased; and yes, a selection procedure significantly related to only one or two job duties can be justified where ''one or two work behaviors are the only critical or important ones.''

It is ironic that the government, in only clarifying its guideline provisions, was adhering to standards which many psychologists were coming to question, indeed abandoning in some cases. The professional basis for the government's technical standards appears to be eroding somewhat. The current situation is perhaps an example of scientific concepts and procedures which are in the process of evolving but which at a certain stage in the development are frozen into governmental regulations. The development goes on; the regulations stay.

In 1980 the Division of Industrial-Organizational Psychology of the APA issued its updated *Principles for the Validation and Use of Personnel Selection Procedures* (the first edition was published in 1975). It was noted, as a reason for the updating, that increased attention had been given to testing in the interim and that greater attention was forecast for the future. As reported by Tenopyr and Oeltjen (1982, 593), there are these major differences between the ''new UGL'' (the Uniform Guidelines with, apparently, the clarifying supplements) and the *Principles*:

Principles	**UGL**
1. Emphasize strategies of validation	Divide validity into three parts
2. Express no preference for strategies	Express a preference for criterion-related validity
3. Do not require search for alternatives to valid selection procedures	Require search for alternatives
4. Do not require fairness studies	Require fairness studies
5. Allow for validity generalization	Make little provision for validity generalization
6. Are flexible in content-oriented test development; recognize that all tests are abstractions	Practically insist on point-to-point correspondence to the job when content procedures are used
7. Do not require special qualifications for ranking on any test	Require justification for ranking on content-developed test

The industrial psychology profession (and other psychologists involved in test theory, construction, and utilization) is currently engaging in a broad reexamination of concepts, terminology, and procedures related to validation. And divergent views are emerging.

The strict division of validation into criterion-related, content, and construct has come under dispute, and a concept of unity of validation is being proposed. Tenopyr and Oeltjen (1982, 590) comment, "In a sense then all validity is essentially construct validity, and the various strategies by which one assesses goodness of measurement of the attribute in question appear to be inextricably intertwined. It would be difficult to conceive of a measurement situation which did not involve all three aspects of validity." Zedeck and Cascio (1984, 490) suggest, "Perhaps confusion would be clarified if we adopted the position that the *procedures* for criterion-related and content validities are reflections of construct validity." The new *Principles* discuss criterion-related validity and content-oriented validity in detail as strategies, but construct validity under the heading of "generality of validation efforts"(1980, 5–16).

In regard to content-oriented strategies, professional differences have been noted in regard to conceptualization of strategies and the procedures for developing a measuring instrument by content-oriented procedures (Tenopyr and Oeltjen 1982, 591). In regard to criterion-related validity, the long-held belief that concurrent validation is not a substitute for predictive validity has come into doubt. There is evidence that predictive and concurrent validations yield the same results (Zedeck and Cascio 1984, 489).

In addition—and as a major product of our reexamination of validation—rather strong support is now being given to the idea of validity generalization, a sharp departure from the long-held view that validation is specific to the situation. The basis for validity generalization is the proposal, which is supported by empirical data, that variations in the outcome of validity studies for similar jobs are due to statistical artifacts. The value to practitioners of a validity generalization model is that it would permit them to generalize established findings to new settings without making new validation studies.

There are cautions to be observed, however, in regard to the degree of differences among situational factors. Similarity of jobs (in tasks or requirements and performance criteria) would appear to be necessary to a significant extent in order to justify the generalizing of findings from other studies. But the prospect of generalization opens doors for practitioners.

Moreover, as Schmidt and Hunter suggest (1977, 537), it can perhaps have an effect on governmental guidelines. Noting that the guidelines (the earlier ones were in effect at the time of writing: U. S. Department of Justice 1976; EEOC 1970) made provisions for limited validity generalization, the authors state, "These provisions may have to be modified in their focus and extended significantly in the future as positive results from the use of this model accumulate" (537). The Uniform Guidelines of 1978 provide in Section 8B that if validity evidence from cooperative studies meet the Guidelines' technical standards, "evidence of validity specific to each user will not be required unless there are variables in the user's situation which are likely to affect validity significantly." Does this statement go far enough to take into account the evolving findings on validity generalization? Perhaps validity generalization will give impetus to a modification of the Guidelines themselves.

The door is not closed to Guidelines changes, as the answers to questions 55 and 57 in the 1979 supplement indicate. The supplement explains that the Guidelines recognize only the content, construct, and criterion-related validation strategies because "they represent the current professional consensus"; but it adds, "If the professional community recognizes new strategies or substantial modifications of existing strategies, they will be considered and, if necessary, changes will be made in the Guidelines." It is further stated that the Guidelines "are not intended to limit research and new developments." But the supplement makes it clear (question 40) that if there are differences between particular Guidelines provisions and validity principles expressed elsewhere, the enforcement agencies would give precedence to the Guidelines.

CONTINUING LEGAL CONSIDERATIONS

Aside from the difficulties with validation techniques themselves, many personnel practitioners are uncertain as to how to confront the related legal issues of feasibility, fairness, and the "cosmic search" for alternative selection devices. In regard to the search for alternatives, they are aware of the absurdities such search can lead to, as, for example, the nonuse of a valid manual dexterity test (that produced no adverse impact) in favor of interview judgments of manual dexterity (Zedeck and Cascio 1984, 498).

Court decisions bearing on personnel practices periodically provide guidance though not always complete clarification. A recent pertinent Supreme Court decision (Firefighters Local Union No. 1784 v. Stotts) held that "under Title VII of the Civil Rights Act of 1964, a court may not order an employer to lay off more senior employees in favor of less senior employees on the basis of race, in derogation of a bonafide seniority system, for the purpose of preserving a specific percentage of racial minority employees" (U. S. Commission on Civil Rights 1985, 1). The import of the case is that the courts may provide make-whole relief for victims of an employer's illegal discrimination but may not order preferential treatment of nonvictims.

The significance of these strictures for personnel selection is that they appear to apply not only to layoffs but to hiring and promotion as well. As expressed in a report by the U. S. Commission on Civil Rights (1985, 49), "Of course, courts may still enjoin the use of discriminatory employment practices, in addition to making actual victims whole. Further, courts still have the authority to order nondiscriminatory affirmative action remedies such as increased recruiting, training, counseling, and education programs. After *Stotts*, however, a court lacks authority under Title VII to approve a consent decree or to order relief in favor of nonvictims of an employer's illegal discrimination at the expense of innocent third parties, whether in the hiring, promotion, layoff, or other context.''

However, in subsequent cases bearing on the composition of the workforce the Supreme Court rendered decisions which bring back into question the argument that make-whole relief should apply only to actual victims of discrimination. In the case of Wendy Wygant et al., Petitioners v Jackson Board of Education (decided May 19, 1986), the Court struck down a Michigan school district plan that sought to protect minority hiring gains by laying off white teachers with more seniority than retained blacks. The decision, written by Justice Powell, found the Board's layoff plan too intrusive a burden on particular individuals and as being insufficiently "narrowly tailored." But Powell appeared to leave the door open for less intrusive means of achieving similar purposes, such as adopting hiring goals. In the case of Local No. 93, International Association of Firefighters v City of Cleveland (decided July 2, 1986), the Court upheld a consent decree that required Cleveland to meet numerical goals for promotion of black firemen to lieutenant and battalion chief. The Court considered the consent decree to be less restricted under federal civil right law than a court order. In the New York case of Local 28, Sheet Metal Workers v EEOC (decided July 2, 1986), the union sought a reversal of a Second Circuit ruling that, as a major provision, required the local to meet a 29% non-white minority membership goal by August, 1987. The Supreme Court upheld the ruling. The majority view was that when "persistent or egregious discrimination" was found, a federal court could order affirmative action to relieve workers who were not direct victims of discrimination.

The recent court rulings do not change the basic governmental requirements as to test validation.

In regard to court attitudes toward validation, Zedeck and Cascio conclude that "the courts apparently still regard content, construct, and criterion-related validity as distinct forms of validation and not as subsets within the unifying and common framework of construct validity" (1984, 494).

A review by Kleiman and Faley (1985) of the 12 criterion-related validation cases adjudicated by the courts since 1978 provides guidance for employers in conducting or defending criterion-related studies, although the indications from the decisions are not entirely clearcut or consistent. The general findings were that judges placed heavy reliance on test-development procedures and that many of them were "reluctant" to accept recent research findings inconsistent with the Uniform Guidelines provisions.

Uncertainties remain, and the survey identified a number of areas of disagreement between the information contained in the courts' decisions and the legal and professional guidelines (829). In three of these issues of particular troublesomeness to practitioners—search for alternatives, "transportability" of validity, and fairness—the decisions of the courts do not give definitive guidance, but court tendencies do emerge, at least in regard to the first two (809–812; 824–827). A formal search by the employer for alternatives with less adverse impact did not occur in any of the seven cases addressing this issue. In two of these cases, this lack drew mild criticism from the judges but did not adversely influence the decisions; in two others the judges ruled that the employers had met their obligations indirectly; and in the others the judges concluded that the burden of the search was unnecessary (one case) or should be placed on the plaintiff (two cases). In three of the four cases dealing with validity transportability (reliance on validity studies conducted elsewhere), the issue rested on whether or not the study adhered to the Uniform Guidelines' stipulations for comparability between jobs. But in the last case (Pegues v. Mississippi State Employment Service), the door to the validity generalization appeared to open a little; the judge, apparently influenced by current generalization research, found not true the plaintiff's allegation that validity is specific to location, tasks, and population. Avoidance of test unfairness (lower scores of a protected group not corresponding to group differences in job performance) remains an unsettled issue in regard both to a test fairness model and the criteria for determining infeasibility of test fairness studies. However, the size of the minority sample (30 used as a standard by one judge) continues apparently to be a major consideration in feasibility.

Taking into account the recent publication by the American Psychological Association of the updated version of the *Standards for Educational and Psychological Testing* (Standards, 1985), Kleiman and Faley supplemented their review (829–831) to consider the possible impact on judicial deliberations of views expressed in the new Standards. Their general conclusion was that a consensus document, though it serves as a guide in assessing validity, will not resolve all disagreements among professionals or provide the clarity a judge would prefer. Therefore, judges are likely to rely on expert witnesses and to reach decisions by resolving the "battle of the experts" (831).

The new Standards did throw additional light on certain issues troublesome to practitioners. In regard to validation strategies, they (1) find as "not possible" rigorous distinctions among content-related, criterion-related, and construct-related means of accumulating validity evidence and (2) recommend decisions based on professional judgments concerning the forms of evidence (more than one may be indicated) that meet the tests of quality and of necessity and feasibility for the intended use of the test (1985, 9). In regard to fairness, the Standards addressed a number of aspects: meaning (using the term "selection bias" or "predictive bias" to apply to differential predictions among subgroups as distinct from fairness as a "larger" issue (13); investigation of predictive bias (seeing it as indicated, where feasible, for groups for which a substantial probability of differential prediction for the particular kind of test has been established by previous research (17); and evaluative techniques (showing a preference for the regression model). In regard to validity generalization, the Standards find generalization to be affected by such major facets as the way the predictor construct is measured, the type of job, the type of criterion measure, the type of test takers, and the time period of the study (12); and the new situation must be similar, in terms of characteristics of the people and job functions, to the situations of the prior studies from which validity generalization is claimed (16–17). The Standards regard the application to new situations as "in large measure a function of accumulated research" (12). In short, they appear to see the claim of validity, through generalization, as often supportable in a new situation but the extent of the claim to be constrained by the available data.

That we experience uncertainties concerning concepts of testing and Guidelines interpretations is not reason enough for abandoning efforts to set test-based selection standards. It does strongly suggest that the efforts would benefit from professional skill and legal surveillance.

DECIDING ON VALIDATION STRATEGIES

A basic decision a company must make in regard to procedures for selection and promotion is whether to use tests. The alternative to the use of tests, since selection and promotion must be made on some basis, is reliance on other less reliable and less valid and probably more discriminatory measures of suitability. Personnel planning would be more difficult. And the economic consequences to a company, particularly one dependent on highly skilled operations, could be severe.

If a company chooses to use tests, it has the ticklish task of applying techniques that are professionally sound (amidst the current reexamination and reformulation); that meet the unmodified (but somewhat clarified) requirements of the government's Uniform Guidelines; and that are practical procedures in the company setting. The challenge to a company is formidable but, fortunately, not insurmountable.

Company practitioners first must recognize limitations forced on them by their own resources and the requirements of the Guidelines. Decisions then become a little more obvious as the practitioners plot their course.

They are well advised to avoid construct validity as an approach to test validation. Construct validation is best left to test constructionists interested in developing instruments that "validly" measure constructs they have in mind. When such tests are developed, there is still the need to establish a relationship with job performance before they are useful as a selection tool.

Criterion-related validation is a route aswarm with cautions but is a passable way to go with judicious guidance. In most companies, the practitioners will be forced to rule out any attempt to use the predictive kind of criterion-related validation because of time requirements and sample limitations. Instead, they should concentrate on concurrent validity with the expectation, supported by research indications, that the results will be similar. There may still be a problem with sample size, but the Guidelines provide solutions, albeit difficult ones: (1) combining jobs within the company that have "substantially the same major work behaviors" (Section 14, B1), taking care that the samples of employees are comparable in terms of such factors as the actual job they perform and the length of time on the job (Section 14, B4); and (2) participation in cooperative studies which meet the validation standards of the Guidelines (question 45, Guideline supplement, 1979).

Content validation, according to the Guidelines, involves the measuring of knowledge, skill, or ability which is a necessary prerequisite to successful performance of critical or important job behaviors. The knowledge, skill, or ability should be operationally defined, and the selection procedure should measure representative samples of them (should, indeed, closely approximate the work situation). The procedure should not, however, attempt to measure knowledge, skill, or ability an employee would be expected to learn on the job. The *Principles* (1980, 12–15) list such requirements for the use of content-oriented strategies as these: The job content "domains" should be defined ordinarily in terms of "tasks, activities or responsibilities or specific abilities, knowledge, or job skills found to be prerequisite to effective behaviors in the domain"; the definition should be in terms of things the employee is expected to do without training or experience on the job; the domain "may be restricted to critical or frequent activities or to prerequisite knowledge, skills, or abilities"; the domain should be sampled so as to ensure that the major and not trivial elements of the defined domain are measured; and the test should have appropriate measurement qualities. In this latter regard, as the *Principles* suggest and the author can attest, reliability is a serious matter of concern with measures of work samples. Work samples seem to have an irresistible appeal for inexperienced test practitioners. As the *Principles* caution, persons engaging in content validity studies should be qualified.

What makes content validity a difficult approach in an industrial setting is that once a practitioner gets beyond obvious skill requirements in a restricted number of jobs, the content domain tends to defy definition, especially in entry-level factory jobs. A typist must have typing skill, a proofreader must know how to spell, a truck driver must have driving ability. These are skills we cannot reasonably expect an employer to teach an employee on the job, and we can employ selection standards for already acquired skills in such cases. The testing device would be restricted to measuring basic skills and not procedures specific to the job which will perforce be learned on the job itself. A typist would be tested for speed and accuracy of typing but not for knowledge of unique forms and set-ups employed by the company. But what does one justifiably test for in the way of prerequisite knowledge, skills, and abilities when selecting employees for entry jobs in a factory, jobs primarily perceptual-motor in nature? Even such basic skills as reading, writing, and performing simple calculations tend in many cases to be trivial requirements not closely related to important job activities. And whatever small degree of such skills is required in the job is possessed in common by virtually all applicants.

For some jobs, content validity is a useful and practical strategy for setting selection requirements, but it does not appear to have a broad enough application to serve as the major strategy in a typical factory. For the development of devices useful for the selection of employees for perceptual-motor jobs, the more pertinent validation technique is criterion related validation; one is dealing in such case with constructs in the form of basic traits or aptitudes (manual dexterity and perceptual speed, for example) little affected by learning.

Achievement in academic subjects may be, increasingly, a legitimate requirement for employee selection as high-technology jobs become more numerous. But when ready indications of academic achievement are available through school records (taking the possibility of overstatement into account), one questions the justification for an exhaustive search for related job content measures.

Content validity of a special kind does have a role to play, however, in the devising of measures for estimating an employee's qualifications for promotion into jobs of higher skill level, especially mechanical jobs, on the basis of achievement in a training program. And the approach can be legitimately used. As stated in the Guidelines (Section 14, C7), "Where a measure of success in a training program is used as a selection procedure and the content of a training program is justified on the basis of content validity, the use should be justified on the relationship between the content of the training program and the content of the job." The 1979 supplement, in answer to question 76, further states, "While the Guidelines . . . note that content validity is not an appropriate strategy for knowledges, skills or abilities which an employee 'will be expected to learn on the job,' nothing in the Guidelines suggests that a test supported by content validation is not appropriate for determining what the employee has learned on the job, or in a training program. If the content of the test is relevant to the job, it may be used for employment decisions such as retention or assignment."

Finally, before a company closes its deliberations concerning the way to proceed with selection tests, it should consider the prospects that validity generalization appears to open to it. The Guidelines do not prohibit the use of tests properly validated in cooperative studies. Nor do they prohibit the use of selection procedures validated by criterion related techniques elsewhere, provided the original study is adequately documented, the work behaviors are the same, the criterion of job performance is relevant for the user, and the sample characteristics are similar (Section 15, E1). It would obviously be of advantage to a company to survey validations studies reported by test manufacturers, the State Employment Security agency, psychological organizations and publications, trade associations, professional societies, other companies, or any other available source; and, if possibly pertinent studies are found, to make the specific comparisons required by the Guidelines. This sort of search is indicated whether a company has adequate samples for its own studies or not. Much time and labor may be saved. If the company's samples are too small for its own studies, the search is even more necessary but should be supplemented by an exploration of the possibility of joint studies under the auspices of the State Employment Security office or professional groups or through direct arrangements with other companies in the same industry.

The question may be raised: Why bother to validate tests at all? The law does not require validity studies to be conducted unless the selection procedures result in adverse impact as determined by application of the "four-fifths" rule (adverse impact generally being regarded as present when the selection rate for any race, sex, or ethnic group is less than four-fifths of the rate for the group with the highest rate). When the selection procedure has adverse impact, a validity study is called for, or, as an option, the user may choose lawful alternative procedures that eliminate adverse impact (1979 supplement, question 31).

The best answer to the question is that eventually a validation requirement appears to catch up with the user. Demonstration of a "rational relationship" (as the term is used in constitutional law) between a selection procedure and a job will not serve (1979 supplement, question 27). The users who want to validate all their selection procedures but are unable to conduct the studies immediately and choose alternative techniques that eliminate adverse impact do so "with a view to providing a basis for determining subsequently which selection procedures are valid and have as little adverse impact as possible" (1979 supplement, question 31). And adverse consequences to the company are likely to ensue if validation efforts are unduly postponed. The 1979 supplement (question 41) states that "validation studies begun on the eve of litigation are seldom adequate" and points out the potential economic costs if a user persists until challenged with a selection procedure having adverse impact (liability for back pay awards, plaintiff's attorney fees, loss of federal contracts, etc.).

In its understandable preoccupation with the admittedly difficult task of meeting governmental selection requirements, a company may tend to lose sight of the benefits to itself of validated selection procedures. Companies recognized the advantages of test validation many years before equal employment opportunity rules went into force. Indeed, the major endeavor of many psychologists employed in industry in the late 1940's was the validation of selection tests. Of course, unfair discrimination must be avoided. But in the process of selecting employees, a company's overriding objective is to develop a competent and efficient workforce and, in the light of contemporary circumstances and pressures, a workforce that is stable as well.

We should get on with it. A company should utilize the validation strategies that fit its circumstances and thereby establish test standards for selection in advance of using them. There is enough flexibility in the Guidelines, though still restrictive, to provide means for the setting of valid test requirements in many job classifications. Modifications in the Guidelines may come later as a welcome event when newer psychological developments are brought to bear on them, but the current Guidelines do not prevent a company from acting now to set up valid selection and promotion requirements. Even under the best of circumstances and with an unlimited choice of procedures, validation studies cannot be expected to produce significant positive results (meeting the .05 level of confidence required in criterion-related studies) in every instance; under the current Guidelines, a persistent program, professionally conducted, should produce valid tests for use in a substantial number of job classifications.

And, of course, a company is required to set up a monitoring system for detection of adverse impact associated with the use of the established test standards (and other selection procedures). The very failure to keep such records gives rise to an inference of adverse impact. The record-keeping regulations, like the validation regulations, may tend to stagger us, appearing, at first glance, to be impossibly complex in the light of the multiplicity of employee groups, job classifications, and selection devices to keep track of. But the operation can be brought within easier compass by taking simplified approaches that are not violative of the guidelines:

1. In regard to selection devices, the "bottom line" approach is pertinent to the assessment of adverse impact; the enforcement agencies will therefore look at the end result of the selection criteria used. The employer would normally be expected to make a yearly analysis of the impact of the total mix of its selection criteria, and adequate records should be kept for such analysis. But sufficient records on components of the mix should be maintained to permit an analysis of the impact of separate components if the "bottom line" impact from the mix is found to be adverse and the impact of separate criteria needs to be examined.

2. In regard to job classifications, a practical approach is to establish "pools" of job titles with the same minimum entry qualifications. Obviously, a small number of employees in a single classification would make an impact study relatively meaningless.

3. In regard to employee groups and between-group comparisons, it would be prudent to focus the analyses first on the most obvious comparisons: females against males, largest minorities against nonminorities.

STEPS IN VALIDATION PROCEDURES

The choice of validation strategies will depend on the size, job structure, and other characteristics of the particular company or plant. For illustrative purposes, let us take a manufacturing plant which employs a large number of workers (enough for sizable samples for test validation purposes in major classifications) in jobs representing roughly three levels of skill: (1) the first level of jobs involving such tasks as supplying machines with material, removing the processed parts, and performing housekeeping and cleaning duties; (2) the second level involving the operation of machines and the making of minor adjustments and repairs; and (3) the third level involving major machine repairs, the rebuilding and modification of machines, and the adapting of machines to meet changes in product specifications. The jobs at the first two levels are considered entry jobs for which new employees could be directly hired. However, an employee hired for a first-level job, if considered qualified, could be moved into a second-level job when an opening occurred. The third-level jobs, because of the significantly higher level of skill and the specialized tasks, are filled by promotion from within.

Concurrent Criterion-Related Studies for Entry Jobs

A reasonable choice of validation strategies for this plant comprises concurrent criterion-related studies for the entry jobs and, for the third-level jobs, a content validity strategy involving a formal prepromotion training program and the development of written and performance achievement tests for measurement of promotional qualifications.

The steps in the criterion-related studies would be as follow:

1. A comprehensive listing and description of job activities. A short statement of duties will not be sufficient; the statement should indicate what an employee does in the performance of the duties.

2. A rather comprehensive listing of worker attributes or characteristics. The list would include such attributes as perceptual speed, spatial orientation, number facility, verbal comprehension, eye–hand coordination, manual dexterity, color discrimination, etc. These should be specifically defined. But it is not necessary for a company to develop its own list of employee attributes and job elements. Material has been developed on the basis of earlier research (McCormick, Jeanneret, and Mecham 1972; Neeb, Cunningham, and Pass 1974; Cunningham, Tuttle, Floyd, and Bates 1974; Cunningham [in press]).

3. An analysis which relates worker attributes to the activities of the particular job. This can be done by personnel having expert knowledge of the job (the immediate supervisor of the operation, the workers themselves, or instructors or trainers, for example) and a firm understanding of the definitions of the comprehensive list of worker attributes. The written job description and the set of attribute definitions should be made available for continuing reference during the analytic procedure.

The procedure can be aided by using cross-sectional paper listing worker attributes on one axis and significant job activities on the other.

The analyst would follow such steps as these:

1. Take each job activity in turn and run through the list of employee attributes.

2. Decide whether the performance of the activity requires a particular attribute in a significant way. If so, make a check mark at the intersection of the activity and the attribute.

3. After completing the cross-sectional checking, take each attribute in turn and scan the chart to determine how many check marks appear.

Some job activities, of course, are more important than others. An attribute required by an important activity would carry more weight in the final summing up than an attribute required by an activity of lesser importance. But the number of check marks will serve as a guide for estimating the total requirement of the particular attribute. Modifications could be made by weighting the involved job activities for importance. Other refinements of the analysis may also be made in arriving at the decision as to the comparative extent of the requirement, in regard to job performance, of the various attributes.

At this point, with jobs defined and possible related employee attributes identified, the project should stop for a search for validation studies performed elsewhere on jobs with similar content and similar employee requirements. When such studies are found, a more comprehensive comparison should be made on the basis of Guidelines requirements, particularly relating to characteristics of the sample of employees in the study and the pertinence of the job performance criteria used.

If the applicability of other studies is not justified, the company's own validation procedure should go forward with step 4. At this point, too, decisions can be made on combining job classifications for validation purposes if samples are small.

4. A search for testing instruments to measure the important worker attributes identified. The best source of information in this regard is the information provided by reputable test developers and publishers. Practitioners should resist the temptation to develop their own tests at this point. The test construction process is complex and lengthy, involving item writing, item analysis, reliability determination, etc. And the emerging test, however accurately it is presumed by its originator to measure the elusive particular construct he is pursuing, must still be found related to job performance statistically. In addition, the proliferation of tests arising from attempts to develop one's own measures of precise attributes can result in an experimental battery of tests too large to be acceptable to the sample of employees we want to test in the project. It is usually possible to find enough pertinent tests, for tryout in our studies, in the catalogs of test manufacturers.

5. Development of criteria of job performance against which to relate the test performance of our job classification sample of employees. This step can be undertaken earlier; it is a crucial one that requires much effort. The criteria should measure important aspects of performance and should be reliable measures. In this latter regard, the employees in the sample should have reached a stable level of performance where further significant improvement is not expected—a stage well beyond trainee status. We want to predict performance "ultimate" for the individual. Performance at intermediate stages in training tends to give unreliable readings and in some cases will depend on aptitudes that will not sustain performance improvements to high levels.

If the job involves a simple motion pattern and skill development time is short, the aptitude(s) prominently relied upon in the early phase—usually dexterity—will probably continue prominently to underpin the continuing performance. But if the job is complex and requires the trainee to advance through a series of developmental stages to achieve full job competence, a number of aptitudes must come into play to carry him through. In many production jobs, for example, dexterity moves an employee through the beginning stage of skill, but the movement to higher levels of skill requires an efficiency in the perception of feedback indications. In multitask jobs an organizational skill (related to intelligence) comes into play in the late learning stages when the employee must bring the total job into compass through the planning and scheduling of activities, preparing for contingencies, and establishing priorities in time allocation. Aptitudes important to early learning continue to work their effects. But in the advanced stages of learning, the mix of aptitudes changes in regard to relative importance of individual aptitudes, and an aptitude may indeed come to the fore which was not required in any significant or measurable way when approximate or intermediate skill levels were attained.

The Uniform Guidelines permit performance in training to be used as a criterion when the relevance of the training is shown (by comparison of training content with important job behaviors or by demonstration of a relationship between training performance measures and job performance measures) (Section 14 B3). But our own standards should go further to rule out training performance as a job performance criterion when the training performance represents intermediate levels of skill development. We are interested in having our criterion measure job performance in important aspects of its advanced manifestations, in having it truly measure job competence rather than, for example, simply task competence or performance representing only interim progress toward job competence. And with such a criterion we can achieve a fuller determination of contributing aptitudes.

In many job classifications, output and/or quality records are available and validly reflect employee performance in important job aspects. The practitioner should reject those measures that are partial indications of the employees' performance but are also significantly influenced by employees in other job classifications (for example, output or efficiency in a machine operator's case may also be the product of the performance of service and maintenance personnel). It is often statistically impossible to partial out the effect of other workers. Practitioners must also resist the temptation to use, as criteria, records of minor aspects of performance simply on the basis of the availability of an objective index. Waste records tend to fall in this category when waste reduction is a relatively minor outcome of performance. When objective records of important job performance aspects are not available, supervisory ratings of performance may have to be relied on as criterion measures. In view of the subjectivity of ratings, it is advisable to tighten them up as much as possible through such means as securing more than one rating (from personnel in position to observe performance adequately) and devising behavior-oriented rating instruments.

6. Administering tests to the samples of employees. Assurances must be given that the testing is simply for experimental purposes in the setting of selection standards, the test scores will be confidential, the records will be destroyed when the study is completed, and the test scores will in no way affect the status of the individual. In no event should test performance be communicated to the employee's superiors or discussed with them. A common experience is to find employees giving minimum effort to the tests and performing below their true

capabilities. Of course, testing should be voluntary and employees should be paid for the testing time, and, on these bases, many will give it their "best shot." But a direct appeal from the test administrator is in order. It is also advisable, in the interest of better ensuring trust and effort, that a manager of high regard involve himself in the explanation of the testing arrangements and purposes. But in no cases should a superior be involved in administering or scoring tests or keeping test records. If confidentiality and the promise of no effect are breached, the total project cannot go forward.

7. Comparing test scores with "scores" on performance criteria by means of correlation techniques. This part of the program should be in the hands of qualified statisticians, although the use of data-processing equipment simplifies the chore. Since differences on the performance criterion measures tend to be small in concurrent studies (the subjects have all "made it" on the job), a statistical correction may be necessary for restriction of range on the performance measures. To be acceptable as a selection device, a test should correlate with job performance at the .05 level of confidence. The issue of fairness should be addressed in this step and the subsequent step.

8. Establishing cutting scores on the valid tests that will separate predicted good performers from poor performers. Again, this is an operation for a qualified statistician.

9. Finally, the tests found valid, with appropriate cutting scores (or ranges of scores), are instituted as a part of the job application and hiring procedure. In companies of significant size, applications are taken and applicant files built up in anticipation of openings rather than at the time openings occur. Applicants should be tested (in groups for efficiency) as part of the application procedure and results discussed in application interviews. It can be anticipated that a limited number of tests will be found to apply to the wide range of entry jobs; otherwise an employee-testing program will place an unreasonable burden on applicants. One testing session should serve to make applicants eligible for consideration for employment in entry jobs for which their test scores qualify them (providing they meet other requirements as well). Retesting should be permitted but advisedly only once and, in the case of written tests, with alternative forms of the tests if available.

In the author's experience, job analyses of an exhaustive kind and criterion-related studies point ultimately to a limited number of basic abilities as pertinent to job requirements in many factory jobs. Dexterity (hand and finger) and perceptual skill appear to be needed for mastery of jobs heavily loaded with motor activities and related perceptions (for feedback information). Jobs in which monitoring is a principal activity especially require perceptual ability. Machine operating in many cases requires a strong combination of perceptual and manipulative abilities. Jobs involving diagnosis of machine problems and the making of adjustments for correction seem to require a combination of mechanical ability, perceptual ability, and manipulative ability. If measurements and calculations are required, arithmetic ability is an added requirement; if manuals are to be used and understood, reading comprehension is important. It is indeed difficult to find a factory job in which one or more of these basic abilities is not likely to be a major requirement for development of job competence.

Content Validity for High-Level Promotion

The content validity approach to the establishment of required qualifications for promotion into the highest-level job in our example would require an employee to demonstrate knowledge and skills of importance in the performance of the higher job itself. Of course, the candidate should have the opportunity to master such job content.

Indeed, all candidates should have equal opportunity to achieve such mastery. In our example, machine operators could pick up minimum pointers by observation of maintenance technicians who work on their machines. One might reasonably require a certain length of experience in machine operating as one prerequisite for promotion. But it is virtually impossible to ensure equal learning opportunities among candidates if they are expected to pick up peripheral knowledge of the higher job while pursuing their assigned duties in a lower job. To give organization to such incidental training is very difficult. The most equitable and most efficient approach is to set up a formal training arrangement which would provide instruction for specified periods in tasks of the higher job itself, on paid time and preferably in a vestibule setting. The training should go far enough to wash out the uneven residue of observational training and permit candidates the opportunity to master the tasks at hand.

In terms of training techniques, this approach would require adequate explanation and demonstration, which could be given to class members in a group, and adequate opportunity for individual practice under one-on-one coaching guidance, which would include cuing and feedback. The individual attention would observe the same time limits from candidate to candidate.

The training would not include all job tasks; much of the job learning would necessarily occur after placement. But the instruction would concentrate on a selected number of important job tasks and related segments of knowledge.

Qualification for promotion would depend on (in addition to other requirements) satisfactory scores in achievement tests. The most appropriate and acceptable kinds of tests seem to be performance tests—the actual assignments of certain job tasks, in which instruction had been given, to candidates for carrying out. Tests of knowledge, related to repair procedures and machine settings, are also pertinent.

Because of ease of scoring, knowledge tests tend to have greater appeal. But accurate and equitable scoring arrangements can be worked out, with advice from supervisors and other personnel experts in the job and with trial runs, for the performance tests. Open-ended questions would appear to be most effective for eliciting genuine knowledge on paper-and-pencil tests, but multiple-choice questions are appropriate when the job situation itself confronts the employee with alternative courses of action (as in deciding on probable causes of a certain kind of malfunctioning).

In an exemplary use (in the author's observation) of achievement testing for promotion to a mechanical job, the trainees were given six work samples to perform, each with a weight related to importance in the job. An employee's performance on each task was rated in terms of how well the individual steps were carried out (each step being weighted), the order of the steps taken, and the length of time required to complete the task. The written test covered knowledge of procedures and machine settings in the full range of the job operations covered in the course. The final course grade gave a weight of 25 to the written test and 75 to the combined performance tests.

Settling on the level of score required as acceptable qualification for promotion is necessarily a deliberative process involving advice from maintenance personnel and supervisors, tryouts of testing procedures with volunteers from among the experienced maintenance technicians, and adjustments based on the performance of early groups of trainees. It is reasonable to place the required score at a relatively high level when testing is intended to measure achievement after strong training and when the training involves a job, like repairing, in which a 60 or 70% performance is unacceptable in operational terms.

Retesting is probably justified once, preferably on an alternate set of job performance and knowledge tests. But permitting a trainee to repeat the training is not advisable. A little pliability is in order, but if the procedure is breached in a significant way to accommodate individual employees or to meet their objections, it will cease to be useful.

Needless to say, the development of the training course, the testing instruments, and the scoring system requires the input and critical review of personnel expert in the job operations. In addition, the actual instruction should be done by someone who is expert in job performance and related knowledge, is recognized as being highly competent, and has the trust and respect of people within the department.

GENERAL PROCEDURES FOR HIRING, SELECTION, AND PROMOTION

Hiring and upgrading requirements should be placed within the context of personnel policies and procedures aimed at strengthening and stabilizing the workforce. Procedures for selection and promotion should involve multiple jobs and rewards and should emphasize the satisfactory assignment and career development of individual employees. In light of the importance to the retention of employees and their commitment to the organization, we should be concerned with developing the employee's competence in a number of job skills within his capability and developing his occupational career in the process.

This objective would require that we provide opportunities for upward movement for qualified employees and for lateral movement among jobs with similar requirements for employees whose promotional capabilities are limited. The goal is to maximize the employee's range of competences, with benefit to the company in terms of a versatile workforce that can adjust to changing production demands and with advantages to employees in terms of increased value to the organization and greater assurance of continuing employment.

A job structure for this purpose would include jobs with different content at the same skill level and jobs at different skill levels. Jobs would be aligned, as far as practical, in simple hierarchies which could serve as pathways for promotion. And they should be strung laterally, as well, to form a framework for cross-training among jobs at relatively the same skill level.

The applicant would be considered for initial placement in keeping with his qualifying scores on the aptitude tests (and the satisfying of other hiring requirements). Jobs may have similar requirements. In many cases, the applicant will be found to qualify for a number of jobs, in which case he would be placed in the first of those jobs that came open. He would have his seniority in a specific job. But an organized training effort, under a system of "cross-training," would be made to teach him other jobs for which he qualifies. For training purposes he would thus be moved for short periods to jobs at the same skill level or higher skill level, whatever his qualifications made him eligible for. If an opening occurred at a higher level, he would be moved into it in line with his seniority. Of course, in a promotion into a high-level job to which separate qualification requirements applied (as the maintenance technician job in our example), he would have to meet those requirements. In our example, he would have to demonstrate satisfactory achievement in a specific formal training program, though as a prerequisite for entering the training program or being considered for promotion, a certain period of time in a lesser but related job may be required. If he qualified on the achievement measures, he would be eligible for the next opening on the basis of seniority. Much training would be needed after the promotion in order to ensure his full competence in the higher job, and satisfactory on-job performance in a probationary period may reasonably be required before job rights are gained.

With such job structure and procedures for movement into jobs, the hiring process can become a semicounseling process, not in terms of offering advice to the applicant but of indicating realistically what might be in store for him. The employment official can indicate what entry jobs the applicant is considered suitable for on the basis of aptitude test scores and other employment requirements. He can also discuss jobs of higher skill but should clearly outline what additional requirements have to be met. He should inform the applicant, too, concerning the training the company would provide to assist the employee to qualify for advancement and to broaden his job competences. In short, the employment manager discusses with the applicant what jobs he can realistically aspire to in the plant and what he must do to qualify for them. Realism is an essential ingredient in the discussion. The applicant should be informed not only of his potential in the plant but of his indicated limitations. Not every applicant will be judged suitable for advancement (indeed, not every applicant will qualify for the entry jobs). But the procedure should be outlined in detail so that the applicant can decide on the basis of accurate information whether or not he wants to cast his lot with the plant. A favorable decision reached through a true perception by the employee of his present and future prospects is likely to result in a stronger and longer commitment to the company than otherwise. And the general effect in the plant as a whole should be a more stable workforce—the ultimate objective.

Of course, follow-up discussions with the employee will be needed to update his prospects and related requirements.

In regard to qualifications for a supervisory job, some minimum experience in a departmental job of high skill (machine operating or machine maintenance) would be required as one indication of technical competence. So, in a strict sense, the hierarchy of related jobs extends to the supervisory job. But many other qualifications are needed for the supervisory assignment, and the possibility of promotion into a supervisory job should not be discussed in terms of promotional routes as part of the beginning counseling, except in the most general terms. Otherwise, we are likely to stimulate unrealistic expectations.

For general education or specific training not connected (or only remotely connected) with job prospects in the plant, the company should provide educational grants and scholarships to employees with a certain amount of service and an acceptable employment record. Those employees who wish to "develop" beyond the scope of job assignments in the plant should be encouraged to enroll. But the decision and effort would be the employee's. The company should simply provide financial help—a common practice in American industry. Qualifications for enrollment would be established by the particular school.

The proposed procedures are intended to ensure objectivity and fairness in assignments and promotions and to provide means by which the individual may achieve broad competences and possibly find a satisfactory career. For those employees who want growth and are capable of it, the opportunity and pathways are here. But as befitting American employees, we cannot expect to march them along in lock step or to do everything for them. Competences and advancement will be gained by individual effort; the company will give opportunities and training, focus the effort, and assume the costs. And in our preoccupation with making provisions, in our job assignments, for individual differences, we should not neglect making place for the employee who finds satisfaction in a specific job and simply wants to remain in it.

Bibliography

Abraham, Katherine G., and James L. Medoff. 1984. Length of service and layoffs in union and nonunion workgroups. *Industrial and Labor Relations Review* 38:87–97.

Adler, Seymour, and Jacob Golan. 1981. Lateness as a withdrawal behavior. *Journal of Applied Psychology* 66:544–554.

Anderson, Kathryn H. 1985. The effects of mandatory retirement on mortality. *Journal of Economics and Business* 37:81–88.

Andreassen, Arthur J., Norman C. Saunders, and Betty C. Su. 1984. Economic outlook for the 1990's: Three scenarios for economic growth. *Bureau of Labor Statistics Bulletin* 2197:9–21.

Arnold, Hugh J., and Daniel C. Feldman. 1982. A multivariate analysis of the determinants of job turnover. *Journal of Applied Psychology* 67:350—360.

Baumol, William J., and Alan S. Blinder. 1982. *Economics: Principles and policy*. 2nd ed. New York: Harcourt Brace Jovanovich, Inc.

Bazerman, Max H., Toni Giuliano, and Alan Appelman. 1984. Escalation of commitment in individual and group decision making. *Organizational Behavior and Human Performance* 33:141–152.

Bendick, Marc. 1984. Worker mobility in response to plant closing. In *Managing plant closings and occupational readjustment: Employer's guidebook*, 47–56. Ed. Richard P. Swigart. Washington, D. C.: National Center on Occupational Readjustment, Inc.

Bierman, Leonard, Joseph C. Ullman, and Stuart A. Youngblood. 1985. Making disputes over dismissals "win-win" situations. *Business and Economic Review* 31(July):26–28.

Breaugh, James A. 1981. Predicting absenteeism from prior absenteeism and work attitudes. *Journal of Applied Psychology* 66:555–560.

Brett, Jeanne M. 1982. Job transfer and well-being. *Journal of Applied Psychology* 67:450–463.

Buchanan, Bruce, II. 1974. Building organizational commitment: The socialization of managers in work organizations. *Administrative Science Quarterly* 19:533–546.

Burge, James D. 1986. Worksharing: A "win-win" concept. In *The job challenge: Pressures and possibilities*, 135–145. Ed. Daniel F. Burton, Jr., John H. Filer, Douglas A. Fraser, and Ray Marshall. Cambridge, Mass.: Ballinger Publishing Company.

Buss, Terry F., and F. Steven Redburn. 1983. *Shutdown at Youngstown: Public policy for mass unemployment*. Albany, N. Y.: State University of New York Press.

Buss, Terry F., and F. Steven Redburn, with Joseph Waldron. 1983. *Mass unemployment: Plant closings and community mental health*. Beverly Hills, Ca.: Sage Publications.

Carey, Max L. and Kim L. Hazelbaker. 1986. Employment growth in the temporary help industry. *Monthly Labor Review* 109(April):37–44.

Cascio, Wayne F. 1982. *Costing human resources: The financial impact of behavior in organizations*. Boston: Kent Publishing Company.

Chao, Georgia T., and Steve W. J. Kozlowski. 1986. Employee perceptions on the implementation of robotic manufacturing technology. *Journal of Applied Psychology* 71:70–76.

Cole, Robert E. 1979. *Work, mobility, and participation: A comparative study of American and Japanese industry*. Berkeley: University of California Press.

Collins, Lora S. 1985. *The U. S. economy to 1990*. Report No. 864. New York: Conference Board.

Cook, Robert F., and Wayne M. Turnage. 1985. The new federal-state program to train dislocated workers. *Monthly Labor Review* 108(July):32–34.

Craft, James A. 1984. Controlling plant closings: A conceptual framework and assessment. In *Plant closing legislation*, 45–57. Ed. Antone Aboud. Ithaca, N. Y.: ILR Press, New York State School of Industrial and Labor Relations, Cornell University.

Cunningham, J. W. In press. The occupation analysis inventory: A quantitative approach to work taxonomy. In *The job analysis handbook*. Ed. S. Gael. New York: John Wiley & Sons, Inc.

Cunningham, J. W., Thomas C. Tuttle, John R. Floyd, and Joe A. Bates. 1974. The development of the occupation analysis inventory: "Ergometric" approach to an educational problem. JSAS *Catalog of Selected Documents in Psychology* 4:Ms. No. 803.

Dalton, Dan R., David M. Krackhardt, and Lyman W. Porter. 1981. Functional turnover: An empirical assessment. *Journal of Applied Psychology* 66:716–721.

Dalton, Dan R., William D. Todor, and David M. Krackhardt. 1982. Turnover overstated: The functional taxonomy. *Academy of Management Review* 7:117–123.

Devens, Richard M., Jr., Carol Boyd Leon, and Debbie Sprinkle. 1985. Employment and unemployment in 1984: A second year of strong growth in jobs. *Monthly Labor Review* 108(February):3–15.

Directory of outplacement firms. 2nd ed. 1982. A Consultant News Publication. Fitzwilliam, N. H.: Kennedy and Kennedy, Inc.

Eisenberg, Philip, and Paul F. Lazersfeld. 1938. The psychological effects of unemployment. *Psychological Bulletin* 35:358–390.

Ferris, Gerald R., Deborah A. Schellenberg, and Raymond F. Zammuto. 1984. Human resource management strategies in declining industries. *Human Resource Management* 23:381–394.

Feuer, Dale. 1985. A world without layoffs: Wouldn't it be lovely? *Training* 22(August):23–31.

Fey, Carol. 1986. Working with robots: The real story. *Training* 23(March):49–51, 56.

Flaim, Paul O. 1979. The effect of demographic changes on the nation's unemployment rate. *Monthly Labor Review* 102(March):13–23.

Flaim, Paul O., and Ellen Sehgal. 1985. Displaced workers of 1979–1983: How well have they fared? *Monthly Labor Review* 108(June):3–16.

Fleishman, Edwin A., and Edwin F. Harris. 1962. Patterns of leadership behavior related to employee grievances and turnover. *Personnel Psychology* 15:43–56.

Folbre, Nancy R., Julia L. Leighton, and Melissa R. Roderick. 1984. Plant closings and their regulation in Maine, 1971–1982. *Industrial and Labor Relations Review* 37:185–196.

Fortune forecast looking beyond the mixed signals. 1985. *Fortune* 112 (October):34–35.

Foxman, L. D., and W. L. Polsky. 1984. How to select a good outplacement firm. *Personnel Journal* 63(September):94–95.

Friedman, Sheldon. 1985. Negotiated approaches to job security. *Labor Law Journal* 36:553–557.

Fullerton, Howard N., Jr., and John Tschetter. 1984. Employment projections for 1995. *Bureau of Labor Statistics Bulletin* 2197:1–8.

Gaylord, Maxine C., and Estelle B. Symons. 1984. Coping with job loss and job change. *Personnel* 61(September-October):70–75.

Goldberg, Marshall. 1985. The UAW-Ford career services and reemployment assistance centers: New ventures in service delivery to unionized workers. *Labor Law Journal* 36(August):526–532.

Gordon, Robert J. 1985. Understanding inflation in the 1980's. In *Brookings papers on economic activity*, 263–299. Ed. William C. Brainard and George L. Perry. Washington, D. C.: Brookings Institution.

Gorlin, Harriet. 1982. *Company experience with flexible work schedules*. New York: Conference Board.

Greenwald, Douglas, ed. 1982. *Encyclopedia of economics*. New York: McGraw-Hill Book Company.

Griffeth, Roger W. 1985. Moderation of the effects of job enrichment by participation: A longitudinal field experiment. *Organizational Behavior and Human Decision Processes* 35:73–93.

Gupta, Nina, and G. Douglas Jenkins, Jr. 1982. Absenteeism and turnover: Is there a progression? *Journal of Management Studies* 19:395–412.

Gutchess, Jocelyn F. 1985. *Employment security in action: Strategies that work*. New York: Pergamon Press.

Hall, Thomas E. 1981. How to estimate employee turnover costs. *Personnel* 58(July-August):43–52.

Hansen, Gary B. 1985. Innovative approach to plant closings: The UAW-Ford experience at San Jose. *Monthly Labor Review* 108(June):34–37.

Harrigan, Kathryn Rudie. 1980. *Strategies for declining businesses*. Lexington, Mass.: Lexington Books, D. C. Heath and Company.

Harris, Philip R. 1985. *Management in transition*. San Francisco, Ca.: Jossey-Bass Publications.

Harrison, Teresa M. 1985. Communication and participative decision making: An exploratory study. *Personnel Psychology* 38:93–116.

Hart, Gary. 1983. *A New Democracy*. New York: Quill.

Hayes, John, and Peter Nutman. 1981. *Understanding the unemployed: The psychological effects of unemployment*. London: Tavistock Publications.

Herold, David M., and Charles K. Parsons. 1985. Assessing the feedback environment in work organizations: Development of the job feedback survey. *Journal of Applied Psychology* 20:290–305.

Hewlett-Packard statement of corporate objectives. 1983. Hewlett-Packard Company, Palo Alto, California.

Hirsch, Barry T., and John T. Addison. 1986. *The economic analysis of unions: New approaches and evidence.* Boston: Allen & Unwin.

Hom, Peter W., Roger W. Griffeth, and C. Louise Sellaro. 1984. The validity of Mobley's (1977) model of employee turnover. *Organizational Behavior and Human Performance* 34:141–174.

Hood, Jane C., and Nancy Milazzo. 1984. Shiftwork, stress and wellbeing. *Personnel Administration* 29(December):95–105.

Howell, James M. 1985. Formula for growth: The New England experience. *Business and Economic Review* 31(January):17–24.

Human Resources Development Institute. 1982. *A union response to plant closings and worker displacement: A program guide.* Washington, D. C.: American Federation of Labor and Congress of Industrial Organizations.

Hutchinson, Frank, and Greg Gilbert. 1985. Readying your company for change. *Training and Development Journal* 39(May):28–30.

Hymans, Saul H., and Joan P. Crary. 1985. The current state of the economy: The facts. *Economic Outlook USA* 12(Autumn):54–59.

Ilgen, Daniel R., Cynthia D. Fisher, and M. Susan Taylor. 1979. Consequences of individual feedback on behavior in organizations. *Journal of Applied Psychology* 64:349–371.

Ilgen, Daniel R., and William Seely. 1974. Realistic expectations as an aid in reducing voluntary resignations. *Personnel Psychology* 59:452–455.

Jagels, Martin G. 1985. Employer with no employees. *Business and Economic Review* 32(October):21–24.

Jamal, Muhammad. 1981. Shift work related to job attitudes, social participation, and withdrawal behavior: A study of nurses and industrial workers. *Personnel Psychology* 34:535–547.

Job sharing: A way to avoid layoffs? 1982. In "Roundup." *Personnel* 59(March-April):58–60.

Kahn, Lawrence M., and Stuart A. Low. 1982. The wage impact of job search. *Industrial Relations* 21(Winter):53–61.

Kanfer, Ruth, and Charles L. Hulin. 1985. Individual differences in successful job searches following lay-off. *Personnel Psychology* 38:835–847.

Kasper, Mirschel. 1984. Unemployment among new entrants to the labor force: A second look at the new unemployed. *Labor Law Journal* 35:475–480.

Kesner, Idalene, and Dan R. Dalton. 1982. Turnover benefits: The other side of the "cost" coin. *Personnel* 59(September-October):69–76.

Kleiman, Lawrence E., and Robert H. Faley. 1985. The implications of professional and legal guidelines for court decisions involving criterion-related validity: A review and analysis. *Personnel Psychology* 38:803–833.

Koch, James L., and Susan R. Rhodes. 1981. Predictors of turnover of female factory workers. *Journal of Vocational Behavior* 18:145–161.

Kokkelenberg, Edward C., and Donna R. Sockell. 1985. Union membership in the United States 1973–1981. *Industrial and Labor Relations Review* 38:497–543.

Komarovsky, Mirra. 1971. *The unemployed man and his family: The effects of unemployment upon the status of the man in fifty-nine families*. New York: Octagon Books.

Latham, Gary P., and Herbert A. Marshall. 1982. The effects of self-set, participatively set and assigned goals on the performance of government employees. *Personnel Psychology* 35:399–404.

Lawler, Edward E., III. 1985. Education, management style, and organizational effectiveness. *Personnel Psychology* 38:1–26.

Leff, Walli F., and Marilyn G. Haft. 1983. *Time without work*. Boston: South End Press.

Lehr, Richard I., and David J. Middlebrooks. 1984. Work force reduction: Strategies and options. *Personnel Journal* 63(October):50–55.

Leonard, Jonathan S. 1985. The effects of unions on the employment of blacks, hispanics, and women. *Industrial and Labor Relations Review* 39:115–132.

Mager, Robert F., and Peter Pipe. 1970. *Analyzing performance, or "you really oughta wanna."* Belmont, Ca.: Fearon Publishers.

Mangum, Garth, Donald Mayall, and Kristin Nelson. 1985. The temporary help industry: A response to the dual internal labor market. *Industrial and Labor Relations Review* 38:599–611.

Markham, Steven E., Fred Dansereau, Jr., and Joseph A. Alutto. 1982. Female vs. male absence rates: A temporal analysis. *Personnel Psychology* 35:371–382.

Martin, Thomas N., and J. G. Hunt. 1980. Social influence and intent to leave: A path-analytic process model. *Personnel Psychology* 33:505–528.

Martin, Thomas N., J. L. Price, and C. W. Mueller. 1981. Job performance and turnover. *Journal of Applied Psychology* 66:116–119.

McCormick, E. J., P. R. Jeanneret, and R. C. Mecham. 1972. A study of job characteristics and job dimensions as based on the position analysis questionnaire (PAQ). *Journal of Applied Psychology* 56:347–368.

McEvoy, Glenn M., and Wayne F. Cascio. 1985. Strategies for reducing employee turnover: A meta-analysis. *Journal of Applied Psychology* 70:342–353.

Michaels, Charles E., and Paul E. Spector. 1982. Causes of employee turnover: a test of the Mobley, Griffeth, Hand, and Meglino model. *Journal of Applied Psychology* 67:53–59.

Miller, Howard E., Ralph Katerberg, and Charles L. Hulin. 1979. Evaluation of the Mobley, Horner, and Hollingsworth model of employee turnover. *Journal of Applied Psychology* 64:509–517.

Mills, D. Quinn. 1985. Planning with people in mind. *Harvard Business Review* 63(July-August):97–105.

Mirvis, Philip, and Edward E. Lawler, III. 1977. Measuring the financial impact of employee attitudes. *Journal of Applied Psychology* 62:1–8.

Mitchell, Olivia S. 1983. Fringe benefits and the cost of changing jobs. *Industrial and Labor Relations Review* 37:70–78.

Mobley, William H. 1977. Intermediate linkage in the relationship between job satisfaction and employee turnover. *Journal of Applied Psychology* 62:237–240.

———. 1982. *Employee turnover: Causes, consequences, and control*. Reading, Mass.: Addison-Wesley Publishing Company.

Mobley, William H., R. W. Griffeth. H. H. Hand, and B. M. Meglino. 1979. Review and conceptual analysis of the employee turnover process. *Psychological Bulletin* 86:493–522.

Mobley, William H., Stanley O. Horner, and A. T. Hollingsworth. 1978. An examination of precursors of hospital employee turnover. *Journal of Applied Psychology* 63:408–414.

Mowday, Richard T. 1984. Strategies for adapting to high rates of employee turnover. *Human Resource Management* 23:365–380.

Mowday, Richard T., Lyman W. Porter, and Richard M. Steers. 1982. *Employee-organization linkage: The psychology of commitment, absenteeism, and turnover.* New York: Academic Press.

Narayanan, V. K., and Raghu Nath. 1982. A field test of some attitudinal and behavioral consequences of flexitime. *Journal of Applied Psychology* 67:214–218.

Nardone, Thomas J. 1986. Part-time workers: Who are they? *Monthly Labor Review* 109(February):13–18.

Neeb, R. W., J. W. Cunningham, and J. J. Pass. 1974. Human attribute requirements of work elements: Further development of the occupation analysis inventory. JSAS *Catalog of Selected Documents in Psychology* 4:Ms. No. 805.

Norwood, Janet L. June 11, 1985. Jobs in the 1980's and beyond. Address presented at the Fifth International Symposium on Forecasting, Montreal, Canada.

O'Reilly, Charles A., and David F. Caldwell. 1980. Job choice: The impact of intrinsic and extrinsic factors on subsequent satisfaction and commitment. *Journal of Applied Psychology* 65:559–565.

Orpen, Christopher. 1981. Effect of flexible working hours on employee satisfaction and performance: A field experiment. *Journal of Applied Psychology* 66:113–115.

O'Toole, James. 1985. *Vanguard management: Redesigning the corporate future.* New York: Doubleday and Company, Inc.

Parsons, Charles K., David M. Herold, and Marya L. Leatherwood. 1985. Turnover during initial employment: A longitudinal study of the role of causal attributions. *Journal of Applied Psychology* 70:337–341.

Personick, Valerie A. 1984. The job outlook through 1995: Industry output and employment projections. *Bureau of Labor Statistics Bulletin* 2197:22–33.

Porter, Lyman W., and Richard M. Steers. 1973. Organizational, work, and personal factors in employee turnover and absenteeism. *Psychological Bulletin* 80:151–176.

Premack, Steven L., and John P. Wanous. 1985. A meta-analysis of realistic job preview experiments. *Journal of Applied Psychology* 70:706–719.

Price, James L. 1977. *The study of turnover.* Ames, Ia.: The Iowa State University Press.

Principles for the validation and use of personnel selection procedures. 2nd ed. 1980. Berkeley: American Psychological Association, Division of Industrial-Organizational Psychology.

Ralston, David A., William P. Anthony, and David J. Gustafson. 1985. Employees may love flexitime, but what does it do to the organization's productivity? *Journal of Applied Psychology* 70:272–279.

Rice, A. K., J. M. M. Hall, and E. L. Trist. 1950. The representation of labour turnover as a social process. *Human Relations* 3:349–372.

Schmidt, Frank J., and John E. Hunter. 1977. Development of a general solution to the problem of validity generalization. *Journal of Applied Psychology* 62:529–540.

Schnitzer, Martin. 1970. *Regional unemployment and the relocation of workers: The experience of Western Europe, Canada, and the United States.* New York: Praeger Publishers.

Scholl, Richard W. 1983. Career lines and employment stability. *Academy of Management Journal* 26:86–103.

Schwarz, John E., and Thomas J. Volgy. 1985. The myth of America's economic decline. *Harvard Business Review* 63(September-October):98–107.

Sehgal, Ellen. 1985. Foreign born in the U. S. Labor market: The results of a special survey. *Monthly Labor Review* 108(July):18–24.

Shank, Susan Elizabeth. 1985. Changes in regional unemployment over the last decade. *Monthly Labor Review* 108(March) 17–23.

Silvestri, George T., John M. Lukasiewicz, and Marcus E. Einstein. 1984. Occupational employment projections through 1995. *Bureau of Labor Statistics Bulletin* 2197:35–47.

Skinner, Elizabeth W. 1969. Relationship between leadership behavior patterns and organizational situational variables. *Personnel Psychology* 22:489–494.

Smith, H. L., and L. E. Watkins. 1978. Managing manpower turnover costs. *Personnel Administrator* 23(April):46–50.

Spencer, Daniel G., and Richard M. Steers. 1981. Performance as a moderator of the job satisfaction-turnover relationship. *Journal of Applied Psychology* 66:511–514.

Staines, Graham L., and Joseph H. Pleck. 1983. *The impact of work schedules on the family*. Ann Arbor, MI.: Institute for Social Research Publishing Division.

Staines, Graham L., Kathleen J. Pottick, and Deborah A. Fudge. 1986. Wives' employment and husbands' attitudes toward work and life. *Journal of Applied Psychology* 71:118–128.

Standards for Educational and Psychological Testing. 1985. Washington, D. C.: American Psychological Association.

St. Antoine, Theodore J. 1985. The revision of employment-at-will enters a new phase. *Labor Law Journal* 6:563–567.

Steiber, Jack. 1984. Most U. S. workers still may be fired under employment-at-will doctrine. *Monthly Labor Review* 107(May):34–37.

———. 1985. Recent developments in employment-at-will. *Labor Law Journal* 36:557–563.

Stogdill, Ralph M. 1974. *Handbook of leadership: A survey of research and theory*. New York: Free Press.

Survey shows rising public resentment to mass layoffs. 1982. *Management Review* 71(October):45.

Sweet, Donald H. 1975. *Decruitment: A guide for managers*. Reading, Mass.: Addison-Wesley Publishing Company.

Tenopyr, Mary L., and Paul D. Oeltjen. 1982. Personnel selection and classification. *Annual Review of Psychology* 33:581–618.

Uniform Guidelines on Employee Selection Procedures. 1978. Equal Employment Opportunity Commission, Civil Service Commission, Department of Labor, Department of Justice.

Uniform Guidelines supplement. 1979. Adoption of questions and answers to clarify and provide a common interpretation of the uniform guidelines on employee selection procedures. Equal Employment Opportunity Commission, Office of Personnel Management, Department of Justice, Department of Labor, Department of the Treasury.

———. 1980. Adoption of additional questions and answers to clarify and provide a common interpretation of the uniform guidelines on employee selection procedures. Equal Employment Opportunity Commission, Office of Personnel Management, Department of Justice, Department of the Treasury, Department of Labor.

Unterweger, Peter. 1985. Appropriate automation: Thoughts on Swedish examples of sociotechnical innovation. *Labor Law Journal* 35:559–573.

U. S. Bureau of the Census. 1984. Geographic mobility: March 1982 to March 1983. *Current population reports*, Series P–20, No. 393. Washington, D. C.: U. S. Government Printing Office.

――――. 1984. Projections of the population of the United States, by ages, sex, and race: 1983 to 2080. *Current population reports*, Series P–25, No. 952. Washington, D. C.: U. S. Government Printing Office.

――――. 1985. Estimates of the population of the United States and components of change: 1970 to 1984. *Current population reports*, Series P–25, No. 971. Washington, D. C.: U. S. Government Printing Office.

――――. 1985. State population estimates, by age and components of change: 1980 to 1984. *Current population reports*, Series P–25, No. 970. Washington, D. C.: U. S. Government Printing Office.

U. S. Commission on Civil Rights Clearinghouse Publication 85. 1985. *Toward an understanding of Stotts.*

Vaill, Peter B. 1982. The purposing of high-performing systems. *Organizational Dynamics* 11(February):23–29.

Wanous, John P., Stephen A. Stumpf, and Hrach Bedrosian. 1979. Job survival of new employees. *Personnel Psychology* 32:651–662.

Waters, L. K., and Darrell Roach. 1979. Job satisfaction, behavioral intention, and absenteeism as predictors of turnover. *Personnel Psychology* 32:393–397.

Weiner, Nan. 1980. Determinants and behavioral consequences of pay satisfaction: A comparison of two models. *Personnel Psychology* 33:741–757.

Wells, Deborah L., and Paul M. Muchinsky. 1985. Performance antecedents of voluntary and involuntary managerial turnover. *Journal of Applied Psychology* 70:329–336.

What you should know about your benefits. 1985. General Motors Corporation, Detroit, Michigan.

Wiener, Yoash, and Yoav Vardi. 1980. Relationships between job, organization, and career commitments and work outcomes—an integrative approach. *Organizational Behavior and Human Performance* 26:81–96.

Wolozin, Harold. 1985. Corporate power in an aging economy: Labor force policy. *Journal of Economic Issues* 19:475–486.

Wolpin, Jacob, and Ronald J. Burke. 1985. Relationships between absenteeism and turnover: A function of the measures? *Personnel Psychology* 38:57–74.

Work in America Institute Policy Study. 1984. *Employment security in a free economy.* New York: Pergamon Press.

Workers without jobs: A chartbook on unemployment. 1983. Bulletin 2174, U. S. Department of Labor, Bureau of Labor Statistics.

You and Kodak: A handbook for employees. 1985. Eastman Kodak Company, Rochester, New York.

Young, Anne McDougall. 1985. One-fourth of the adult labor force are college graduates. *Monthly Labor Review* 108(February):17–23.

Youngblood, Stuart A., and Gary L. Tidwell. 1981. Termination at will: Some changes in the wind. *Personnel* 58(May-June):22–23.

Zedeck, Sheldon, and Wayne F. Cascio. 1984. Psychological issues in personnel decisions. *Annual Review of Psychology* 35:461–518.

Zemke, Ron. 1985. Stalking the elusive corporate credo. *Training* 22(June):44–51.

Index

About the Author

JAMES E. GARDNER served for many years as corporate Training Manager with Fieldcrest Mills. He has written four books in the field, including *Training Interventions in Job-Skill Development*, *Helping Employees Develop Job Skill*, and *Training the New Supervisor*.

DATE DUE